A
PRIVATE
WAR

Herr Bronisław Szatyn, *Kennkarte*
photo, Cracow, 1941.

Bruno Shatyn

A PRIVATE WAR

Surviving in Poland on False Papers, 1941-1945

Translated by Oscar E. Swan

Foreword by Norman Davies

WAYNE STATE UNIVERSITY PRESS   DETROIT 1985

Some believe the incredible, others do it.

Library of Congress Cataloging in Publication Data

Shatyn, Bruno, 1911-
    A private war.
    Translation of: Na aryjskich papierach.
    1. Szatyn, Bronislaw, 1911-   . 2. Jews — Poland — Biography. 3. Holocaust, Jewish (1939-1945) — Poland — Personal narratives. I. Title. DS135.P63S44713 1985   940.53'15'039240438   84-21905 ISBN 0-8143-1775-8

Publication of this book has been assisted by a grant from the Polish Culture and History Publication Fund of Wayne State University.

Originally published in Poland as Na aryjskich papierach *(Cracow: Wydawnictwo Literackie, 1983); copyright ©1983 by Bronisław Szatyn.*

To the memory of millions of people tortured to death by the Nazis

Publisher's Note

Professor Norman Davies, the historian of Poland, kindly consented to our request to provide a Foreword for the English-language edition of *A Private War* in order to provide the reader with the historical context in which Mr. Shatyn's narrative takes place. The views he expresses are not necessarily those of Mr. Shatyn.

Foreword

During the Second World War, Poland became Europe's Golgotha, the most terrible killing-ground in the long history of a continent well versed in violence. It was chosen by the German Nazis as the laboratory of their racial theories and as the site for their most extravagant death camps—Auschwitz, Treblinka, Sobibor, Majdanek. In a country which had already lost well over a million people amidst the rigors of the Soviet occupation of 1939-41, and in conditions of terror which far exceeded those of any other part of occupied Europe, the Nazis organized the systematic murder of the world's largest Jewish community and the forcible enslavement of the non-Jewish majority. Mass arrests, mass reprisals, mass executions, mass starvation, mass deportations were the order of the day. The Jewish Holocaust was but the blackest chapter in a black chronicle of horror which engulfed the whole nation. In the end, Poland's war casualties totaled more than six million men, women, and children, or almost 19 percent of the population. (This compares with 11 percent in Yugoslavia and the U.S.S.R., 7 percent in Germany, 2.5 percent in Japan, 0.9 percent in Great Britain, and 0.2 percent in the U.S.A.) Of the victims, the overwhelming number were defenseless civilians, and very nearly half were Jews.

Until that time, Poland had traditionally given refuge to persecuted Jews from all over Europe. In the days of the old Polish-Lithuanian Republic, before 1795, Polish Jews had enjoyed both religious freedom and communal autonomy. In the period of Tsarist rule, the Russian

vii

partition of Poland and the Jewish Pale of Settlement in Russia were essentially one and the same area. In the period between the two world wars in the twentieth century, notwithstanding massive emigration, Poland still remained the principal haven for European Jewry. It was the home of Hassidism, and of the best established centers of orthodox Judaism. It saw the flowering of both Yiddish and Hebrew literature and the growth of all the main currents of modern Jewish politics from the Socialist Bund to the Zionist movement. In the last years before 1939, it witnessed a great upsurge of Jewish dynamism in most walks of life, from theater and the arts to education, publishing, the press, and social welfare. Polish Jewry had its hard moments, but in the words of an old Hebrew pun, *Polin* (Poland) stood for *Poh-lin*—"Here one rests."

Polish-Jewish relations over the centuries cannot be easily simplified, but they are often misrepresented. There were periods of growing optimism and assimilation, as in the mid-nineteenth century, and periods of growing pessimism and tension, as in the 1930s. There were many straightforward social, cultural, and economic reasons why intercommunal animosities should be sharpened, just as there were sound political and psychological reasons why both Poles and Jews should have shared the same insecurities and rivalries. In the era of Nationalism, there were Poles of the National Democratic persuasion who treated all Poland's ethnic minorities, including the Jews, with undisguised hostility, just as there were growing numbers of Jews of the Zionist persuasion who treated Poland as a country fit only to turn their backs on. Equally, there were people of goodwill on both sides who were devoted to the cause of harmony and conciliation. There was an important sector of the population, especially in the numerous intelligentsia, who thought of themselves both as Poles and Jews. In a land where the Jews formed one tenth of the total population and in cities such as Cracow, Wilno, Lwów, or Warsaw accounted for 30, 40, or even 50 percent of the citizens, a certain degree of prejudice and discrimination was only to be expected; and it would be idle to pretend that the Polish record was unblemished. But it would also be inaccurate to suggest that Poland ever experienced the same level of pathological racism which has reigned at various times in neighboring Germany or Russia. Polish philo-Semitism is a subject not without its merits. What is more, one has to remember that the Zionist viewpoint, which has since become dominant in world opinion on Jewish affairs, always had a vested interest in inflating Jewish grievances in the land where most Jews then lived. It stands to reason that no

Foreword

right-minded Zionist, committed to the creation of Israel, could ever have publicly admitted that life for the Jews in Poland was perfectly bearable. Yet in the words of a British ambassador to Warsaw, Sir Horace Rumbold, at the start of the inter-war period, "It is of very little service to the Jews to single out for criticism and retribution the one country where they have probably suffered least."

Similarly, as Professor Władysław Bartoszewski has recently emphasized, one has to take account of official propaganda emanating from People's Poland since the war. Having taken control of a country in which they had virtually no popular support, the Polish communists took pains to embroider the memory of prewar and wartime Poland with all the calumnies and innuendoes which they could invent or exaggerate; and the Jewish issue with all its painful emotions lay at hand to be manipulated. Hence, not only the so-called Government of Colonels but also the principal Polish resistance movement, the Home Army, with its unmatched record of struggle against the Nazis, could be conveniently labeled as "Fascist," or "undemocratic," or "anti-Semitic," or whatever. Western opinion, appalled by the fate of the Jews and uneasy about the western Allies' own inertia on the Jewish front, was eager to find yet another scapegoat. In reality, the Polish Communist Party, while occasionally advertising its own allegedly liberal and pro-Jewish proclivities, has not refrained on other occasions—notably in 1956 and 1968—from unsavory campaigns of exactly the opposite kind. With a monopoly of all media and information under its control, it could tailor Polish history to its own ends. It is highly ironic, for example, that Warsaw was rightly endowed in 1948 with an imposing monument to the Heroes of the Ghetto but has never been granted the compliment of an official monument either to the Home Army, which launched the tragic Warsaw Rising of 1944, or to the Polish soldiers who died defending their capital against the Nazi invasion of September, 1939.

Above all, one has to remember the distortions which derive from the horrors of the war and the Holocaust. Everyone's memory is selective to some degree, and people who have lived through traumatic times tend to select those facts which hurt them least. Poles, scarred by the experiences of the Nazi and Soviet occupations, and proud of their country's refusal to collaborate, are understandably outraged when careless commentators talk of alleged Polish assistance in the Nazis' Final Solution. At the same time, they are prone to exaggerate the assistance which Polish civilians might have given to fugitive Jews. For their part, Jewish

ix

survivors of the Holocaust, preoccupied with the tragedy of their own people, are apt to look on all wartime Gentiles in Poland with hatred and suspicion. For them, it is all too easy to believe that no one cared a fig for the fate of the Jews and that the Nazis' Final Solution was the natural conclusion of centuries of inbred European hostility. When recriminations of this sort begin to fly, both Poles and Jews can forget that the true authors of their common misery were to be found among Poland's foreign invaders, and in particular among the minions and battalions of Adolf Hitler.

One might have believed, in fact, that a balanced, credible, and authentic description of Polish-Jewish relations in wartime Poland is beyond our reach. The horror of the camps and the ghettoes, where the Nazis had segregated the Jews from the non-Jews, may have been extensively described—and no modern child should grow up without knowing something about it—but the wider realities of life in the towns and countryside of occupied Poland are less well known. Historical accounts are often befogged by tendentiousness and controversy. Honest reporting on this subject is a rarity, which makes Bruno Shatyn's memoir a gem of real worth.

Bruno Shatyn is uniquely qualified to present an eyewitness account of wartime Poland. Although he lived in disguise "on the Aryan side," he was a Jew who maintained close contacts with his relations in the ghetto and was able to discuss with them the dilemmas of their fate. At the same time, he came into everyday contact with German petty officialdom and with Poles of all classes, and was able to observe their attitudes and actions at close quarters. What emerges is a human panorama of great variety, where not all the Jews are heroes or victims and not all the Gentiles are monsters or bystanders. One could read *A Private War* simply as a vivid adventure story, as a gripping chronicle of ingenious escapades, rescues, dangers, and triumphs over adversity. But it is also a valuable social record, explaining many facets of the occupation—the details of how the Polish Jews were concentrated for deportation, how Nazi labor policies worked, how the progress of the Eastern Front could be deduced from the freight traffic on a local railway line. It is most memorable, however, as a human document, faithfully recording the reaction of individuals, weak and strong, to the pressures of an appalling disaster.

Foreword

Of course, one man could only be in one place at one time, and if Shatyn escaped from the ghetto, he also avoided many of the worst occurrences beyond it. Although he vividly describes the death and destruction which descended on the civilian population during the September war of 1939, he did not directly experience the Nazis' terrible resettlement and pacification campaigns in the Polish countryside, and he did not see the Warsaw Rising of 1944. From the Jewish perspective, Shatyn was incredibly fortunate, but he was relatively well sheltered within the overall Polish context as well.

At one point in the war, Shatyn meets a humorous Polish squire, who has a fund of tall stories about big game hunting in Africa. One can feel the bond of sympathy, and a skeptical reader is bound to wonder whether some of Shatyn's passages do not belong in the same category. It is enough for one man to have survived the Nazi occupation, and to have played the Scarlet Pimpernel successfully on numerous occasions, without deciding at the end of the war to walk unharmed through the middle of a Nazi-Soviet tank battle, or to push his ailing mother-in-law in a wheelbarrow over the flooded ice floes of the frozen Vistula. What is important is that the whole picture rings true; the observation of human psychology is sharp and convincing: the narrative is brisk and clear. The book is eminently commendable to all who wish to know and feel what the Nazi occupation was really like for a man who was at once very ordinary and very exceptional.

Norman Davies
School of Slavonic and East European Studies
University of London

Contents

PART II
Przemyśl and Cracow: Childhood and Youth

Author's Note

I have left many incidents out of my narrative, considering them to be too wild and improbable. Even now, after so many years, they seem fantastic to me; what am I to expect of the reader who has never had similar experiences, who does not belong to my generation, and who has difficulty re-creating in his mind the spirit of those times? Everything I have discussed here is true. No names, dates, or places have been changed, with the exception of a single name, where I yielded to the request of that individual. If some inaccuracy has crept into my story at one point or another, this can be attributed to the length of time that has passed since these events and to the fact that, until I wrote this book, I had never returned in my thoughts to those days, not wishing to poison the present with the past.

Bruno Shatyn

Translator's Preface

As I am neither Jewish nor Polish, ethnic or national background was not a factor in my interest in bringing Bruno Shatyn's story to the American public. I became involved with this book partly through a personal connection with the Shatyn family—their daughter Irene was my Polish teacher and became my good friend at the University of California at Berkeley—but mainly because, when Mr. Shatyn sent me his manuscript, I recognized that it was a valuable record of human triumph over adversity, as well as a well-written suspense thriller (I should add that this was long before the book was published in Poland and became an overnight sensation).

A number of memoirs of Jews in the ghettos of Poland have appeared recently, but Bruno Shatyn's *A Private War* is the first account of civilian life in Poland during World War II written by a Jew who survived not in hiding or in a concentration camp but in the open, under an assumed identity. Shatyn was one of very few Jews in Poland sufficiently Polish in appearance and habits—and sufficiently lucky—to be able to slip through the German net and lead a more or less "normal" life (though readers may well call life in Poland at this time something other than "normal"). Throughout his six-year ordeal, with its moments of terror, its narrow escapes, and its quieter periods of despondence, despair, and futility, he does not lose his fundamental objectivity, his ability to assess situations instantly and react appropriately, nor even his ironic sense of humor.

Because of his unique situation, Shatyn is able to see events around him from a dual perspective—as a Pole and as a Jew—and his story significantly broadens one's conceptions about Polish-Jewish relations during the war. For this reason alone, his book deserves the widest possible dissemination. Saturated as Poland is with reminiscences about the war, Shatyn's book came as a revelation when it was published in Cracow in 1983, in large part because of the author's uncommon willingness to give credit where credit is due. Through Shatyn's eyes the Poles emerge—not so surprisingly, after all—as decent people, good neighbors, and trustworthy friends who exhibit normal human concern for those in distress, qualities all the more striking in those trying times. Polish reviews have stressed the book's "balance," and indeed the work is remarkable for its lack of politicizing and settling of accounts. The Germans are not all bad, the Jews not all good; the Poles come in various shades and stripes. If any group is criticized here, it is the Jews themselves, for their short-sightedness, lack of resourcefulness, and unwillingness to face facts and take action. It is a German official who encourages Shatyn to hide his Jewishness and go underground, and who then reinforces this advice with a three-month advance on his wages. When Shatyn's cover is eventually exposed, it is by a Jewish girl, herself in hiding among the Poles, who cannot resist gossiping even when other lives depend on her discretion.

The author's employers, Count Antoni Potocki of Olsza and the younger Potockis, Count Jerzy and his wife, are accorded particularly warm treatment. Even after learning that he is a Jew, the Potockis keep Shatyn on their estate as administrator, fully aware that in so doing they are endangering their own lives. Nor are they alone in sharing Shatyn's secret: we hear of many other Poles who, at the risk of their lives, help him and his family to survive. For Shatyn thinks not only of himself. He rescues his parents and many other members of his and his wife's family from the ghetto and sets them up in various new lives "on Aryan papers" (as the book is titled in Polish).

Shatyn's book is first a war memoir, but it is also much more than that. Before the war the author was a doctor of laws and a successful young Cracow attorney. In recalling his youth in Przemyśl and Jarosław, and later at the university in Cracow, he describes in fascinating detail the milieux in which he lived. A dilatory pupil, he eventually managed to graduate from the gymnasium in Jarosław, whose instructor of religion, Father Szypuła, he came to love, as he says, like a father. It was Szypuła who encouraged him to go to Cracow to study law, giving him a five-złoty piece as a parting gift. Shatyn's early years at the university are lean ones; his mother's well-connected relatives in Cracow turn their backs on the poor relative from the provinces. Later, having acquired a reputation as a distinguished student, he lives well by cramming his fellow students for their examinations. He tells of his professors, of the various Jewish milieux (one of the most intriguing parts of the book), of his legal practice.

When the Germans invade Poland, the young lawyer, with a horde of others, flees to the east and makes his way to Przemyśl. There he soon perceives the nature of the emerging German policy toward the Jews and obtains "Aryan papers" with the help of Polish friends. He eventually settles his wife and daughter in the Cracow suburb of Borek Fałęcki, himself obtaining the position of estate manager on the rental property of the Potockis in Borek Szlachecki ("Nobles' Woods"), near Skawina, a town about twenty-five miles from Oświęcim (Auschwitz). It is as estate manager that he conducts the bulk of the maneuvers in his "private war," although he waits out the final days of the Soviet offensive and German retreat in a hamlet in the mountains.

So successful is Shatyn's masquerade that he actually acquires the reputation on the Potocki estate of an anti-Semite. This cover allows him to accomplish such improbable feats as rescuing a Jewish girlhood friend of his wife from Skawina under the noses of the SS. Later he sets up his brother-in-law and his wife as counterman and waitress in a German army canteen in Krosno; another brother-in-law is placed in the post of director of the German State Labor Office (Arbeitsamt) in Kalwaria Zebrzydowska. His mother masquerades as his brother-in-law's mother-in-law; a young cousin becomes the brother-in-law's live-in kitchen maid. When his mother dies, of natural causes, her Catholic funeral is attended by a contingent of local Nazi officialdom in full panoply, and so on. So fantastic are such details that one would hesitate to accept them in a work of fiction.

In the United States, with its tradition of rapid cultural assimilation, it may be difficult for the reader to imagine the tremendous gulf separating Polish and Jewish society in Poland in the 1920s and 1930s. Although the Jews can be described as one of several disadvantaged minorities, the situation was not as bleak as it is sometimes depicted (our American use of the word "ghetto" to mean "black slum" is misleading here). Then there were the "Litvak" Jews, recently arrived from the east and speaking little or no Polish, and the Orthodox Jews, who had kept their own dress, language, customs, religion, and schools, resisting even a modicum of accommodation to the prevailing culture. Thus Poland was quite different from most other countries of Europe, where a much larger proportion of Jews were "assimilated." Despite the inevitable sharp social tensions created by such a situation in this fiercely Catholic country during the economic hard times of the 1930s, and despite growing anti-Jewish sentiment, demonstrations, and clashes at the universities, in labor unions, and in other areas of public life—often enough fomented by the Nationalist element among Polish politicians—most urban Jews in Poland before the war lived in peace and relative prosperity.

The vibrant life of the Warsaw Jews before the war is captured particularly well by Isaac Bashevis Singer in *Shosha*, a novel to which Shatyn's memoirs bear comparison in more than one respect: one may mention Shatyn's direct yet highly selective way of narrating the story, his indulgent irony, his taste for conveying character through a detail of physiognomy, and his equal treatment of events great and small, comic and sublime. For many readers in today's Poland, raised in an atmosphere of an irrational postwar anti-Jewish backlash, where "anti-Zionism" has been a ringing propaganda theme in almost every period of government crisis and the history of the prewar Jewish community has been almost a forbidden subject, Shatyn's colorful description of Cracow's Jewry no doubt comes as a revelation; for many, it is probably their first positive introduction to Poland's lost Jewish heritage. Undoubtedly it is as much as anything the realization of this irretrievable loss, and a revived interest in this now extinct part of the Polish cultural landscape, that attracts the Polish reader of today and accounts for the book's tremendous success there.

Bruno Shatyn wins his private war, but like all "happy endings" connected with the war, this one too is clouded: for millions more, including members of the Shatyn family, the war was not a personal triumph or success story in whose afterglow one may bask from the vantage point of forty years. It was almost forty years before Shatyn could confront these traumatic memories and write about them, and one wonders how many other equally dramatic stories must be locked in the recollections of those still living, still unable to discuss their experiences openly. The dark background that must be a part of any work dealing with the fate of the Jews in Poland during World War II cannot diminish the significance of Shatyn's work as witness to individual life-affirming experience during a time of general cataclysm. It is its truth, combined with its message of courage, optimism, and humanity, that makes *A Private War* unique among war annals of this type and gives it the right to stand alongside other great literary and documentary memorials to this tragic episode.

The success of this book in Poland encouraged me in my search for an American publisher, and I feel that I made a fortunate choice. Mrs. Jean Owen, of Wayne State University Press, assumed the most active possible role in all aspects of this book's preparation, ranging from matters of format, clarity, and consistency to a veritable creative role in portions of text.

Oscar E. Swan

Illustrations
and
Maps

Guiding a tourist around the castle, 1933.

Entrance to Wawel Castle, Cracow, where the author and other guides waited for the tourists' custom. (Photo Andrzej Mokrzycki, Polonia Society of Cracow, 1983)

Collegium Novum, the main building at Jagellonian University, which houses the faculty of law. (Photo Andrzej Mokrzycki, Polonia Society of Cracow, 1983)

The author on his way to classes, 1933.

Doctor of Jurisprudence, June, 1938.

The author and his wife on their honeymoon at Rytro with their landlord's dog, Rex, in July, 1939, just before the invasion of Poland.

Forged Kennkarte in the new name of Herr Bronisław "Szatyn," resident at 53 Wolność St., Prądnik Czerwony District, Cracow, 1941.

Krakau, den 18. 7. 1941

Nr.- Z-S-110/41

Es wird bestätigt, dass die nebenstehende
Photographie den E. Szatyn Bronisław röm-Kat
geb.am 8.III.1911 in Krakau, wohnhaft in Krakau-
Urzędnik Czerwony Wolnoscigasse 53 darstellt.

Szatyn Bronisław
Eigenhändige Unterschrift

O. MIEJSKI w KRAKOWIE
i Urząd Obwodowy VIII

STADTVERWALTUNG
KRAKAU
ZARZĄD MIEJSKI
w KRAKOWIE
87

Amtsleiter
Kierownik Urzędu:

Bochenek Karol

Count Antoni Potocki's manor house at Olsza,
outside Cracow, in 1982.

Count Jerzy Potocki's manor house at Borek Szlachecki, near
Skawina, in 1982.

Maria Friede's house in Skawina (1982 photo).

Skawina marketplace and town hall, where the Jews were assembled by the SS (1982 photo).

The Polanka-Haller manor house, next to the Potocki property outside Skawina (1982 photo).

Farm girls dressed for the harvest festival at Borek Szlachecki, August, 1943.

Marta, leader of the Polish women workers at Borek Szlachecki, at the festival.

Count and Countess Jerzy Potocki posing with the harvest wreath.

Kennkarte *obtained by the author for his sister Krystyna in the name of "Janina Górnik," April, 1942.*

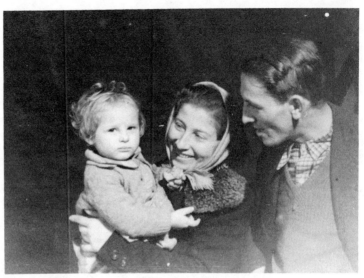

The family in Przemyśl, 1941.

Krakau, den   9.12.43

Fernruf: Sammelnummer 151-20

Generalgouvernement
Distrikt Krakau

Der Kreishauptmann Krakau-Land
Amt für Polizeiangelegenheiten   Bescheinigung
AZ.:./S

Es wird hiermit bescheinigt, daß Herr Bronislaw S z a t y n ,
geb. am 8.3.11 in Krakau, wohnhaft in Borek Szlachecki Nr. 1,
als Verwalter auf dem Gute Borek-Szlachecki, Kreis Krakau=Land,
beschäftigt ist.

Diese Bescheinigung gilt nur in Verbindung mit der poln.Kenn-
karte Nr. X/98248 ausgestellt vom Stadthauptmann der Stadt
Krakau am 2.4.1942 .

Gebühr: 5.-- Zloty.

Reg.Ob.Insp.

Generalgouvernement
Gebührenmarke

*Author's identification paper as manager of the Borek Szlachecki
estate issued by the* General Gouvernement, *Cracow, December,
1943.*

Isaak and Gusta Neulinger, Basia's parents, in a prewar portrait.

The author with his daughter Elizabeth, eleven months old, at Borek Falecki.

Photo of author taken for identification papers in 1942 while employed at Borek Szlachecki.

Rózia Neulinger Singer, Basia's oldest sister, in a 1942 Kennkarte *photo.*

Ewa Schatten's Kennkarte *photo as "Ewa Nowak," 1942.*

Joachim Schatten's Kennkarte *photo as "Jan Nowak," 1942.*

Samuel Singer, Rózia's
husband, 1942.

Ewa Schatten's grave in the Catholic
cemetery at Kalwaria Zebrzydowska,
September, 1943. The Polish
inscription reads: "Passing along life's
sad trails, guided always by kindness
and goodness, no wonder we all
mourn your loss, beloved mother."

Elizabeth, aged five, and Irena, aged two, with their mother at
Zakopane, 1945.

Gusta Neulinger and her
daughter Helena
Neulinger Stein at home
in Israel, 1950.

The Shatyns at a Polish
ball in Caracas,
Venezuela, 1958.

*Elizabeth Shatyn Lipsey
and her husband, Robert,
Huntsville, Alabama,
1959.*

*Irene Shatyn Pastor and her husband, Manuel, Berkeley,
California, 1962.*

The author's father at the age of eighty-five, at home in Caracas, 1959.

Memorial photograph of Jerzy Potocki on his death, January, 1983.

The family in Caracas, 1959: left to right: *Emil Schatten, Barbara Shatyn, Ernestyna Schatten, Joachim Schatten, Józef Krulig, Krystyna Schatten Krulig, her son Edward, Rela Schatten, Ewunia Schatten* (in front), *Leszek Krulig* (seated, with Capri).

Barbara Shatyn today,
Palo Alto, California.

The author.

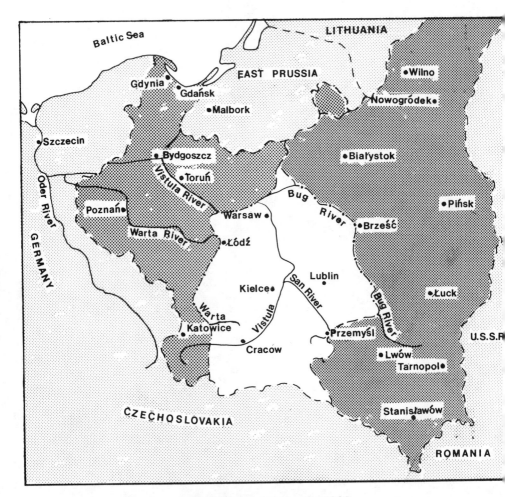

Partition of Poland, 1939.

Key: *white, General Gouvernement* area;
light gray, Polish territories under German control;
dark gray, Polish territories under Soviet control;
dotted and dashed line, border marked by river.
(Drawn by Ron Kolenda.)

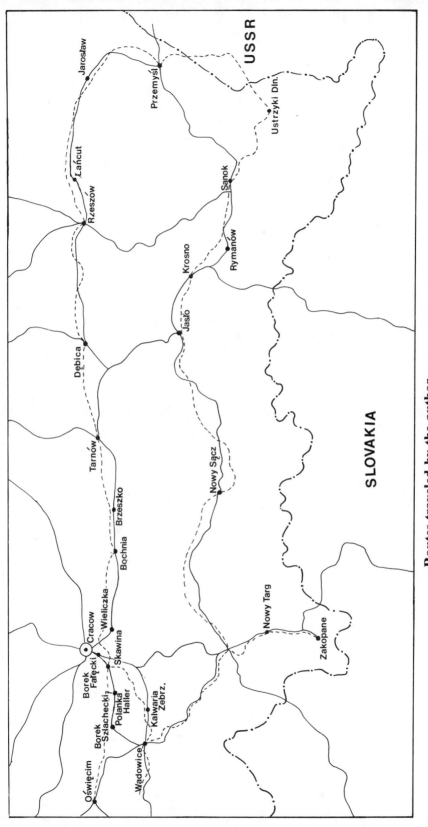

Routes traveled by the author.

Key: *solid line, highway; dashed line, railway.*

(Drawn by Ron Kolenda.)

PART I

The Estate of Borek Szlachecki, 1942

Chapter 1

Old Count Potocki

It was the beginning of 1942, the third year of the war in Poland. At that time I was working as an agricultural engineer, managing the estate of Borek Szlachecki ("Nobles' Woods"), located in the district of Cracow, not far from the little town of Skawina on one side and the city of Oświęcim (Auschwitz) on the other. The property belonged to Count Antoni Potocki, although the count himself lived on his estate in Cracow, in the Olsza district. The Olsza property was not large, but because the city of Cracow was expanding in that direction, its value had been increasing by leaps and bounds. These acres were really no longer agricultural fields, even though Potocki used them for farming: they were lots awaiting urban development—in fact, before the war Potocki had sold small parcels from time to time for this purpose.

The count and his wife lived alone in Olsza. Their two sons were both married and were living elsewhere. The manager at Olsza was a certain Miętka-Mikołajewicz, a long-standing employee of the count. Potocki himself, a man past sixty, gray-haired, lean, with fine aristocratic features, was a typical representative of his class. Not overly talkative, when he did speak it was with authority, commanding the respect and attention of his listeners.

I came to the Potocki residence in Olsza twice a week to give detailed reports on Borek Szlachecki and to receive instructions. I usually stayed for dinner. The dinner ritual was fixed and immutable.

3

Dinner was served promptly at twelve, and the meal was consumed in silence and concentration. The countess almost never spoke. When dinner was over, she remained in the dining room, while the count and I retired to his study for cigarettes and brandy. To the count I was nothing but a clerk and did not merit a seat at his table. However, practicality took precedence over such considerations because in this way, right after dessert, we could sit down in his study to discuss business.

Right from the start the count did not conceal the fact that we were beset by hard times—very hard times. The Nazi requisitions were completely ruining Olsza. He had trouble just scraping together enough money and farm produce to pay the help. In the past he had been able to sell some parcels of land, but now, in wartime, this was no longer feasible. Besides, to sell land now would mean disaster for the entire estate. He was trying to institute the most stringent economies at Olsza, and he expected the same from me at Borek Szlachecki. Manor policy was aimed not at making a profit but simply at getting through the war. The count made me personally responsible for seeing that his orders were carried out to the letter.

I understood Potocki's situation perfectly; nevertheless, it put me in a very delicate position. The count's younger son, Jerzy, recently married, lived with his wife on the estate at Borek Szlachecki. Both were in their twenties, modern in outlook, full of life, refined and generous in the extreme. It was not easy for them to adjust to the rigorous regime instituted by the old count. To combat the tedium of living in the country they would invite their friends to the estate: the Zbąszynskis, Lubomirskis, Radziwiłłs, and others would come calling, and we had to receive them in a certain style. The young Potockis would themselves be invited to other estates, and they couldn't go with empty hands. All this took money, and in the meantime the old count was demanding that we keep expenses to a minimum.

Military Levies

Borek Szlachecki was reeling under the burden of awesome military levies. We were in no shape to meet the needs of the Nazis and at the same time pay our workers. Before the war it had not mattered whether a farmhand was paid in money or in kind: for money he could buy whatever he needed. However, during the war, money became next to

4

worthless; one had to pay for almost everything in produce. We were unable to pay our farmhands entirely in kind, however, because the Nazi requisitions were so huge that the estate was left with barely enough to survive. In addition, Nazi regulations carefully spelled out how much we were allowed to pay our people in that way. At first the situation seemed hopeless, but with time, because of my efforts and, I have to admit, the considerable goodwill generated by the young countess, we at last got the manor economy on an even keel.

German supervision over our estate was of a rather cursory nature. The Nazis hardly ever looked in on us, and when they did, it was mainly to load up on food specialties which they could not get in Germany at any price. We owed this good fortune to the ancestral name of Potocki. Before the war, Hermann Göring, the German field marshal and economic dictator of the Reich, used to visit Count Alfred Potocki at Łańcut for "hunting," as they called it. After the outbreak of hostilities, Göring made it clear to the invading Nazi forces and the occupation authorities that "Graf Potocki" was under his personal protection. Fortunately for us, the Germans were not very well informed about the family connections of the Polish aristocracy; they did not know that there were many branches of the Potocki family and that our Count Potocki was not related to Count Alfred of Łańcut. To be safe, they preferred to handle all Potockis with great circumspection and to stay as far away from them as possible.

We had to deliver our military levies to the German occupation authorities through the agricultural cooperatives—one in our town of Skawina, for milk delivery, and another in Cracow, for all remaining commodities. These Polish cooperatives, well established before the war, now belonged to the Nazis, who occupied all the supervisory positions, leaving Poles only the low-level jobs. The cooperatives had few customers with whom to carry on illegal business. Most of the larger estates had been taken over by the Nazis and were administered by Germans. The manors remaining in Polish hands were too modest in size to absorb large amounts of this or that commodity. Because of the size of our estate and because we were rarely inspected, we made an ideal partner for black-market dealings. For example, at one time the cooperative in Cracow had a twenty-ton carload of saltpeter (used for fertilizer) to sell. Saltpeter on the black market was worth even more than wheat, so the cooperative prepared papers showing the transfer of the saltpeter to our estate; in actuality, the cooperative sold it to another buyer. In return for our signature on the receipt for the saltpeter, we received a share of the proceeds, which came to a sizeable amount of money. After this first successful business venture, relations between the Cracow cooperative and our manor became more intimate. I outlined our economic problems to their Polish managers, who promised to give our situation serious thought. (Naturally, by helping us, they intended to help themselves as well.)

The Germans had released certain properties from the obligation of supplying military requisitions if they agreed to operate as stock facilities. Such manors raised cattle and also cultivated grain or potatoes as seed crops. The crops were taken for distribution elsewhere, and the producing estate received food and other consumer goods in exchange. The Germans considered their own agricultural products superior to those of the Polish farmers. They claimed, for example, that German wheat sown over a given area would have a greater yield than the same amount of Polish grain. By the same token, their potatoes were more productive. The people at the cooperative therefore suggested that our estate be converted to a stock farm; they assured me that it would be profitable for both of us, and they were not mistaken.

Not long after this conversation, a German evaluation team drove up, examined our fields, and declared them admirably suited to seed crops. Soon we received word from the cooperative that our first shipment of German seed grain had arrived. The grain was in perfect condition. Before being turned over to us in Cracow, it was to have been sprinkled with chemical additives and poisons at the cooperative to protect it from local pests and diseases. After that, of course, it would no longer be fit to eat. No one, however, sprinkled the grain with chemicals. It arrived in the purest form imaginable, wonderfully suited for consumption. I signed a receipt for a large amount of this treasure, but I actually received less than half as much. Under the supervision of the cooperative's German employees, who of course were in on the hoax from the beginning, the Polish workers sold the rest on the open market. The grain allotted to us was then mixed with other varieties. We planted the mixture, and as soon as the heads of grain were tall enough to determine the variety, the German inspectors arrived, examined the crop, and declared it to be impure, of no value as seed.

The inspectors' job was to examine the grain and nothing more. What happened to it afterward was not their concern: that was somebody else's affair. We had been released from the obligation of meeting military quotas, and our grain had been disqualified as seed crop. The cooperative saw to it that no one else checked up on it. It stayed on the estate, and now we had enough grain to meet the needs of the manor and to pay our workers, and even some left to sell on the open market. As it turned out, the cultivation of pure German grain, especially imported from Germany, could be profitable for us, for the employees of the cooperative, and for a small band of Nazi operators as well.

A similar procedure was adopted in the cultivation of potatoes; we never had to release any of them. The cattle and hogs were marked for breeding purposes only, so we were released from meat supply quotas. In return, we were to provide young pigs and cattle as breeding stock. By an amazing twist of fate, from the very moment that our cattle and pigs were designated as breeding stock, the cows became barren and the pigs stopped growing. Later I learned that the Nazi supervisor of the cooperative, one Krüger, a relative of the chief of security in the *General Gouvernement* (the Nazi name for that part of occupied Poland not incorporated in the Reich), was at the head of all these so-called inspection teams, or at least they answered to him. They worked as a group, a band of get-rich-quick artists onto a good thing.

The clerks in the Cracow cooperative put me in touch with the Skawina dairy cooperative, in which Poles worked for starvation wages. We soon struck a deal: they would regularly report the amount of milk which we were to supply, but instead of delivering it we would pay them twenty groszy (one hundred groszy to one złoty) for each undelivered liter. From time to time, so as not to arouse suspicion, we would send down to the cooperative a horse-drawn wagon loaded with milk cans, but the cans would be filled with water instead of milk. We took first place in the entire district for the punctual supply of the required amount of milk; indeed, we received prizes from the occupation authorities, in the form of ironware, fabrics, and alcohol. The value of the prizes exceeded the amount we paid to the cooperative for the non-delivery of milk, and to add to the beauty of the arrangement, once a week we received a bonus of a five-liter jug of pure cream from the cooperative.

The only person on the estate who knew about our supplies or, rather, our non-supplies was the driver who took the water to the dairy. He was an elderly man who had worked on the estate for many years and was very reliable. He had lost his only son in the war, and he hated the Nazis with a passion. I suspected, and not without reason, that instead of well water, he filled the milk cans with pond water. Once I even joked

7

with him on the subject. He looked at me in all sincerity and said, "Even pond water is too good for those sons-of-bitches."

Near our estate was a large firebrick factory (firebricks are bricks that have been specially treated to withstand high temperatures). These bricks played some role in German war production, and so the factory had been placed under the control of the SS. Before the war, it belonged to a Czech company, and the manager, a Czech by the name of Wasenda, still occupied his former position. The SS troops were housed in the modern administration building, but they did not interfere much with the manufacturing operation, considering this to be someone else's concern. The factory constantly received shipments of the raw materials necessary for brick production. At the station in Skawina I often saw carloads of first-class coal being shunted onto the sidings leading to the factory. We too received a small coal allotment, but of the worst quality, very dirty, more like peat than coal, with a low burning point. However, farm produce is worth something too, especially during a war. Before long we had established a trade arrangement with the brick factory. We gave the brick-makers food in return for all manner of industrial products necessary for running the estate—quality coal, kerosene, fuel and oils for running our equipment, and many other essential items.

Farm Workers

Our most urgent concern was the procurement of an adequate work force. During the war labor was hard to come by, and without the right workers, even the most favorably situated farm could go under. We employed both full-time help and seasonal labor hired for early spring through harvest time. The full-time help included the house servants, such as the head cook, her helpers, and the chambermaids; and farm workers such as grooms, stable boys, livestock girls, ploughhands, field hands, the blacksmith, gardener, clerks, apprentices, and steward.

Some of the workers lived in the farmhands' living quarters on the estate; others, if they were from the neighborhood, lived at home. The steward, apprentices, head cook, and chambermaids lived in the lower apartments of the manor house. I lived in a nearby apartment rented from a farmer, but I took my meals and had my office at the manor house. My wife, Basia (Barbara), and my two-year-old daughter, Elusia (Elizabeth), lived in Cracow in the Borek Fałęcki district, on

Chapter 1

Zakopane Street. Every Saturday I visited my family for the weekend, returning to Borek Szlachecki on Sunday evening; and whenever I went to the city on business during the week and had a little free time, I also dropped by to see them.

Our seasonal labor was hired each year through the local Arbeitsamt, or German labor office. The director of the Arbeitsamt, Joachim Mann, was a German of Silesian extraction who knew Polish. His assistant was a Pole, Tadeusz (Tadek) Słomka. Słomka hated the Nazis with his whole heart and soul. He couldn't stand the German guttural way of speaking. At the very sound of a German voice, his face became contorted with rage. He could read no German, and whenever his superior was out of the office, which happened quite often, and some piece of German correspondence arrived, festooned with impressive seals in various colors and marked *Dringend* ("Urgent") or *Wichtig* ("Important"), his hatred would get the better of him. Germans have a particular way of writing official documents. They love to compose terribly long, complex sentences, difficult for a foreigner even to read through, let alone understand. Słomka was able to make out the first part of a word with the help of a dictionary, but to understand any long or complex expression was beyond his capabilities. He would agonize over such a document for a long time, growing angrier and angrier, until finally he would fling open the drawer of his desk, pull out an old tennis ball, and hurl it over and over at the portrait of Hitler thumbtacked to the wall until his pitching arm gave out.

Once I was present during one of these outbursts. I noticed that the portrait seemed to be in rather good shape, for all its ill treatment, and I commented on it. "I have enough of this trash to last a lifetime," he replied. "Probably more than fifty of them. They sent a whole package to hand out. But why bother? One person hangs it up, and another tears it down. As for me, I'd rather have him hanging up there in place of his portrait."

Słomka constantly cursed the fate which doomed him to sit in a Nazi office sending Poles to work in the Reich. Whenever he had to assemble a list of workers to be sent to Germany, he would round up the dregs of society, in defiance of the Germans' instructions, and put them first in line. The Nazis set the number of workers to be sent, of whom three-quarters were to be farmhands. Słomka kept elaborate notes with the names of likely candidates. When the time came to compile a list, he would whip out his notes and, with immense satisfaction, enter at the

9

top the names of those whom he considered the worst elements: criminals, prostitutes, girls who went out with Germans, and the like. As a final touch, he would give their occupation as "agricultural laborer." As for the decent young men and women in the district, he tried to settle them locally in some kind of respectable work, this being his own small attempt at sabotage.

Słomka handled the labor supply for our estate. At first our relationship was polite but official; later it took a commercial turn, as we traded him produce for workers; finally it became quite cordial, as we took a liking to each other and became close friends. Słomka gave me a lot of good advice outside the range of his official duties. For example, he advised me to send several rings of sausage to the mayor of Skawina; to the German military police (Gendarmerie); to the head of the local police, the so-called Polish or Blue Police (composed of Poles enlisted by the Nazis and wearing the same color uniform, navy blue, worn by the prewar Polish police force); and even to the local stationmaster whenever possible. His reasoning was simple: "In case anything happens, they can't do much to help, but you have to have them on your side because any of them, if they want, can do plenty of harm. They'll all pay less attention to you, which can only be for the best. The less they know about you the better. Sometimes they actually can be of help or can find something out for you. You never know." Słomka's words were prophetic. The good relations with the stationmaster turned out to be quite useful. Thanks to him I made contact with the railway employees, who were at that time one of the best sources of information in the country, as I will explain later on.

Labor Shortages

In 1942 I needed about forty seasonal workers. The ideal would have been to hire girls from the country—strong, healthy, used to hard work—but I knew that was impossible. The Nazis were looking for country girls too. Even if Tadek had wanted to give me the kind of women I needed, his superior would not have authorized it, and Tadek's job could be in jeopardy. We sat down at the table like two conspirators, calculating all possibilities, trying to determine how many country girls I could get and how many city girls without any farm experience the

Arbeitsamt would add.

We agreed that I would hire, and the Arbeitsamt would approve, eighteen able-bodied village girls, and, in consideration of the fact that city folk were not worth nearly as much to us, instead of twenty-two more he would give me about thirty, but they would all have to be Jews. The Poles could be sent to Germany, and the Jewish girls could not; the Jews received smaller wages; and they were not to be paid in kind. So Tadek could get me the extra number. They would even give me one Jewish man who was a real farmer—and hence a skilled laborer—from a nearby village, as well as his elder brother, a townsman.

Before the war there were few Jews living in Skawina, but now there were more and more. The settlement of Jews there began in 1940, when the Nazis established their "capital" in Cracow. Governor General Frank set up headquarters in Wawel Castle, the ancient seat of the Polish kings. At first the Germans wanted their capital *Judenfrei*, free of Jews; later they decided to leave twenty thousand in the city. The rest were to be evacuated. They issued orders that any Jewish resident who left the city voluntarily before September 15, 1940, would be allowed to take whatever possessions he wanted with him. After this date the Jews who evacuated were allowed to take only a limited number of possessions.

Many Jews took advantage of this "opportunity" and left the city before the deadline. The Nazis locked the rest into the ghetto on the other side of the Vistula River, in the Podgórze district. Even after the deadline, however, many other Jews escaped to the country, preferring to live in a small town in freedom rather than walled into the Cracow ghetto. The Jewish population that decided to leave Cracow before the fifteenth was not permitted to move just anywhere. The Nazis published a list of eighty-six towns and cities where Jews were forbidden to settle. Skawina was not among the forbidden towns, and it was only a short distance from Cracow, so many families settled there. Each able-bodied Jewish man or woman had to register in the local Arbeitsamt to be assigned to various occupations. Some worked in factories, others on the roads; still others, with a special skill or trade, tried to find work in their own or some related area. Many tried to get work on our estate, partly because it was out in the fresh air and partly because they expected to receive decent treatment and to benefit from the proximity of food—although in theory it was forbidden to pay Jews in kind.

Our Jewish Workers

I had no choice but to agree to the proposal of the Arbeitsamt. I hired eighteen village girls, and in addition the Arbeitsamt assigned me twenty-eight Jewish women and two men. The leader of the Poles was a girl named Marta, vivacious, full of life, with a keen sense of fair play. She was always ready to stand up for her rights and would never put up with the slightest injustice to herself or to any of her girls. As a worker she had no equal. The Jewish women assigned to us ranged in age from seventeen to twenty-four. Some of them had been at the university. Their leader was twenty-three-year-old Herta, a brunette with large brown eyes and a serious expression, greatly respected by those in her group. She came from Bielsko and had a degree in philosophy and a fluent command of Polish, French, English, and German. She was alone; her parents had already been taken by the Nazis.

The two groups of girls were separated by the gulf created by the invaders. The Jewish girls had to wear armbands with the Star of David and were paid downright miserable wages. The Poles had the right to receive payment in kind, while the Jews did not. The Polish girls were used to field work; the Jewish girls were not. The Poles, accustomed to hard physical work, were strong and sturdy, while the Jewish girls tired easily and were short on resourcefulness. All this gave the impression of two classes, the privileged, competent Poles and the downtrodden, good-for-nothing Jews.

However, if at first the two groups of workers had nothing to do with one another, they gradually became acquainted. The Polish girls showed the Jews how to perform certain tasks, and they in turn benefited from the society of the educated city girls. Their work, age, common language, and mutual curiosity drew them closer. At last it got to the point where in many activities not demanding special skill they no longer worked side by side but together, as a single unit, and it must be admitted that both sides were pleased with this arrangement.

We on the estate were not overjoyed at the prospect of having so many city girls working for us. I was resigned to trouble sooner or later. The country girls had spent many seasons working on estates; they knew what was expected of them, and for this reason they were easier to work with. The city girls were an entirely different proposition. They had their own notion of what farm work was like, and they soon grew weary of it. Besides, because of the Nazi regulations and the constant harassment by the invaders, the Jews were exceedingly touchy and inclined to take everything as an attempt to humiliate them.

As I already mentioned, the Arbeitsamt assigned to us two Jewish men, brothers from a neighboring village. The elder, a squat, swarthy, shifty-eyed forty-year-old, was a townsman, but not completely. As a youth he deserted his family and native village, converted to Catholicism, and found employment in a customs office on the Czech-Polish border. He never returned to his village. Of course, after the Nazi invasion, he had to wear the Star of David and was treated like any other Jew. Now he remembered his native place and returned home. His parents, farmers for generations, were no longer alive. He found that his younger brother had inherited the land from his father and was also a farmer.

The younger brother did not look the least bit Jewish. He spoke in the local peasant dialect, when he spoke at all, and was rather timid. When he came to the manor he worked as a groom, going to the horses in the morning when it was still dark, cleaning their stalls, feeding and watering them, and then riding out into the fields to complete his other tasks. He knew his business and was respected by everyone. After work he returned home and worked on his own small farm until late at night. He was an excellent addition to the estate, and we never had any trouble with him.

The elder brother, who had spent his adult life in a customs office, was a different story. He knew nothing of farming and had no desire to learn, doubtless hoping to get some kind of supervisory position. He slouched around the manor yard, talked as much as ten others, and, worst of all, liked to play informer. A typical convert, he could not stand Jews. He was constantly going on about "us Catholics" and "those Jews," and was always telling the steward in a contemptuous tone that "the Jews aren't working; you can see for yourself they're not doing a thing." At first I paid no attention to his complaints, but before long I realized that sooner or later I would have to put a stop to them. We were not accustomed to having workers inform on one another; it only led to bad feelings and disrupted work.

One day he stopped me in the yard and "informed" me that the steward had sent several Jewish girls to do some kind of work but that, instead of working, they were just sitting around on the grass gossiping. He must have caught me at a bad moment, for I let him know in no uncertain terms that this was none of his business, and that if he knew what was good for him he would get back to the work the steward had given him. I also forbade him once and for all to hang around the manor yard. "It seems, sir," he said in amazement, "that you forget that we are both Catholics, men of the same faith. It's true I wear a Jewish armband, but that's just Nazi regulations."

This made me even angrier. I made it plain that to me he was just another Jew, that I had hired him as such, and that if I caught him idling about any more I would fire him on the spot and inform the Arbeitsamt. He went off into the fields in a fury and told the other workers what I had told him—his own version, of course. He added that there was no longer any doubt that I was not merely an anti-Semite but an unadulterated racist, that I didn't go by faith, only by blood and ancestry. This version spread quickly among the workers and soon got back to me.

Shortly afterward I had a confrontation with the Jewish girls. One day we were to cart cow manure into the fields. The steward had divided the workers into three groups. The first was to load the manure onto the wagons, the second—the drivers—was to cart the manure to the fields, and the third was to spread it out carefully and pack it around the plants. Spreading manure is fairly arduous work and, in addition, requires a certain amount of skill, since it is easy to scorch the young plants with too much fertilizer. However, loading the manure onto the wagons was something anyone could do. The steward assigned the Polish girls to spread the fertilizer around the plants, while the Jewish girls were to load it into the wagons.

The Jews were simply outraged at this division of labor. They deliberated among themselves and finally decided to appeal the steward's decision to me. Their leader, Herta, came to my office and bitterly protested what she considered to be the unfair treatment of the Jewish girls. They had already suffered enough at the hands of the Nazis; they had signed up for work on a Polish farm voluntarily, expecting to be treated like humans; and here we were, sending them, fresh from the city, into this muck that stank to high heaven. On top of it all, they were going to ruin their dresses, for they had no choice but to undress in front of everyone or to climb into the manure pit, filled to the brim with this foul-smelling, runny goop, with their good clothes on. On behalf of her girls, she earnestly requested that I rescind the steward's orders.

I tried to explain that they should try to see the other side of the problem. A manure pile is no bed of roses, and I could understand that its smell could be particularly loathsome to girls from the city, but for us

14

farmers the manure was precious, and one got used to the stink. I was unable to countermand the steward's orders in any case, I told Herta, because he was responsible to the count, who was not on the estate that day. I was only an administrator, with no direct authority. Besides, I said, I doubted that the count would have changed the steward's plan because it was clearly the most logical arrangement for getting the work done. I asked her to get the girls to work as quickly as possible, since everything had come to a standstill because of their protest. The other girls were waiting in the fields, the drivers were standing idle, and here we were dickering instead of loading.

Herta saw that it was no use, and got up to leave. At the door she turned around, looked me straight in the eye, and said, "I know that you don't like Jews. We can't do anything about that, but I was at least hoping that your sense of justice would outweigh your prejudice." Then she turned and left. I had a feeling that the girls would not go back to work and that the results would be unfortunate. I would have to inform the Arbeitsamt that I had fired them and then ask for new workers. But these workers were already assimilated into our system, and that was one loss; the other was that any delay was always costly.

I went out to the barn. The drivers were standing by their carts waiting, and the Jewish girls were standing alongside, with no intention of getting down to work. I sent for the stable girls to help us. I then undressed, taking off my boots, pants, and shirt, until I was standing there in my underwear. Our steward did the same. We two then picked up pitchforks, crawled into the manure pit, and started forking manure into the carts. The stable girls now tucked up their skirts, got into the manure with us, and began loading it quickly and skillfully onto the carts. The Jewish girls looked on in amazement for a moment. Herta was the first to hitch up her skirt, take a fork, and step gingerly into the pit. The others followed, grimacing all the while, but in they went and began to help. The job went quickly, and the crisis was averted.

The Apprentice Steward

Sometimes misunderstandings with the workers were more serious, though, and despite the best intentions, we had no choice but to fire someone. One day I received a call from Miętka-Mikołajewicz, the count's manager in Cracow, saying that Count Antoni had hired a boy as an apprentice steward and was sending him out to us. I was rather surprised, for it was not the custom of the old count to engage workers for us. Later I learned that the boy had been taken on by way of protection. He was from around Poznań, where his parents had a large farm. After their property was expropriated by the Nazis, the family moved to Cracow. The boy was an only child, and his parents were worried about his safety in town. One way or another they had gotten in touch with the old count, and he had hired the boy and sent him to work for us.

Right from the start it was clear that this fellow was going to be of no help, but was staying with us only because Cracow had become dangerous. Around nineteen years old, he was tall and well built, with light blond hair, a pug nose, and tiny blue eyes. He was used to having his way in everything, pampered and spoiled by his rich family. He was insolent to everyone, treated his visit to the country as a joke, and had no intention of altering the dissipated habits to which he had grown accustomed at home in Poznań and later in Cracow. He was also something of a sadist, as we later discovered. He had a habit of disappearing right after supper, probably riding into Skawina or some other town in the vicinity and spending the entire night there. In the morning he would reappear, bleak and bleary-eyed, tumble into the nearest haystack and sleep off his escapade—to the disgust of everyone. He never did his work and was never where he was supposed to be. He soon became the object of universal ridicule.

We could see that the boy was good for nothing, but we had to humor the old count, so we settled on a compromise: we let him stay at the manor and gave him as little to do as possible (he would have ignored any orders of ours anyway). Of course he was quite pleased with this arrangement. As for us, we didn't know what to do with him, for his existence made a mockery of our authority and undermined discipline.

Fond of fast riding, he gave the animals themselves no thought, but cared only for the pleasure of the ride. Rubbing down the horses after a gallop in the country was no concern of his; that was someone else's responsibility. In short, he played the young master. He brought with him a trained German shepherd dog, and the neighboring farmers brought a constant stream of complaints against the two of them. At his command his dog would chase their ducks, geese, and other barnyard fowl. In the same way he would set his dog on wild game—rabbits, wild ducks, and other birds.

Chapter 1

He treated the workers with open contempt. He dare not lay a finger on the Polish girls, for he knew that their leader, Marta, despised him and mocked him to the others. More than once she let him know that if he made a move in their direction he would have to answer to all the boys in the village. However, the Jewish girls were defenseless, and he could give full rein to his sadism without fear of reprisal. Hardly a day went by without some complaint against him, but he was a coward and cunning as well, always able to explain how each new incident had been someone else's fault. When the evidence against him was overwhelming, he would become contrite, and solemnly swear that such a thing would never happen again.

One Monday morning he went into the field where the Jewish girls were working. He was in a bad mood; someone had pulled some hay off the stack where he lay sleeping as usual and wakened him. In a nearby field our groom was cutting grass with a mowing machine. The boy left his cap and jacket in this field and commanded his dog to guard them. The dog lay down in the uncut grass, completely hidden. The boy then went to the field where the Jewish girls were raking grass and asked one of them to fetch his jacket and cap. One of the girls, unsuspecting, went to get them. The dog watched her coming closer and closer, but she didn't notice him until she bent down to pick up the jacket. Then it was too late. The shepherd sprang at her with a snarl and sunk his teeth into her thigh.

The groom heard the dog's snarl and the girl's scream, and in an instant was off the mowing machine and running toward her with a pitchfork. She was lying in the grass, still held by the dog. Suddenly the dog noticed his new adversary. He abandoned his prey and started to run at the mower, but when he saw the deadly pitchfork aimed at him and realized that the mower was interested only in the girl, not in the jacket, he withdrew diplomatically, growling and snarling, and lay back down in his original spot. The mower lifted the half-conscious girl. Her skirt was torn and her thigh was bleeding. After some cursory first aid, she was carried to the manor, where the wound was washed, disinfected, and bandaged. Still in shock and shaking uncontrollably, she was put in a room next to the kitchen.

At this dramatic moment, the young count arrived from town. He saw the commotion and got the whole story straight from the groom. The count was furious and ordered the girl taken to a doctor, releasing her from work for the rest of the week with pay and directing that if she still was not well after a week she was to return to the doctor's office until the wound was completely healed.

We then went to my office. The count told me that he had been hearing about the behavior of the apprentice for some time and that it had gone far enough. He simply could not bear the sight of him any longer and wanted me to get rid of him, to give him notice then and there. I was in something of a dilemma. It seemed to me that if the young count himself fired the boy the old count would not overrule his decision, but that if I did so, and the apprentice had a chance to tell his side of the story, the count was sure to annul my decision, if only because I did not have the right to fire someone whom he had hired. One way or another, the boy would stay on the farm. Accordingly, I decided simply to reprimand him and to warn him that we could lose our workers if the Arbeitsamt found out about his goings-on. At the same time I threatened that if there were any further incidents I would go to the old count in person, and then nothing could save him.

The farm workers were scandalized by my mild resolution of the affair. The Jews took this as further proof of my anti-Semitism, and young Count Potocki apparently felt the same way. "Do you really dislike the Jews so much?" he asked. I explained why I had acted as I did. He did not reply, and I do not know whether he believed me or not. I could see that the tension on the estate had increased to the point where steps had to be taken. The apprentice had to be fired, but in a way the old count could accept.

Two weeks passed. Again on a Monday, the apprentice steward, as was his custom, was snoring on a pile of hay in the barn. Noon arrived, and the workers were assembled in the manor yard awaiting instructions for the afternoon's work. I sent someone into the barn to wake up the apprentice and fetch him into the yard. He came out half-conscious, disheveled, his head covered with straw, blinking and half-blinded by the bright afternoon sun. Obviously hung over, his face was red and blotchy; in short, he looked a mess. The farmworkers couldn't help laughing out loud. The young count, who was present, was disgusted. He said nothing but turned and stalked away. I could see that he was trying to control his temper. Later, after the evening meal, he called me to his room and ordered me to fire the boy immediately. He was to be off the estate that very day. The boy took his pay, his dog, his traps, and was gone.

Chapter 2

Concentration of the Jews

My contact with the outside world was rather limited. I traveled once or twice a week to Cracow on business or to visit my wife and daughter. All the information I needed was obtainable in Skawina. The successes or failures of the Germans in North Africa or even around Moscow or Leningrad did not interest me. All that belonged to another world and could not affect my immediate future. I had no interest in whether the Americans had recovered from the shock of having their fleet sunk at Pearl Harbor, or whether Stalin was going to move his capital east of Moscow. I felt like a man on top of a volcano watching to see which way the lava is flowing so as not to be carried away.

I gathered information here and there—in the town offices, in the Arbeitsamt, at the train station, even from the parish priest. The priest knew almost everyone in Skawina, and his impressions of the inhabitants were usually remarkably astute. We grew to respect each other. Before the war I had gone on pilgrimages with friends to Kalwaria Zebrzydowska, and I had visited the famous shrine in Jasna Góra in Częstochowa a number of times. I often attended church services. I was an expert in church liturgy and administrative structure, and I knew canon law by heart. In 1929 the state of Italy had signed an agreement with the Holy See known as the Lateran Concord, creating the Vatican City State, an independent entity. I loved to discuss the provisions of this concord with the priest. More than once he shook his finger at me as if to say, "Hey, my boy, what seminary did you escape from?"

19

I: The Estate of Borek Szlachecki, 1942

I sorted and classified the information thus gathered, trying to decide what was certain, what was probable, and what was only hearsay. As noted earlier, on the advice of Tadek Słomka I had made the acquaintance of the Skawina stationmaster and, through him, the railway workers, especially the conductors. We shared a common language, for I had worked on the railroad for a while and was no stranger to its network and terminology. The conductors were an invaluable source of information. As I gained their confidence, I learned many things unknown to the population at large.

Of late I had become interested in a certain phenomenon. More and more Jewish families were moving from neighboring villages to Skawina. All these people gave the same reason for leaving their former homes: a representative of the local authorities—a policeman, mayor, or other official—had come to each family and informed them that according to a new German order Jews were to leave the area, for in the future it was to be free of Jews, *Judenfrei*. Whoever failed to leave his home before the appointed date would be handed over to the German secret police, the Gestapo. The Jews could take whatever possessions they wished, or they could sell them or give them away, as they preferred. As a rule they were given from a week to ten days to leave.

The local government in Skawina was instructed not to interfere with Jews attempting to settle there. The local Arbeitsamt could register the newcomers for work, although no particular pressure was to be applied. The newly arrived Jews were free to live wherever they could find a place, as long as it was within the boundaries of the town.

No one knew why the Jews were being evicted from their homes, nor why they were being allowed to settle in specially selected localities: was it only a coincidence that these localities were situated near large railroad junctions? The most puzzling aspect of this policy was that the resettlement was not accomplished in typical Nazi style, in that the occupation forces used neither violence nor terror.

The inhabitants of Skawina were not pleased with this influx. They had not yet recovered from the arrival of the Jewish masses from Cracow two years before, and now a new drive was under way. It became very crowded in town, but there was a rumor that the whole business was to be short-lived, as the Germans were planning to settle the Jews in their recently acquired immense empty territories in the Soviet Union. There they would be free to live and work in peace. No one knew

20

the source of this rumor, but everyone was familiar with it. Some held that the Nazis had softened their stand on the Jewish question because they were experiencing setbacks on almost all fronts; others denied this.

I myself placed no trust in the Nazis and looked with growing suspicion on this concentration of Jews in a single place, accomplished in such an untypically mild manner. Evidently the Germans did not want to spread panic among the populace. I determined to investigate the matter more closely. I felt sure that the workers on the German Eastern Railway (the Ostbahn) would know whether the transportation of the Jews to the east had begun in other localities. However, whenever I tried to raise the subject, the railwaymen were silent. It was clear that they did not wish to discuss the matter with me. Before long, however, by piecing together answers to various questions, I formed a picture of what was happening—something which was on everyone's mind but which everyone was afraid to speak of because what they knew, or suspected, was so hideous, so preposterous, that it was easier to remain silent.

The Polish conductors had been accompanying the transports of Jews to the east—the "resettlement of the Jews," as it was called. For the most part they were taken to Małkinia Górna on the Bug River, to Sobibór or Bełżec in the former district of Lublin, or even to Lublin itself—to the southeastern district of the city called Majdanek. The transports carried from five to ten thousand people each. The Polish conductors were not allowed to ride to the final destination. At the final stage of the journey the trains were taken over by SS troops, assisted by the volunteer armies of the Baltic countries and the Ukraine.

According to our conductors, something happened shortly thereafter. The cars returned empty and thoroughly cleaned. The passengers did not go on farther east, or the conductors would have known about it. They did not stay at their point of arrival either, for there was not enough room in these districts to accommodate so many people. Why weren't the conductors allowed to travel to the final destination? What happened there? Where had all these people gone? The same answer occurred to everyone, but no one wanted to be the first to state the obvious—that these people were simply being exterminated, not just by the thousands but by the hundreds of thousands. There could no longer be any doubt. Under the guise of transporting the Jews east for resettlement, the Nazis were sending them all to specially constructed extermination camps.

Silberman and the Sacred Scriptures

One morning the maid came into my office to report that there was a farmer outside waiting to see me. I asked him to come in, and he timidly entered the room. He was a man of around seventy named Silberman, tall, lean, with close-cropped hair still rather abundant for his years, darker on top but completely white around the temples. His face was thin, his eyes were bright, and his nose was long with a slight crook. Everything about him bespoke a quiet dignity and the soundness of body which comes from a lifetime of work in the open air. His hands, with their long, work-worn fingers, caught my particular attention. He wore his pants tucked into his boots peasant-style, and in his physiognomy, general appearance, and manner he was indistinguishable from any other local small landholder. Even his manner of speaking was typical of the local peasants. He entered, as I said, very timidly, crushing his cap in one hand and holding a ragged cloth sack containing some shapeless object in the other. He stood in front of my desk, frowned, and began speaking with evident difficulty.

As I looked at him, I recalled that I had done him a favor some two or three weeks earlier. One evening as I was returning from a field next to his farm, our Jewish farm girls were returning by the same route from a meadow where they had been raking hay into stacks for the night. Each of the women carried a rake on her shoulders. I saw Silberman and his wife raking hay and piling it in stacks in a field next to their house. "Why don't you help your countryman over there rake his hay?" I called over to the girls. "It's nothing for you, there are so many of you, but there are only two of them, and old folks at that." Silberman, as I noticed, was pleasantly surprised, but no more so than Herta; in fact, she was amazed, but without a word she quickly led the way to Silberman's field, followed by the other girls.

Now Silberman was standing in front of my desk shifting from one foot to the other and trying to start a conversation. Peasant-style, he began with the weather—nice weather we're having, rain won't spoil the crops, and the like. I could see that something important was on his mind and that he was deeply agitated, but he didn't know how to speak of it. Obviously he had not left the fields in the middle of the day to come to talk to me about the sun and the rain. At last he summoned up his courage and explained what had brought him.

22

Chapter 2

He was not much of a talker and had trouble coming to the point. Jews had been living in this valley for several hundred years, he began. Before the war there had been about ten Jewish families here. Some had moved to town and others had been driven out by the Germans, until he was now the only one left. This morning a Blue Police officer came to his farm and told him that he had to leave his home within a week, for the vicinity was to become *Judenfrei*. He was not yet sure where he would go, but probably to Skawina. He did not much want to move there, but it was the only town where he was not a stranger. He had friends there and thought they might help him find a place to stay, although he realized that this would be difficult as more and more Jews were evacuated from their villages and were settling in Skawina.

But this was not why he had come to see me. For a number of years he had been the head of the local Jewish community; they gathered at his home for prayers. He was the keeper of the Torah, which had been in the village longer than anyone could remember. Now he had to abandon his village. This didn't bother him, he said; his life was almost over in any case; but he was concerned about the fate of the Sacred Scriptures. He felt that I was a good Catholic and that we both believed in the same God. He asked me in the name of that God to take the Torah from him for safekeeping. He asked me to promise by whatever we both held holy to deliver these scriptures to the Jews if peace ever again returned to the earth.

His eyes filled with tears as he continued to speak, but I was no longer listening. I sat at my desk with my head bowed. After a while he fell silent, perhaps thinking that I had fallen asleep. When he saw that this was not so, he too fell silent. After a while I rose from my chair, walked around my desk, and placed my hand on his shoulder. "I swear that if I survive the war and there are still Jews on this earth I will carry out your wish," I said. Before I knew what he was doing, Silberman had seized my hand and was kissing it. Then he pushed his sack into my arms, turned on his heel, and left the office. I stood there for a while trying to think. Finally I hid the Torah in an office cabinet; that night I took it to the granary and buried it deep beneath the wheat. Silberman left the village several days later, and I never saw him again. He undoubtedly perished in an extermination camp.

Soon after the arrival of Soviet troops in Cracow in 1945, a Jewish committee was formed, and I carried Silberman's treasure to committee headquarters on 38 Długa Street. One of the committee workers opened the sack. The Torah was on a long strip of parchment rolled up in equal parts onto two wooden rollers with handles on either end, one for holding and the other for attaching ornaments. Both rollers were bound with tape, and over everything was drawn a dark green protective velvet covering; all this was wrapped in a white linen cloth of the sort Jews use for burying the dead. There were also two richly decorated silver knobs with little bells, to be placed on the upper ends of the rollers. Each bell was carefully wrapped in tissue paper to prevent it from ringing. From the color of the parchment one could see that the Torah was hundreds of years old. The clerk put everything back in the bag and put it together with some other Jewish relics. Then he opened a large book, entered the date and registration number, and noted that it was a Torah; finally, he asked my name and how it had come into my possession.

When I saw the indifference with which Silberman's spiritual treasure was treated, even though common sense told me that it could not be otherwise, I felt that he had been done an injury. When I compared the emotion, pride, and tenderness with which he had described the Sacred Scriptures to the indifference with which it was now received, I felt a great revulsion. I gave the clerk no details, nor did I leave my name. I merely said that I had been asked to deliver the Torah to the committee. The clerk did not press me further, and I felt that I would be abusing Silberman's trust if I described that last meeting with him. These holy scriptures had remained in the same little village for hundreds of years, witnessing the birth, growth, and passing of generation after generation. Now they had become an item on the clerk's list of similar dead things. They would pass into history—without a history.

The Visit of Hans Zwickel

Toward the end of June a high functionary of the Arbeitsamt in Cracow, Hans Zwickel, visited our estate, advising us of it in advance by telephone. Officially he was coming to see whether we had enough workers for the approaching harvest. He added that he would be able to spare only a moment because he was very busy getting ready for a vacation trip home to Germany. We translated this to mean that we were to prepare a hefty package of foodstuffs, even bigger than usual, for him to take home with him. Such was the time-honored custom.

Chapter 2

Herr Zwickel drove up that afternoon in an official car, managing to time his arrival just at the hour of our early supper. An elaborate table was spread for him, including white bread, butter, sausage, ham, and, most important, a large quantity of vodka flavored with fruit syrup. He did not have to be pressed to stay for a meal but immediately made himself comfortable and began gobbling up the good things on the table, washing the food down with copious amounts of vodka. The day was quite hot, and when he had stuffed himself to the limit, he became drunkenly expansive. Slapping me vigorously on the shoulder, he confided that the real reason for his visit was a concern for our well-being. He knew that we had many Jewish workers on our estate who would soon be taken, and we could easily be caught with the harvest to bring in and not enough laborers. I replied that I did not understand why those workers were going to be taken. We were satisfied with them, they were settled in their work, and they would be all we needed until the end of the season. He looked at me out of the corner of his eye.

"These are orders, and orders must be obeyed," he drawled. "The Jews have to be evacuated."

"Where to?" I asked in spite of myself.

"To the disposition of heaven" ("Zum Himmelskommando"), he replied sarcastically.

Noticing the incredulous expression on my face, and wanting to convince me that what he said was true, with the dogged determination of a drunk he took from his pocket a thick, well-worn notebook and began to drone out the names of the towns from which the Jews would be taken and the dates of the deportations. Of the various towns he mentioned, only a few stuck in my memory, such as Cracow, Skawina, and Przemyśl. The date for Skawina was August 29. I was alarmed at this news but tried not to show it, asking about his trip home. Finally he got up, said his farewells, and left, not forgetting, of course, his parcels.

I knew that I had come across a piece of extraordinarily important news, but what was I to do with it? It occurred to me that I once knew an officer in the Holzer Bank in Cracow; as far as I knew, he still worked there. One day, while on an errand in Cracow, I decided to pay this person a visit. Before the war the Holzer Bank was one of the country's more important private financial institutions, with offices in several foreign countries. The currency exchange office was located in the Sukiennice Pavilion on Market Square by Mariacki Plaza. The bank officer I knew was a certain Rosenzweig, whom I had met once by chance. I also knew that a relative of his by the same name was the head of the Cracow ghetto council, so I felt that he would probably be the most responsible person to entrust with my newly acquired information.

I found Rosenzweig in his office. The occupation forces had allowed him to stay at his post even now for the sake of institutional continuity and for his foreign exchange contacts, for he was well known in financial circles abroad. He was quite old and gray-haired, slight in stature. I introduced myself, and he remembered me. I told him that I had obtained authoritative information, from a high-ranking German official, that the Cracow ghetto was to be liquidated, and that I knew from other sources that the deportations were not, as the Germans stated, to the east for work in the former Russian territories but to specially constructed extermination camps. I emphasized over and over that I had my information from the most reliable sources, that he must not ignore my warning but pass it on where it might do some good. I kept repeating: deportation meant certain death.

Rosenzweig received my warning with an indulgent smile. He said that he had been working in the bank with the Germans since the beginning of the war. He was on good terms with them; they valued and respected him; if any such thing were being planned, he would be the first to hear about it. He was used to wild rumors; no one knew who started them and why they spread so quickly. During the first war people had also spread various improbable stories, he told me. "I appreciate your good intentions," he concluded, "and I thank you for going to so much trouble to see me, but I advise you not to concern yourself further with these fabrications. Why frighten people unnecessarily?"

Plainly, I had not convinced this banker, and I did not know what other arguments to make. Rosenzweig was the epitome of respectability. He lived in the ghetto, and each day a Latvian soldier accompanied him to the bank, waited for him there, and walked back with him again at the end of the day. He worked in the bank without an armband, for customers would not have understood what a Jew was doing working in a German bank. The other bank officials were kind and well disposed toward him; he may even have had one or two good friends among them. Perhaps they were perfectly upright and were also in the dark. After all, their business was finance, not murder. I could understand Rosenzweig's attitude: it was simply beyond his comprehension that there were madmen at large engaged in mass extermination.

I was unable to keep my news from the young Potockis, although

I tried to present it in as neutral a way as possible and did not tell them my source. The Potockis were not in the habit of asking questions unless I volunteered information of my own accord, for it was best not to be too curious in these times. I said, in brief, that it was likely that all the Jews would be deported from Skawina, but I did not know where. So we were about to lose our farm workers, and if the deportations occurred before harvest time I would have to go to the Arbeitsamt in Skawina to see about procuring other workers.

The young count and his wife were visibly upset. It was not easy to deceive them, even by speaking circumspectly. The count looked at me sharply and asked, "Is that all you know? Is that all you can tell us?" I gave an evasive answer.

The countess took the news especially badly. For some time she and Herta had been drawing closer. Herta was tutoring her in foreign languages; she would come in from the fields one or two hours before the other girls, change clothes in the manor house, and sit down with the countess in the drawing room. They were both about the same age; they had developed a great respect and affection for each other, and the countess was plainly shaken by the news that Herta was about to be deported. She had no faith in the Germans and knew that any change could only be for the worse.

I told the old count much the same story, in a business context—it looked as though we might have to find more workers soon. I did not suspect that he would be so upset. It was never possible to deceive him, and now, in his customary matter-of-fact style, he put a direct question: "When is the deportation in Skawina going to take place?" he asked. "On the 29th of August," I answered without hesitation.

He too did not press me for the source of my information but was evidently turning something over in his mind. At last he rose and brought our meeting to an end, adding that he would return to the subject again shortly, but that in the meantime I was to say as little about it as possible.

In the middle of August the Arbeitsamt telephoned from Skawina to ask me to call at the office. When I went there the following day, I was informed that the central Arbeitsamt in Cracow had ordered that all Jews be released from existing employment. Those employed in occupations considered vital to the war effort (*Kriegswichtig*) were to be replaced with Polish workers. Our estate belonged to a group designated as vital to the war, so we would have to exchange our workers for others

27

as early as the following week. Since no skilled agricultural labor was available for the moment, I would have to make out as best I could; in any case I could count on having the Jewish workers only until the end of the week.

In addition, I learned that a few days earlier two SS dignitaries had arrived in Skawina and established their quarters in the Franck factory. They had paid a visit to the mayor and informed him that they had no intention of interfering with his affairs but that, as far as the Jews were concerned, they were forthwith released from his jurisdiction and placed under that of the SS. The town was to continue to let in all Jewish settlers. In the course of further conversation at the Arbeitsamt I heard again what I already knew, that both the mayor and the Arbeitsamt expected the imminent deportation of the Jews, although no one knew where they were to be sent.

I returned to the estate and told young Potocki about the order. He advised me to have the final wages ready for the Jewish workers by the end of the week; meanwhile, his wife began wondering how to protect at least Herta from deportation. At her urgent request one of the nearby convents agreed to shelter one person until the end of the war. The countess herself was to take her there at night. She asked me to present this plan to Herta.

Accordingly, toward the end of the week I called Herta into my office and informed her that the Arbeitsamt had directed all Jewish workers to be released that very day; at the same time I set forth the countess' plan. She was not surprised at the first piece of information, for evidently workers had been released from other places even earlier. She did not react immediately to the rescue plan but stood there for a while in silence. At last she began speaking slowly, almost at a whisper, as though talking to herself rather than to me. "It is wonderful of the countess to try to help me," she said. "Please thank her for her kindness and good intentions, but I don't think that I can take advantage of her offer. I came to work here together with the other girls as their leader, and I cannot abandon them now. My parents and fiancé are already dead, killed by the Nazis. These girls are the only family I have, and I must share their fate."

I could think of nothing to say, and she too remained silent. Still she stood there. After a moment she went on: "I have wanted to say something to you for some time, but I haven't had the chance till now. This is probably our last conversation here on earth, and I want to tell

28

you something that has been on my conscience for quite a while. My co-workers and I have been sure that you were a cold, heartless anti-Semite. We thought we could see how you felt about us. But for the past two months, since I have been coming to the manor house to study with the countess, I have seen things more clearly. The Potockis have nothing of the anti-Semite in them, and they would never respect you as they do if you did. An anti-Semite doesn't ask Jewish workers to help an old Jewish farmer rake his hay, and what I have just heard from you makes me certain that we were mistaken. We were deceived by appearances. You see, we Jews have been persecuted for so long that if we meet someone with a different outlook we take it as a sign of prejudice."

I sat there looking at her without knowing what to say. After a moment she said, "I want to leave you some kind of keepsake, but I don't know what. I have nothing." After a moment's thought she unfastened an earring and stretched out her hand to me. I accepted her gift, and she went away. I never saw her or any of her girls again. The earring I have to this day.

The Old Count and the Horse Trader

Several days later I was at the old count's giving him my weekly report. He listened attentively. The deportation of the Jews looked rather suspicious to him. He said he was sure that in their new place of habitation they would have an even harder life than here, perhaps even in concentration camps. No one could predict what the Nazis would do; they were capable of anything, and he did not trust them one inch.

The count always came to the point without beating around the bush. He said that he was interested in seeing a certain Jew in Skawina before the deportation. His name was Schneiderman, a horse trader by profession. "I have bought horses through this Schneiderman," the count said thoughtfully, "and I am convinced that he has always cheated me right and left. But none of that is important now; we are both old men. I would gladly pay any price to save him from deportation. Perhaps we could get him out of Skawina and into the Cracow ghetto."

I told the count that his plan was unrealistic. Skawina was occupied by special SS troops brought in from somewhere else. Jews were no longer allowed to leave the town, and no one had a contact within these new units. The count sat brooding, and I decided to leave. On parting he asked me to find out Schneiderman's exact address in Skawina and promised to visit us the following day.

Before leaving I stopped in to see the count's manager, Miętka-Mikołajewicz, to find out something about this Schneiderman. The Jew was the same age as the count and a most expert judge of horseflesh. When southern Poland was still part of the Austro-Hungarian Empire, he would travel to Hungary to buy horses for the count, and the count had always been proud of having the very best. He never bought or sold a horse without first consulting Schneiderman. They both loved horses and spent hours together talking about their favorite subject. They respected each other sincerely, despite the fact that the count never failed to refer to Schneiderman as "that old swindler." It was hard to say whether this was out of admiration for Schneiderman's expertise or whether his pride did not allow him to admit his liking for Schneiderman. (In the count's circle, it was not customary to praise Jews.)

Next day the old count appeared at Borek Szlachecki. He always drove a black carriage drawn by two beautiful matched Arabian horses, dapple grays, with a liveried coachman. Both the carriage and the horses' harness bore the Potocki arms. He stopped at the estate only for a moment to drop the coachman and pick me up. I took the reins, and we set out for town. I had located Schneiderman's little cottage the day before and drove to his tiny street. We drew up, the count stepped out, went up to the cottage, and knocked on the door. A tiny old Jew, gray as a dove, opened the door. He stood there for a moment blinking in the sunlight and didn't recognize the count, but in a moment his eyes became wide with amazement. He bent to kiss Potocki's hand, but the count raised up his head, hugged him, and kissed him on the cheek. The sight of the two old men crying, embracing, and kissing was deeply moving. A number of passers-by stopped and watched from a distance. There was the carriage, the magnificent horses, the Potocki crest, and the distinguished old man in his dark suit holding an old Jew in a tight embrace. They realized that they were witnessing a human tragedy. At last the count tore himself away, returned with a rapid step to the carriage, and ordered me to drive off. Schneiderman still stood there on the sidewalk sobbing, watching the carriage drive away. On the way back the count spoke not a word, but sat hunched in his corner, lost in thought. He said nothing to anyone on the estate but returned directly to Cracow.

Chapter 2

After this meeting the count fell ill. For many weeks he lay in bed and was said to have "caught a chill." He did not even receive me with my reports. I did not see him again for several months. He was pale and much thinner, his hair a shade grayer, and was even more reticent than before. I never again heard him speak the name of the old horse trader; it was as though he had never existed. The count knew that all the Jews had been deported, and by that time it was common knowledge that the "deportations to the east" were really to the extermination camps.

Chapter 3

Rescuing Maria Friede

Several months before the events described in the last chapter, I met one of our Jewish girls walking with a friend, also a Jew, on the street in Skawina. I recognized the friend's face but could not remember where I had seen her. Several days later, out of curiosity, I asked our worker her friend's name. Though she could not understand my interest in a Jew, she said that it was Maria Friede and that she was from Cracow. The name sounded familiar, and one Sunday, when I was at home, I asked my wife whether the name Friede meant anything to her. She was astonished, and reminded me that Maria was her high school classmate, that I knew her too, and that she had paid us a visit after our marriage. I told my wife that her friend was now living in Skawina. She was deeply concerned and wanted to know more, but I knew nothing further. One day in Skawina I again saw Maria coming out of a small house; later I learned that she lived there. After that I saw her on the street fairly often, although she did not recognize me and I had no desire to renew our acquaintance.

The old count's farewell visit to Schneiderman took place four days before the deportation of the Jews from Skawina. The Jews knew the date of their departure, and the town was in commotion. Everyone watched with grim apprehension as events unfolded. Many Poles had friends among the Jews and were greatly concerned, for it was known that their fate was uncertain.

Many Jews left most of their belongings with friends, expecting to reclaim them after the war, though some sold everything they owned in order to raise the money they thought they would need to start life all over again in a new place. The German regulations specified that they could take with them whatever they could carry, so everyone wanted a rucksack, which held a lot and was easy to carry. Everyone was possessed by this rucksack mania; everyone was looking for one and gazing enviously at the lucky few who had been able to obtain one.

Peasant wagons from nearby villages clogged the streets. The farmers, learning that the Jews were selling their belongings, came to town and bought everything imaginable for practically nothing. Wagons drove along loaded with tables, chairs, beds, mattresses, stoves—even brooms and pots and pans were tied onto the ladder-sided carts. Still other wagons carried Jewish property to friends for safekeeping. The town was bustling with activity, but the atmosphere was far from festive.

I lay awake at night staring at the ceiling. All this was more than I could bear. Were these old men, women, and children—the sick as well as the able-bodied—all, without exception, going to their deaths? Was there no power on earth strong enough to stop it? Perhaps this was only a nightmare from which I would soon awake.

Unfortunately, this was no dream. These representatives of one of the most advanced peoples on earth were preparing the extermination of another, equally advanced culture with all the precision, fussy attention to detail, and cold-blooded efficiency for which the German nation is noted.

Something drew me to Skawina. I had to be a spectator. If I survived the war, I could bear witness to this genocide. Scholars might later disagree as to the number who perished and the reasons for the greatest mass murder in human history, but would there be any person left to describe the lives, feelings, fears, and sufferings of these people? And even were I to describe all this, who would believe me? People would say that what I had seen was impossible, the delusions of a diseased mind. Nevertheless, I determined that human disbelief would not keep me from my account.

Since I could enter and leave Skawina without difficulty, I went there daily. I saw more and more SS troops arrive, members of a special detachment. After the war I learned that these detachments were called "Einsatzgruppen" and had been formed the previous year, in 1941. When Hitler invaded the Soviet Union, these specially selected troops, consisting of Germans and volunteer detachments from the Ukraine and the Baltic countries, followed the invading armies into the heartland of Russia, murdering the entire Jewish population. Now, a year later, they were engaged in transporting the Jews of Poland to the extermination camps.

The unnatural commotion in town had been in progress for two days. August 27 arrived, two days before the deportation. More and more SS troops poured into town. Two soldiers walked past me, and I heard them speaking Ukrainian. The exits from town were manned as usual by a group of SS accompanied by a local Blue Police officer. I left my carriage at the miller's and walked around town alone, trying to take in everything. I stopped in the town square. The sweet shop was closed, and the owner, a woman I knew, was standing outside on the street. I asked whether she had been ordered to close her store, but she shook her head; she just did not want to open it and give these dogs anything to eat.

I headed for the part of town where Maria Friede lived. A blond-haired, thin girl with a tear-stained face, perhaps seventeen years old, was coming out of Maria's house in the company of a somewhat older boy, his head completely shaved. I went up to them.

"Does Maria Friede live in this house?" I asked.

"Yes," the girl replied, bursting into tears again. "She is my teacher. I went to say goodbye to her. I would give anything to save her." She was unable to say more, her every word smothered in sobs.

I told the two young people that I was the manager of the estate in Borek Szlachecki and that I did not know Maria personally, but friends of mine who did know her had asked me to see whether I could do anything to help her. I had no idea what help I could give, but if they wanted to help her too, perhaps they could come out early next morning to our estate. In the meantime I would try to think of some plan.

I returned to Borek Szlachecki. After supper I went to my room and opened the window. The evening was lovely, warm, and peaceful. Even today, I can remember what a beautiful summer that was. I sat by the window and thought back over the events of the war, about my decision to live on the sidelines of these momentous events, to play it safe and look after my own skin. Now I had to re-examine these principles. The very idea of trying to save Maria was contrary to every rule by which I had been living. The chances of success were minimal, and the price for failure was so terrible that I could not contemplate it. Wasn't this too high a price to pay for trying to save one individual? On the other hand,

Chapter 3

I thought, had I really grown so insensitive to human suffering? These madmen were condemning thousands of people to death; was I, who had a chance to do something, to remain aloof only because I had vowed to do so? I felt that I had to try something. I could not just stand by and watch.

Once I had made my decision, I felt quite calm. The price for failure was death, and I had to spell this out to Maria's young friends. They seemed to view things a little too romantically; they might not realize the price they would pay if things went wrong. Next I realized that I would have to work out a detailed plan to see whether a rescue operation was feasible. How would Maria's friends behave? How would she herself react? How long would the operation take? What time of day would be best? Where could we take her when we got her away from Skawina? How would we obtain new identification papers and employment somewhere for her where she would be safe and secure until the end of the war?

It was sunrise by the time I had worked out a scheme that seemed not only simple but also to have the makings of success. I had breakfast and then took to my office a scarf and a duster which the young countess usually wore in the summer when she rode to town in the open carriage. I told our groom that I would be taking the carriage to Skawina shortly after nine o'clock and asked him to hitch up two fast horses. I told the maid that some people would be coming around nine o'clock to see about doing some work for us, and that she should show them in directly, since I had to go to town.

I then sat down at my desk and wrote two long letters. One was to the young Potockis, explaining that I had decided to rescue a certain person in Skawina. I asked them to look after my wife and daughter, to see that they had enough to eat, if I were to be arrested or killed. I also asked them to forgive me for taking such a rash step; it was too late now to discuss the matter with them in any case. Then I drew up a detailed summary of the business affairs of the estate up to that date, including a list of the names of my business contacts, both personal and institutional, and attached it to my letter. The second letter was addressed to my wife. I asked her, too, to forgive me for what I was about to do, and told her that it was difficult to explain my state of mind but that, in order to keep up the struggle for survival, I had to have respect for myself. It was no longer possible to stand by and watch others go to their deaths. If I did not act now, I would be unable to carry on in the future.

I realized that it would not be easy for her to understand my decision; I simply felt that I could not act otherwise.

I walked across the yard into the horse barn and showed the groom the horses I wanted to take to Skawina at nine. Then I inspected the granary, locked the door, and pocketed the key. I walked through the other barns and stopped to examine one barn completely filled with straw. None of this was necessary; I was just killing time, waiting until nine and wondering whether the couple I had met yesterday would appear. Perhaps they had had second thoughts. My entire plan depended on their help.

They came at nine exactly and I wasted no time. I told them that I had worked out a plan which might work, but one could never be sure. Something unexpected might happen, and we could be caught. I asked them whether they realized that failure might well mean death. I asked them to swear that if we were successful, and ever met again, in Skawina or anywhere else, they would never speak to me, much less suggest to anyone that we shared a secret. For as long as the war lasted, they were never to try to find out what had become of Maria Friede. They went out of the barn to talk things over privately. After a few minutes they returned and told me that they understood and agreed to everything. Then I outlined my plan to them.

Shortly after nine o'clock the groom drew the carriage up in front of the manor house. I told him that I would drive myself to Skawina and take these two people back with me, for they had come here on foot. He was not surprised, for I often drove to town alone. Once off the estate, I took out the countess' duster and long white scarf. The girl put on the coat and pinned the scarf over her head. Next to her sat the boy, attracting attention to his shaven head. I was on the driver's box. As we entered town we passed the guard next to the Franck factory. Two SS men and a local Blue Police officer were standing guard. The Polish policeman knew me, and I waved to him and drove onto the bridge that crossed the river into town. The carriage halted on a quiet little street not far from the house in which I expected to find Maria. I got down, and the boy moved over to my place and took up the reins. The girl and I went up to the house; I knocked and without waiting for an answer we opened the door and stepped inside.

Maria was standing by the window. At the sound of the door opening she turned and cried out in fright. I could not blame her, for I was not too encouraging a sight. My trousers were tucked into my boots peasant-fashion, my shirt was unbuttoned, and my hair was tangled from the wind. It would have been easy to be frightened. Maria quickly bent down to one corner of the carpet on the floor—perhaps she had poison there. I did not reflect on the possibility but caught hold of the arm stretched out toward the carpet and said, distinctly and calmly, "Maria! Basia sent me—your school friend—I have come to save you!" I don't know whether she heard all I said, but she did hear the words "Basia, your school friend."

"Basia? Where is she?" she cried.

I promised that I would tell her everything later. Her pupil in the meantime tore off her duster and scarf, dressed Maria in the coat and tied the scarf on her head exactly as she had worn it. Maria and I rushed out of the house, leaving her pupil behind. She was to return home quietly once we were safely away. I led Maria to the carriage and put her in the rear seat. The boy got in beside her, and I took my place on the box. With a crack of the whip we were on our way back toward the estate along the same road. The whole thing had taken ten minutes at most.

We crossed the bridge over the river again and passed in front of the Franck factory. The guards were still standing by the entrance, where the road turned right. The Blue Policeman left the group of guards and walked toward the oncoming carriage. In another moment he would see that it was not the countess: he would discover our trick. I prayed for the end to come quickly and painlessly. Instead of turning the horses to the right along the road as I should have done, I barely tugged at the reins. My arms felt paralyzed. Perhaps I didn't turn the horses at all—perhaps they themselves veered to the right toward home. They almost brushed against the approaching policeman, who jumped back out of their way. Now I tried to pull up, but he waved us on. All this time the SS men were paying not the slightest attention.

I gave the horses their heads, and they trotted on briskly. Five hundred meters further on we entered a woods; only now did a reaction set in. I was seized by an uncontrollable fit of laughter, or maybe sobbing. My passengers had not even noticed our near-disaster. I stopped the carriage and told the boy to walk back to town, as we had planned. Then I took the duster and scarf from Maria, and she rode on as a regular passenger.

As long as I live I will never forget that bridge, the bend in the road, the startled face of the policeman, my fit of laughter, and the sudden change in our situation. We had made it! We were alive and well and on our way home. We drove to the granary. I took out the keys from my pocket, opened the door, let Maria inside, then locked it up tight. Then I returned the countess' duster and scarf to their usual place, entered my office, and resumed my daily routine. That evening I transferred Maria to the barn and made her a hiding place on an enormous stack of unthreshed wheat.

After dinner I told the Potockis that I wished to speak with them. They were intrigued by the fact that I wanted to talk to them at such an hour in the evening; this was completely unheard of. They were even more surprised when I said that I would prefer to talk outside, where we could be sure of not being overheard. They assented, and we strolled along in silence. I hesitated to break the silence, and they waited for me expectantly. Before long we came to the barn in which Maria was hidden.

It was not easy for me to begin, but finally, without further ado, I told them that in the barn, at the very top of the wheat, a friend of my wife's was hidden, her best friend from high school, a Jew. I asked them to forgive me for presuming to hide her there without their knowledge and permission, but it had all happened so suddenly that there had been no time to seek their advice. In two days' time I promised to take her to my house in Cracow, but for the time being I had no choice but to keep her hidden here, and I thought that I had chosen the best hiding place. I could stand guard at night to make sure no one entered the barn, but during the day it would appear suspicious for me to hang around there. I asked them both to see to it that no one removed anything from the barn during the day. Next day the deportation of Jews from Skawina would be over, and the woman would be gone.

I had said all that I had to say, and the Potockis did not ask for more information. Doubtless there were many questions they would have liked to ask. When and how had I gotten her to the estate so that no one saw and no one knew? What was my wife doing with a Jewish friend, with such an anti-Semitic husband? Did I realize that I was endangering not only myself but also them and the entire estate? We slowly turned toward the house. As we parted, the countess gave me her hand.

"Never fear," she said matter-of-factly. "Jerzy and I will watch the barn." Jerzy nodded his head in agreement.

Two days after the deportation of the Jews from Skawina, I took Maria to our house. I didn't want to keep her on the estate any longer, for sooner or later someone would discover her. I knew that the SS men had already left Skawina, and life in the town had returned to normal, if one could call it that.

Before dawn Maria crawled down off the stack of wheat, washed up, and had some breakfast. Before four o'clock, when people began to stir on the estate, we stole away to the Wielkie Drogi train station in the carriage driven by our trusted coachman Żmuda. We waited until six o'clock for the passenger train from Oświęcim to Skawina. I knew from the schedule that there would be a fifteen-minute layover in Skawina while we waited for a connection from Wadowice. That stop would be dangerous; Maria would have to be hidden someplace. As we rode to Skawina I had her go into the lavatory and lock the door. I took up a position in front of the door, as though waiting my turn. Luck was with us; no one tried to use the lavatory during the stop. In any case I was ready for such an eventuality: I was here first; you can go to another car. Several minutes later we were at the Cracow-Swoszowice station, and here we got off and walked for a few hundred meters across the fields to my little house on the main road on Zakopane Street.

When we came in, Basia stared at us in amazement. She did not expect me, nor did she know that I had had any contact with Maria. In fact, she knew nothing about the Jewish deportation and had no idea why Maria was suddenly here in our house. This is not to say, of course, that she wasn't delighted, but she was also consumed by curiosity. I told her that unfortunately I had to go back immediately, for the train from Cracow to Skawina left in fifteen minutes, but that Maria would tell her everything. I said goodbye and left.

On the way back I had to laugh at my assurance that Maria would explain "everything." What, after all, would Maria be able to explain? She had just learned that I was Basia's husband: what was I doing in Skawina? Where had she been hidden for the past three days? What was my present position? How had I learned of her existence? She had no answers to any of these questions; most of them Basia herself would have to answer.

Maria learned the details of her rescue only thirty-five years later, when I began writing this book. This woman must have been born under a lucky star. When everyone in Skawina was getting ready for "resettlement to the east," and the rucksack mania was breaking out, her friends wanted to know whether she had found herself a rucksack yet. Maria replied apathetically that she hadn't. She somehow had a presentiment that she wouldn't be needing it.

I: The Estate of Borek Szlachecki, 1942

As I took Maria to our house I said not a word about the deportation of the Jews in Skawina which I had witnessed and which is described in the following chapter. Maria stayed with us for about two weeks, after which she left for the west, to the vicinity of Częstochowa, by this time provided with new "Aryan" papers. There she lived through the war as governess to the children of the Częstochowa District forest inspector. Her new birthday was to be August 28, a date which she celebrates to this day.

Chapter 4

The Deportation of the Jews

On August 29, 1942, the day after Maria Friede's rescue, the deportation of the Jews from Skawina began. I drove to town first thing in the morning, wanting to see everything at first hand. The evacuation was already in full swing. The preceding evening a special train for transporting the Jews had drawn up to the station, made up of closed boxcars with barred windows as well as passenger cars. The passenger cars were for the troops responsible for running the deportation—additional detachments of SS shock troops. The floors of the boxcars were covered with straw, under which quicklime had probably been spread. The train was diverted onto a siding some two kilometers from the main station.

In the morning one SS division sealed off the town in order to prevent last-minute escapes, while other troops took part in the action proper. The Jews had been instructed to assemble in the marketplace at nine o'clock. Each could bring whatever he could carry. They began to assemble at the appointed time. In the meantime, the SS, assisted by the Blue Police, searched all Jewish homes. They turned everything inside out—apartments, pantries, storerooms, shops, barns, courtyards, even nearby fields. Of course, they did not find anyone. No one was going to hide even in the best of places, only to come out several hours later to be caught and shot. While this house-by-house search was taking place,

41

other soldiers formed the victims into columns and started them toward the station.

The town appeared to be under complete evacuation. The columns of Jews moved along slowly, weighed down with bundles, rucksacks, and suitcases—each person carrying whatever he considered most valuable or essential. One old man pushed a two-wheeled cart with his sick wife in it. A two-year-old girl carried in her tiny hands her most important possession, a little chamberpot. Here and there the stronger helped the weaker. Some people, struggling under the weight of heavy bundles, had further burdened themselves on this hot August day with heavy winter coats, since the east, where they were to be resettled, was known for its bitter winters.

The columns moved along in silence; the people walked quietly and with dignity, as though sensing that this was, for them, a final journey. At their side marched the grim-faced SS troops. The Poles lined the sidewalks, looking on in absolute silence, as though frozen in place. Not far from the depot a narrow dirt road wound along beside the railroad tracks, and it was along this path that the SS marched the Jews to the boxcars, ready for the deportation. I ordered our coachman to turn the carriage around, and we drove back through the town to the estate.

The Eyewitness

Several weeks later I met an acquaintance who worked on the railroad and lived not far from the tracks where the final act in the drama of the Skawina Jews was played. He and his wife peeked out of a little attic window to see what the "deportation" looked like.

The Jews, he said, were drawn up alongside the train and ordered to lay down all their belongings by the side of the road. Then, from the direction of the train, another contingent of SS appeared armed with rifles and clubs and holding frenzied German shepherds on leashes. As if on command, they suddenly rushed on the crowd and began to drive them into the boxcars. The frightened people, driven along by screams and blows from all sides, desperately tried to climb into the cars. Those who fell along the way were bludgeoned to death by SS clubs. The rest were packed into the cars as tightly as was physically possible; the children and those killed on the road were then thrown in on top. The car doors were bolted. This hellish scene, accompanied by piteous wailing

42

and shrieking, was enacted next to each boxcar until at last all doors were shut and locked. The precious packages, rucksacks, and suitcases put down by the roadside were tossed into the last two cars.

Although the cottage of the railroad worker was a slight distance away, he said that the cries, screams, and moans of the condemned were as clear as if they were next to his house. By afternoon the cries were weaker; by evening he could hear nothing. That night a locomotive was hooked up to the train and took it away. Although this was over two weeks ago, the railroadman trembled and shook as he related his story. It was a sight he would never forget.

I have left out many details of this man's story to spare both myself and the reader the pain, shame, and humiliation of knowing that the perpetrators of these deeds were fellow human beings. I had seen these "select" SS individuals at close quarters many times. Each time I wondered where in the world such men had been found, and who could have turned them into such beasts.

On the estate work went on, as it had to, but one could feel the tension in the air. Everyone knew about the deportation and what it meant. We were too near Oświęcim not to know. Almost everyone had a friend or relative from that area, so we knew that the stench of burned human flesh hung over the entire district.

We had lost thirty workers, almost half our work force, and the Arbeitsamt had not replaced them; they had no more to give. The Jews had filled many sorts of jobs, and now all employers were demanding replacements. With the beginning of September, we did not need as many hands as before, but we could not run the estate without any extra help at all, so we made do with whoever we could. The farmhands brought their wives, the seasonal workers brought their sisters and friends, and several Polish girls from Borek Szlachecki applied to us for work. However, the atmosphere had changed. A feeling of sorrow and emptiness settled over our estate, which once had been so lively. Perhaps the Jewish workers had not been the equal of our village-trained girls, and perhaps now and again we had laughed at them for their clumsiness, but they were, after all, young people who talked, laughed, and even joked. Now, wherever we turned, there was emptiness; really, their absence was more keenly felt than their presence had been. Thirty young healthy beings had suddenly ceased to exist, had become a memory.

Betrayal

The countess' maiden name was Straszewski. Her mother and three younger sisters lived in Cracow; I knew nothing of her father. Not a week went by without the countess visiting her family, and the sisters often dropped in at the estate too. The eldest of the three sisters, Teresa, was a rare beauty, smooth-skinned, with rich blond hair, dark eyes, and heavy eyebrows. She spoke little and smiled rarely. Evidently very capable, she was really the head of the family in spite of her age—only twenty-one. The middle sister, nicknamed Kika, was her opposite— plump, merry, talkative, always laughing, and adored by everyone. The youngest was only twelve—a thin, lively, inquisitive girl, always asking questions and wanting to know about everything that went on at the estate. They were all delightful company, and I liked them very much. Their mother never came to the estate. Whenever I was in Cracow on business I would look in on them, at the countess' request, bringing them something or taking something back, picking up news or passing on something of interest. I enjoyed these visits.

One day, as I was setting out for the city, the countess, as usual, asked me to deliver some small package to her mother, admonishing me not to forget. The Straszewskis lived in a rented apartment on the second floor. The youngest sister would usually race to the door and, when she saw me, would shout at the top of her voice, "Mr. Szatyn is here!"

This time when she opened the door she was silent, but I paid no particular attention to it at the time. I came in, went down the long hall, and turned into the brightly lit drawing room. Mrs. Straszewski was there, together with Teresa, Kika, and some other girl with dark hair and an olive complexion. I noticed her large, dark eyes, in which I could see a trace of fear. All of them except the mother looked at me intently while introducing the girl, who mumbled her name under her breath. Then everyone fell silent.

Oh ho, I thought to myself: I have come at a bad time, evidently interrupting some argument or discussion, for everyone just sat there looking at me as though I were in the way. As usual, I started chatting in a casual way, but when this got no response, I handed over my package, asked whether they had anything to send the countess, and made the excuse that it was late and I had to be getting back. They made no attempt to detain me, so I said goodbye and drove back to the estate.

We were right in the middle of the harvest, and I spent almost every day in the manor yard. I noticed something strange: the count hardly spoke to me at all. Normally he would greet me effusively, ask about news or the schedule for the day, and often suggest that we ride into the fields or into Skawina, but now he seemed to be avoiding me. I thought to myself, not without smiling, that there must be some tempest brewing in Cracow at the Straszewskis, and now it had reached us here on the estate. Evidently they were in some kind of trouble, but it was none of my business, especially if they were not going to tell me about it.

Then one day, when the count and I were together in the barn, he grew irritated at the steward. "What sort of Jew's business is this?" he snapped. I was taken aback. I knew that he did not like the steward and even intended to replace him sooner or later, but what did that have to do with "Jew's business"? Jerzy had never used this expression before. Was he still feeling the effects of the deportation of the Jews?

Two days later in my office he again suddenly lashed out at me. "You're wriggling like a Jew!" he said. I was sitting on the windowsill discussing some business or other, and his comment simply made no sense in the conversation. I could see that he was upset, so, making no reply, I got up and walked out the door, leaving him alone in the office.

I walked into the fields, at first unable even to ask myself what had happened. Then I began thinking over the events of the past two weeks, especially my visit to the Straszewskis. First, as I was leaving for Cracow, the countess had reminded me to call at her mother's, something she had never done before, for she knew that I was not forgetful. Next there was the behavior of the sisters, even the youngest, and the business of this strange girl with those frightened eyes. I was sure that I had seen those eyes somewhere before. Who was she? Had that meeting been some kind of confrontation? Jerzy's behavior, his avoidance of me, his earlier remark, completely out of character, and now his recent jibe, "You're wriggling like a Jew"—suddenly everything became clear, and I was overcome by a great sadness.

I turned back to the house and went to my office to think. The cook brought me dinner on a tray, but I told her to take it away and to send the chambermaid to me. When she came, I asked her to go upstairs and ask the count to come down to my office, for I had something important to say.

I stood next to the open window and looked into the distance. It was fifteen minutes or more before the count came down. The door to my office was open; I turned around as I heard him enter. "What is so important that it can't wait until morning?'' The count was shrill. When he was upset his voice rose, and he was speaking in just such a voice. I took firm hold of the windowsill and made a tremendous effort to control myself. "Count Jerzy," I said, "you suspect me of being a Jew. You are right: I am. I have put my whole heart into this estate because I loved it and because I felt safe here, but no longer. Please accept my resignation. I can leave tomorrow if you like, or I can stay until you find someone to replace me. That is all that I have to say.''

One could have heard a pin drop. The count stood there dumbfounded, his mouth open. He certainly had not expected such an outburst from me. Finally he asked me to stay right where I was until he came back. He ran upstairs to his rooms and returned in a few moments, still agitated, with the countess. The countess began, "My husband has told me what happened a moment ago. I think that he has behaved badly and in poor taste, and he feels it himself. I apologize for his behavior. In his defense I can only say that he took it amiss that you had not told him who you really were. It was that girl at my mother's who revealed that you were a Jew, a lawyer from Cracow.''

As I made no attempt to reply, she continued: "In my opinion, your reaction to what has happened, while it is understandable and might seem reasonable, is simply not practical. If you are really concerned about your safety and the welfare of your family, which I do not doubt for a moment, then resigning from your job here would be the worst thing you could possibly do. Locally it would attract attention, and wherever else you went you would be a stranger, under constant surveillance. Here everyone knows you and no one suspects a thing. As far as we are concerned,'' she continued, "we would be very sorry to see you go, for we wouldn't be able to explain it even to our own father without telling the truth, and that would be letting more people in on the secret. No, I feel that you ought to stay here, and I speak for both of us in swearing that you will never again experience any unpleasantness. We would like you to consider that the incident never happened.''

I thanked both of them for their kindness but asked them to be patient. I had an important decision to make, and I preferred to wait until the next day before making up my mind. They agreed and went back to their rooms, while I went outdoors into the cool night to gather my thoughts. The moon was shining brightly, undimmed by a single cloud. The stony ground and wheat stubble in the fields were as clear as in daylight. Somewhere in the distance a dog was barking; here and there birds settling down for the night were twittering; the crickets had begun their night-time conversations; and from a nearby pond frogs were making a din. An immense sadness came over me at the thought of leaving all this behind. I had come to love these meadows and fields, the pond and the far-off forest. After years of turmoil I had come to know peace here—peace in which I could concentrate on saving those closest to me.

The countess was right: my sudden departure from the estate would set people talking, possibly with fatal consequences. On the other hand, my situation on the estate had changed radically. I would no longer be able to work as before. The friendship of the Potockis had been my mainstay; now, in spite of all their reassuring words, I felt that my job could no longer be the same to me.

If I did leave, I thought, as I walked along, I really would not have to worry about finding work. Next to us was the Polanka-Haller estate, which before the war belonged to General Stanisław Haller.* It had been seized by the Germans and was now run by them. It was much larger, richer, and better outfitted than ours, with first-rate farm machinery, high-grade cattle, fertile land, ample forests, and water. The Germans had installed their own Treuhänder, or commissar, to run it, a man named Kepper. He was an East Prussian farmer no longer fit for service at the front. I often visited him, as neighborly custom demanded, and found him an unhappy man. He knew no Polish and so could not talk freely with his Polish workers; he saw and felt the hostility of everyone around him. To make his situation worse, night after night the estate was raided by armed bands of Polish partisans. He would sit locked up in his rooms while they calmly rifled the storerooms and took whatever they needed. It was only because he put up no resistance that he remained alive and brought no harm to others. He was sick of the whole business and longed for his far-away home and wife, but each time he requested return to Germany, his superiors refused on the grounds that they had no one to replace him. Whenever I visited him he tried to convince me to take charge of his estate; this would be an important step up for me, he argued. Each time, I explained that it was true that the Polanka-Haller property was magnificent, but that my family

---

*Stanisław Haller (1872-1940), a general under the Austrians and later in the newly formed Polish army following World War I, perished in Soviet captivity at the outset of World War II.

had served the Potockis since time immemorial; were it not for that, I would have made the change without hesitation, I assured him gravely.

Now I remembered the German's offer. I knew that my stay in Borek Szlachecki was, despite the Potockis' arguments, at an end. Until now they had had no reason to think of danger connected with Jews. Now they would tremble whenever a German inspector stopped by. Hiding a Jew was punishable by death, and it would be only a matter of time before the count and countess would feel acute relief at the prospect of my departure. As for what people would say, my transfer to Polanka-Haller would be understood as a desire to improve my status, an excellent pretext, and appearances were all-important here. Perhaps the Potockis would be strong enough not to be concerned about the fact that they were hiding a Jew; perhaps not. I finally decided that it would be better to leave matters as they stood for now, and not to take impulsive action.

I still did not understand exactly how my secret had come out. I learned the details several weeks later. From my behavior and my clear dislike of close contact with our Jewish workers, the Potockis had concluded (and they were not alone in this) that I did not like Jews—I did them no harm, but I did not like them. At the same time they saw me as a calm, rational person, someone who would never act rashly, so they were doubly astounded when I took a step which could easily have brought about my own ruin and that of my entire family. To save someone from the jaws of death, and on top of it, a Jew! That was beyond their understanding. On the other hand, they were proud that a Pole had managed to find a chink in the German armor and, under the very noses of the SS, in broad daylight, without force or bloodshed, to rescue a person condemned to death. They were consumed by curiosity, wondering how I had done this, but they were too tactful to ask, and I did not volunteer the information on my own.

As for the countess, she had tried to be discreet on the estate, but at her mother's and sisters' house rumors and tales got started. At this time a girl from Cracow was working as a seamstress for Mrs. Straszewski. The Straszewskis knew that she was Jewish and was using false papers. As bad luck would have it, she was there one day while the countess was telling the amazing story of the Jewish woman who had been snatched from the middle of Skawina, filled with Germans, and taken to the estate. Of course, my name, Szatyn, came up again and again. The seamstress listened quietly, but finally she said, "I know that man. His name is Dr. Schatten.* He's not an agricultural engineer at all. He's a lawyer from Cracow, a Jew. He was a friend of my brother.''

She was right. She was the younger sister of Doctor Liebeskind, whom I knew quite well. When I last saw her she was still a child, and so I hadn't recognized her. Everyone laughed at her remark, for I had been working on the estate for a long time—I had been there even longer than the Potockis. However, Miss Liebeskind kept insisting that she was right, and went on to describe my appearance exactly. At this point the sisters became alarmed, and the countess, to settle the matter once and for all, sent me to her mother's on that errand. Then the girl acted stupidly a second time: instead of calmly saying that she had made a mistake, she began to cry and passionately denied everything she had told them earlier. Her outburst of tears and violent denials, of course, only served to convince the sisters that her first statement was true.

Count Jerzy still had a faint hope that it was all a mistake; he couldn't believe that someone with whom he talked and worked every day could have so deceived him. He went about the estate upset, and as he could not resolve the matter honorably, he began trying to provoke me. At first his attacks were mild, but when he saw that they had no effect, he increased his efforts, finally rousing me to anger. Once that did happen, he was frightened at the consequences. I could see that both he and his wife really wanted to forget my whole story and put things back as they were. Unfortunately, their discovery of my secret had changed our relationship drastically. None of us could turn back the page.

My thoughts raced. My life had completely changed. Not one soul on the estate had known I was Jewish until now. Those Polish friends and acquaintances whom I knew and trusted did not know where I lived or worked. Now, at one stroke, so many people had found out about me—the count, the countess, her three sisters, her mother, even Miss Liebeskind. My personal danger had increased a thousand-fold, but, strangely enough, I wasn't brooding about that. I was thinking about our Jewish workers who had been taken away to the extermination camp, and about old Silberman with his Torah. When I asked our Jewish workers to help him and his wife rake and stack their hay,

---

*The girl's identification depends in part on the virtually identical pronunciation of "Schatten" (in German, "shadow") and the author's assumed Polish name, "Szatyn" ("auburn"). The present spelling, "Shatyn," was adopted when the author became an American citizen in 1968.—*Tr.*

I: The Estate of Borek Szlachecki, 1942

Silberman was too grave an individual to show surprise, but he did remark to his wife in Yiddish, "Look, what a decent fellow!" I had also noted Herta's surprise at my suggestion. That had been reckless of me, and because of that incident Silberman had chosen me to keep his holy books. When he stood behind my desk that day while I sat with my head lowered, he thought that I was asleep. He had no glimmering of my inner tribulation.

And the girls? They had taken me for a racist. When they wanted to talk about me to my face, they spoke Yiddish. One day one of them had evidently been sent to straighten my room, for as I was out in the fields not far away I heard one girl say to another, "Look at the great lord! He can't abide Jews but he doesn't mind sleeping under a Jewish quilt." My quilt, pillow, and pillowcases were covered with a light blue satin fabric bearing the hand-sewn monogram of my wife. It was a Jewish custom that when a girl married, her parents outfitted her with such things. Only a Jewish girl would have noticed it. No wonder that I avoided them; they were dangerously observant.

And Herta—we could have rescued her. Why didn't she want to fight? She had gone to her death in the name of solidarity, but what had she accomplished by it? And our laborer, the converted Jew? Changing his religion was his own affair, but adopting Christianity merely to get a post in a government office was despicable. I despised him for being a toady and for talking disparagingly about the Jews. His own brother, with whom he lived and whose generosity he exploited, was a Jew. He never tired of defaming the Jews to the workers, knowing full well how offensive this was to the Jews among them. Of course, he did this only to emphasize his separation from them. He was indeed contemptible, but in no way did even he deserve to perish in the extermination camp.

I looked up again at the clear, bright sky. The flickering of thousands of tiny lights in the firmament always comforted me; I always found them in the same place. The North Star was my constant companion at night whenever I wandered in unfamiliar surroundings. It was my most faithful friend, never abandoning me; I could trust it to set my direction. I had no fear of the stars and expected no dangerous surprises from them. Each and every one was a true and faithful friend. It was people here on earth that I feared; from them I always expected "surprises." I could see that my struggle for survival thus far had been a trifle compared to what lay ahead.

50

PART II

Przemyśl and Cracow: Childhood and Youth

Chapter 5

My Father

My father came from a family of farmers that had settled at the foot of the Carpathian Mountains near Ustrzyki Dolne. The land grew oats and not much else. Most people worked in the lumber business, cutting down the trees on the slopes of the mountains in summer, and carting them to the railroad junction in Ustrzyki Dolne in winter. There they would be shipped around the world.

From his earliest years my father was captivated by lumbering. For him it was a symbol of his beloved forests and mountains. He could not abide enclosed spaces and felt comfortable only in the outdoors. When he was thirty-two years old he left Ustrzyki Dolne to marry my mother and settle in the vicinity of Przemyśl, in the lowlands, where he sold farm equipment. His customers were for the most part Ruthenians (as Ukrainians who were Austrian subjects were called) from the Carpathians. He loved to return to Ustrzyki Dolne and breathe the brisk mountain air, walk the crooked, narrow roads, plunge into the wild, dark, mysterious forests with their familiar fragrances. I inherited this love for the mountains and forests from him.

Logging in the Carpathians

In 1923, when I was twelve, my father took me with him on one of his trips back home. It was winter, and all the local farmers were busy

53

carting the logs to the nearest railroad junction. No one who has not seen it can possibly imagine the experience and skill required to bring logs out of the mountain forests. The forest blend there was varied and abundant; plenty of oak, maple, hornbeam, willow, and larch, with beech and fir predominating. The beech, when it was mature—that is, when it was over one hundred and twenty years old—was a particularly valuable and sought-after export commodity. Gray alder, on the other hand, was considered a weed. Some called it the forest's herald, or the outpost of the woods, for it secured the land first, to yield later to sturdier and more valuable types over hundreds of years.

Trees were cut and trimmed of their branches in the summer and left to lie until winter, when it was easiest to transport them. My father and I helped in the logging operations on this particular trip. Each log was at least fifteen meters long and one meter across and weighed over ten tons. The loggers used small strong runners. One set of runners was placed under each end of the log, which looked like a long, thick pipe. The snowy roads down the mountain, even though smoothed by the loads of previous parties, were very dangerous, for they were steep and narrow, and there was a sheer drop at the edge. One driver sat on the front of the rig and guided the horses. The turns had to be taken with great precision because it was easy to snag a log on a tree growing along the roadside, and then all the loggers' trouble was for nothing. The log had to be cut loose and sent crashing down the precipice at the edge of the road. In the rear, on the end of the stump, sat two more drivers. Their task was to help steer with the rear runners and to brake, for this massive load could skid on the slick steep trail at any moment and hurtle down the mountain like a torpedo, crushing the horses under its enormous weight and smashing to pieces on the first turn. The rear drivers sat on the stump back to back, each of them looking after one side of the stump, each with a stout pole ending in a steel spike. Whenever the road grew steeper, the front driver would call out "Ho-ho!" which meant that the road was steep but straight. Then each rear driver would dig into the snow on his side with his pole at the same time and with the same force. This was simple braking; the force with which the cutting edge of the pike dug into the snow was proportional to the steepness of the slope. If the road dropped off and turned to the right, the driver called out "Hetta-ho!" which meant, "Down and to the right!" Then one rear driver braked less strongly and one more strongly, and thus helped the load make the turn. Finally, the call "Wiśta-ho!" announced a drop-off and a turn to the left, requiring the opposite operation. These three words—*hetta, ho,* and *wiśta*—sufficed for all possible situations. I sat proudly on the log up front, while my father, holding a pole in his hand, was a rear driver. The log moved quietly, quickly, and menacingly down the steep trail. The biting cold air stung our faces. My father's hair was blowing in the wind; his eyes shone: he was in his element, entrusted with an important and responsible job. How he loved to work in that wintry mountain air!

From that day on I began to understand my father. He was a typical child of the mountains; just being there made him happy. He had no fear of anything, was kindly toward everyone, lent a willing hand where it was needed. He was erect as a pine, and just as thin, with a thick shock of beautiful hair.

My Mother

My mother was a completely different sort of person. She was a Katz, a family well known for its priests and rabbis. According to family tradition, the Katzes could trace their origin to the first priest of Israel, Aaron. After the fall of the Jewish state, they immigrated to Toledo, Spain. They left Spain in the fifteenth century because of religious persecution and settled in Poland. They had lived in the Przemyśl vicinity for four centuries, and the rabbinical profession was passed from father to son until the end of the nineteenth century. At the family's special request the Hapsburg court in Vienna gave the family the name of Katz, an abbreviation for "Kohen-Tzedek," or "judge of peace." The Katzes performed the office of justice of the peace together with that of rabbi. My mother's father was the first to break with tradition, retaining the title of justice of the peace but not that of rabbi, performing the lay functions of his office but not the religious duties. He founded the local Jewish synagogue and represented the local community before the state government and even before the court in Vienna. He was also well-to-do, and enjoyed the respect and trust not only of the Jewish population but also of the neighboring Gentiles.

I do not know how much legend is mixed with truth in this story, but certainly the Katzes had been rabbis and representatives of the local Jewish community in Przemyśl for centuries. My mother constantly stressed her noble origins, considering that she had married beneath herself; instead of marrying into a rabbinical family she had taken a man of the plebeian caste.* She was a small woman, and from her earliest years fate placed on her shoulders more weight than she could easily bear. In 1915 the Russians captured the Przemyśl fortress, and my father, a sergeant in the army of Emperor Franz Josef I, was taken prisoner and was released only after the war through the efforts of the Danish Red Cross. During the war my mother had to care for her children alone. The Austrian armies were retreating, and the population was being removed from the war zone, so we were evacuated to Vienna. There the poor housing and food undermined my mother's health. After the war we returned to Przemyśl, but times were still hard. Nothing remained of the Katz family's former prosperity. Our own home had been burned to the ground, and we had no place to live.

My mother had a particularly sensitive nature. She never thought of herself but was constantly looking after the well-being of her own children and even her friends' and neighbors' children. Always weighed down by some grief or worry, her health slowly deteriorated, and she looked for help: if the people around her could not help, then who could? Perhaps some holy man, some miracle worker. She became more and more interested in this sort of thing.

The Thirty-Six Righteous Ones

Among the Jews there is a legend the world is supported on the backs of thirty-six righteous men. They are scattered throughout the world. No one except these men themselves knows that they are among the Thirty-Six. They never hold any important or conspicuous office but labor at some humble task. Should the secret that one of them belongs to the *Lamed Vav* ("thirty-six" in Hebrew) accidentally be discovered, that person dies immediately and someone else is born in the world to take his place. Their task is to teach justice, to perform good deeds, and to give aid and succor to the downtrodden. There was a local belief that one of the Thirty-Six Righteous Ones was buried in the old Jewish cemetery in Przemyśl. It was said that in life he had been a butcher's assistant. One day a large, violent bull was led into the slaughterhouse. It kept

---

*The Jews are divided into three castes. The highest, Kohen, to which my mother belonged, is the priestly caste. My father belonged to the lowest, or plebeian, caste, Israel.—*B.S.*

bursting its traces and running about, and no one could do a thing with it. However, as soon as the Righteous One entered the slaughterhouse the bull became quiet, and the butchers had their way. The Righteous One quickly left the shop and went out of the village into the forest. The villagers followed and found him beneath a tree bent in prayer, a halo shining about his head. "He is holy! One of the Righteous! One of the Thirty-Six!" people began to shout. The man did not deny this but instead walked slowly home, got into his bed, and died. He was laid to rest in the local cemetery, now known as the "old cemetery," not used for years.

When I was a boy this grave was already more than two hundred years old. On it lay a small, tumbledown stone marker, darkened with age, with an almost obliterated inscription. A niche had been carved in the stone, and in it people placed notes with their requests, in the belief that the Holy One would help them. Beside the grave a kind of Jewish "learned man" had set himself up in business, and for a small fee he would write a request in Hebrew on a roll of parchment. Whenever my mother felt that her troubles had grown too burdensome, she visited the grave to request the help of the Righteous One. This visit always helped; she would return home calm in the knowledge that someone stronger than herself, a holy man, shared her troubles.

Troubles at the Gymnasium

There were four children in our family. Helena was the oldest, then Christina, my brother Emil, and finally myself. At home I was considered a black sheep, and I accepted this opinion as correct. As I had said, I inherited my father's love for nature and the outdoors, for freedom and independence both physical and emotional. I also had a goodly amount of perceptiveness and a critical attitude.

I was enrolled in the local Ukrainian classical gymnasium. The school system in those days consisted of four years of grade school, followed by eight years of gymnasium, the rough equivalent of American junior high and high school. From the first year we studied rules of grammar and vocabulary and enough languages to keep us busy— Polish, Ukrainian, Latin, German, and, beginning in the third year, Greek. If these languages had been taught in a modern way they might have aroused my interest, but our teachers followed a thoroughly old-fashioned method. They were not interested in how words were pronounced or what sentences sounded like; for them the only important thing was the ability to recite grammatical forms fluently, to know all the irregular declensions, conjugations, and forms, all the grammatical rules, and all the exceptions.

I found all this very boring. The world was so beautiful; outside the sun was shining and spring was bursting forth in full blossom, and I had to recite grammar and vocabulary. I didn't even try to understand what my teachers were saying. I either slept during my language classes or played hookey. My teachers finally had enough, and in my fourth year I was told to get out, for I was a "born loser." This by no means gracious judgment was uttered by my class master, Professor Grech, who advised me that I would do better to become a tailor's apprentice than to continue wasting time in school. In short, the teachers were sick of me and I of them. They breathed a collective sigh of relief when I left the school, and I was happy to be freed of the torture of learning the three Rs on a hard wooden bench. My parents were not happy about the arrangement, but as they had repeatedly been told by my teachers that I simply did not have the ability to learn, they came to believe this, and I was certainly willing to agree with all of them.

Here I will digress slightly. In 1938, when returning one day by train to Cracow after a fine holiday in the eastern Beskid Mountains, I got into a compartment occupied by only one other passenger. After a few moments I took a closer look at the man seated opposite me and with amazement saw the same person who had advised me to become a tailor's apprentice. I greeted Professor Grech in Ukrainian and we struck up a conversation. At first he did not recognize me, but then something clicked. "Don't tell me your name!—I'll recall it in a second!" He put his hand over his eyes, then looked at me again, and suddenly his face brightened. "You're Schatten!" he almost shouted, happy that he had remembered me after all.

"Yes," I replied; "The same Schatten whom you once advised to become a tailor."

"Well? And did you?"

"The tailors didn't want me, so I had no choice but to finish gymnasium, then university, and at present I am a lawyer in Cracow: not a bad one, some people say." He was utterly mortified.

"I think, though, professor, that your advice was sound," I told him. "I really did not belong in the classical gymnasium. I completed my studies in a mathematics and natural sciences gymnasium, but I must admit that I like law very much and am quite happy with my choice." We began to laugh at my academic vicissitudes and said friendly farewells as he disembarked.

After leaving the Ukrainian gymnasium, I attended a sort of private school in Dobromil for a while, the student body of which was composed mostly of the rejects of other schools. Evidently the burden of these "undesirables" was too heavy for the poor little school, for shortly after my arrival the Lwów school superintendent took away its license and disbanded it, momentarily bringing my educational career to an end.

Summers

I made friends with other boys of my age regardless of nationality. For the most part my pals loved the outdoors as I did. We went on long walks into the nearby forests and mountains. My best friend was Ores R., the son of a Greek Catholic priest from a nearby village (celibacy was not required of these priests). I often stayed with Ores' family during summer vacations. His mother was a warm hospitable woman; the priest remains in my memory as a kind and wise, though somewhat coarse, man. I felt very close to Ores and his younger sister Olga. They had a beautiful farm, and I felt at home there helping them with the chores.

The greatest joy for us children was to wash the horses. The priest had three of them, beautiful and very well cared for. Their coats gleamed; they were fed plenty of oats and were constantly curried and washed. Giving the horses a swim was our special chore and pleasure. We would ride bareback to the San River, about two kilometers away. There we stripped down to our underwear and, remounting our "chargers," rode them into the river. As long as the horses had ground beneath their feet, we rocked back and forth to the rhythm of their gait, but in a minute we could feel them swimming. Their bellies and then their backs would disappear beneath the water; this was the moment to slide off. The horses swam along with the current, following their instinct without any interference from us, and exhilarating in their bath. Ores and his sister were excellent swimmers. Sliding off the horses into the water, they would grab their tails. From time to time they would let go, swim in a big circle, and again grab the horses' tails and drift along with the current. I was not so bold and preferred to swim next to my horse holding on to his mane.

A perfect silence reigned; here and there a fish jumped, a sheep bleated, or a dog barked, but this did not disturb the peace of the countryside, baking in the hot rays of the sun. When the horses once again found land beneath their feet, they clattered up out of the water, and we mounted again and rode to our favorite spot, a small, narrow island formed by the forking of the river. There we drove the horses back into the water while we stretched out in the sun. They swam across the river and slowly wandered home, stopping to graze along the way, leaving us basking on our little island.

The hours passed and the sun was low in the sky when a rowboat appeared from the other side of the San bearing some of Ores' friends and a guitar. Together we built a fire and sat around it, moving closer and closer together as the heat of the setting sun faded and twilight embraced the land. Now it was time to sing. The sad strains of the melodious Ukrainian *dumy** of the steppes and the Dniepr River drifted through the still, starry night. At such moments time no longer existed for us, but the faraway peal of the church bell would remind us of the time. Our friends rowed us across the river and we trudged home, still under the spell of the enchanting evening. Right after vespers I would stumble into the barn, where I loved to sleep, and in five minutes would be dead to the world.

Two months at the farm passed like the crack of a whip, and I returned to Przemyśl healthy, sunburned, and more in love with nature than ever. In town there was a completely different atmosphere. Pupils were getting their uniforms ready for the coming school year and buying notebooks and texts. All conversations revolved around the same subject—school. I alone took no part; gradually I came to feel as though I were a pariah; the bonds of schoolboy communication and friendship had been broken.

The Jarosław Gymnasium

One day on a walk in the fields outside of town I met an older boy who was studying law in England. Out of habit, to explain my position

---

*Dumy, the plural of *duma*, are Ukrainian folk ballads, usually with a historical theme.—*Tr.*

as a non-student, I began to complain of the old-fashioned and repellent manner of instruction at the Ukrainian gymnasium. This boy listened seriously and did not contradict me; he even admitted that there was a lot of truth in what I said. On the other hand, he said, it was difficult to get by in the world without that little slip of paper known as a graduation certificate. As far as he was concerned, he went on, he had finished school only to get this piece of paper. He did not argue or return to the subject, but his comments made a strong impression on me. For some time I had felt that something was not quite right with me, and here was a person who not only did not criticize my behavior but, on the contrary, agreed that there was truth in what I said. It seemed necessary to swallow a bitter pill in exchange for that certificate. After that—the devil take all schools!

Without fanfare I submitted a request to the school superintendent in Lwów asking to be admitted by examination to the eighth year of gymnasium. I believe that such requests were rare; at any rate, mine was accepted. I was assigned to the A. Witkowski School of Mathematics and Natural Sciences in the city of Jarosław, a place known for its rigorous academic standards. For entrance I had to pass examinations in seventeen subjects.

My arrival caused a stir at the gymnasium. It was unheard of for someone to gain admittance to the eighth year by examination. The teaching staff had no desire to grant a diploma to someone from outside who had not spent years in their institution acquiring its "patina," but they had no say in the matter, since the school superintendent had accepted me for examination. This did not prevent them from looking on the whole affair skeptically.

I crammed as hard as I could until examination day. The examinations were both written and oral, spread over three days. I passed sixteen subjects faultlessly; in the seventeenth subject, drawing, I belonged in the second year, according to the examiner. The teachers met and deliberated at length. Finally they arrived at a compromise: I was to be set back by one year and placed among the seventh-year students. This decision met with opposition from an unexpected source: Father Szypuła, the teacher of religion, refused to sign the minutes of the faculty meeting. He maintained that if my drawing was on the second-year level then I belonged in the second year, which was obviously impossible because I was nineteen years old. An alternative was not to admit me at all, which would be contrary to the results of the examination. A third choice was to allow me into the eighth year, for which, in his opinion, I was prepared. As far as my drawing was concerned, it was true that I was no Matejko,* but what could one do? It was no use trying to budge Father Szypuła: he was the specialist in catechism, noted for his stubbornness (or determination, depending on one's point of view), and too important a figure in the school to fight. The other professors had no choice but to accept me into the eighth year.

My acceptance into the gymnasium did not mean that I was *definitively* accepted, however. I had to pass a second examination—that of my classmates. I was already something of a celebrity, but they knew nothing about me personally. Most of them had been at the school for eight years and were good friends, but I was not even from the same town. They were reserved at first, but after a month or so they allowed me to join their "set." From them I learned the details about my placement examination, described above, and also about general conditions at the school.

Father Szypuła

Father Szypuła was tall and stout, with a large head, a bass voice, and a dignified manner. He looked like a pastor among his flock, especially in his long black cassock, which made him appear even larger. His physical appearance alone commanded respect and obedience. When he was with the other teachers, one noticed him first of all; the others receded into the background. One day on the street I met him walking home. I began to thank him for helping me get admitted to the eighth year. He cut me off at the start. "My son," he said, "it is neither to your credit nor to your detriment that they are fools." "They" meant the other instructors. That day I walked all the way home with him.

From that day on I began to visit Father Szypuła, at first only occasionally, then more and more frequently, until I was seeing him regularly every other week. I had plenty of time, for the eighth year consisted of a review of the material learned in the preceding years. The priest had his regular duties to carry out, but he gave freely of his time when it came to advising me about my future. A feeling of trust and respect grew up between us, and I came to love him like my own father. I

---

*The renowned nineteenth-century Polish painter.—*Tr.*

told him all about myself—about my family, my initial failures in school, my decision to get my certificate, and so on. He always listened attentively. My descriptions of my father's personality—his longing for his native mountains and forests, his loyalty to his beloved Austrian emperor—appealed to this priest immensely: Father Szypuła even expressed a wish to meet him. He laughed heartily when I told him of Professor Grech's advice that I become a tailor's apprentice. "Yes, that's just like Grech," he roared, almost choking with laughter. It appeared that he knew Professor Grech well, for before coming to Jarosław he had been the religion instructor at the classical gymnasium in Przemyśl.

By and by he began to direct our conversation to the subject of my future. In retrospect I see that he studied my personality carefully before trying to steer me in the right direction. "Well, fine," he said one day. "Let's suppose that you have your diploma. What then?"

"What then? I don't know. I suppose the whole world will be open to me." I really had no idea.

"Don't talk too much about the world opening," the priest said in response, "or you might fall in. A diploma is no window to the world. It is rather a key to the door; beyond that door is a struggle and competition for the attainment of knowledge. It all depends on you; you can open the door with the key and enter, and then you will either become someone or no one. If you work, you'll get somewhere; if you don't, you'll be wasting your time."

"What could you study?" he continued. "You'll never make it into the academy of fine arts, that much is clear. Not physiology either, for you have no predilection for cutting up bodies. You're too smart for pharmacy, and they'll never make a language teacher out of you; probably all that's left is law. There's a professor in Cracow called Vetulani who'll teach you canon law; one day you'll know more than I do," he said in a lightly mocking tone, "but never fear; law is a worthy profession: after that, all doors really will be open to you. You'd best go to Cracow, for it's a decent town." (I knew that he himself had taken a degree in theology in Cracow and was well acquainted with the city and the university.) "Of course, it won't be easy to get in. For one thing, you'll need Latin."

"But I know Latin," I protested.

"It's one thing to know it, another to prove it on paper, and Latin is not one of our subjects. I don't suppose the idea would delight you, but why don't you arrange for tutoring in Latin after the class day? There is a person here who teaches it."

And so I began studying Latin again. It was taught by an old man who probably did not himself understand what he was doing in a mathematics and natural sciences gymnasium. There were four pupils "eager" to take his course, and he was quite pleased to have a fifth. When he learned that I could quote from Caesar and Ovid and knew pentameters and hexameters, he was transported with delight. And so, when I completed the gymnasium, my diploma stated that I had taken Latin as an extra subject and had passed with distinction. I had spent barely ten months in the Jarosław gymnasium, and now I had that famous slip of paper which was to open the world to me. With the blessing of my beloved Father Szypuła and a five-złoty piece in my pocket, which he had given me "for an emergency," I set out for Cracow.

My bonds of friendship with Father Szypuła remained unbroken. I wrote him often, reporting in detail on the progress of my studies (he insisted on this), and never failed to send him greetings on holidays and at the New Year. I never spent his five-złoty piece but kept it as a good-luck charm. Long after the war, somewhere between Montevideo and Buenos Aires, I lost my suitcase and, with it, my lucky talisman.

Chapter 6

My Arrival in Cracow

I fell in love with Cracow the moment I first saw it. When I arrived there in 1931, it had over two hundred thousand inhabitants; to me that was a big city. I had been to Lwów several times to see the eastern trade fair, but Cracow was something special. To sum up the difference between these two towns, I would say that Lwów was all bustle, Cracow all tradition.

I had imagined the city as a collection of large apartment buildings standing in rows like soldiers, but in fact it struck me as pleasant and picturesque. No building was like another. The mixture of styles, proportions, shapes, decorations, and architectural features somehow created one beautiful symphony. Each street and alleyway, each corner, facade, portal, or cornice, bore the stamp of originality, and everywhere were parks and boulevards filled with lush and magnificent greenery. In later years I got to know almost all the interesting buildings and monuments better than the native Cracowians themselves, but even then I was always finding something new. The only jarring sight to my eye was the Phoenix building, on the corner of the A-B line and St. John's Street. (The main street along Market Square in Cracow was called the A-B line, and on it the Phoenix Insurance Company had built a modern concrete building completely out of character with the others.) I could not understand why the city had allowed this company to build a three-story building of reinforced concrete and glass next to such venerable buildings as the Cloth Hall, St. Mary's Church, the palaces, and the other marvelous centuries-old burghers' houses. It looked like a *nouveau riche* intruder at a party of aristocrats.

The Cracowians

Even the inhabitants of the city were completely different from what I had imagined. Two societies lived here side by side, I discovered. First there were the true Cracowians, people who had lived there for generations, with their own habits and customs. Practically all of them knew each other. They called anyone from outside Cracow a "provincial," whether he came from Katowice, Poznań, Warsaw, or Lwów; to them he was "from the provinces," a second-class citizen. As they put it, "No one knows where he comes from." The other society was made up of precisely these "provincials," of course.

The Cracowians and the special architecture of the city blended into a harmonious whole. Their traditions were ancient and unbending. A Cracowian was defined not by personal characteristics but by family connections. For example, in response to the question, "Who is Mr. X?" the answer would invariably be, "Mr. X is the son of Lawyer Y, whose uncle is Councilman W; his aunt is the chairwoman of the Z Society," and so on. Thus one could find out all about the personal relations of a given individual without learning anything whatsoever about the person himself.

That's just the way it was in Cracow. The natives cultivated relationships exclusively among themselves; they were polite, but not excessively so; and they always had more time than they knew what to do with. They were never in a hurry—at least not during the day. At night, however, no self-respecting Cracowian would be caught dead on the streets of the town. One had to be safely at home before "tipping time," that is, before the gates of the apartment houses were locked by the custodian. As a rule apartment houses had an entry gate with a little building just inside called the annex. Here the custodian ruled supreme, taking it as a mortal insult if anyone referred to him as the "watchman." He was the *custodian*, and that was that. One of his duties was to clean the stairs and hallways of the apartment house and to keep the sidewalks clear of ice and snow in the winter. He also kept the register of tenants, noting who moved in and out and in whose name they were registered. He saw to it that no unauthorized person was living in his building.

The custodian's quarters were usually located near the entry gate, and he locked that gate at the stroke of ten o'clock in the winter and eleven o'clock in the summer. If a tenant returned home after closing time, he had to pay a tip. Cracowians raced to get home before closing time. It was not so much a matter of the fifteen-groszy tip; it was simply not considered decent to return home after your gate was locked. Citizens lept onto a trolley, flagged down a cab, or simply ran to avoid arriving home late. They would argue with the custodian that it was not yet ten o'clock, that he had shut the gate too soon; they would display their own watches to make the point; but the custodian, with stoic calm, would produce his own enormous alarm clock to prove that he had actually locked the gate three minutes after the hour. These quarrels took place daily with one tenant or another. The custodian received all complaints with unruffled serenity and continued to lock the gate according to the time on his own clock. It was possible to avoid paying the tip by renting a gate key from the custodian for three złotys a month, but for some reason few people took advantage of this opportunity.

People of a "worse" sort—that is, the "provincials," particularly the students—led a completely different existence. They were unconcerned by "tipping time"—indeed about coming home at any set time—about living where they were supposed to be registered, or about the Cracowians' opinion of them. They led their own separate, colorful life. The came from all over: from Pomerania, Poznań, Silesia, or the east. They rose whenever they liked and went to bed when they were tired; they were Cracow's Bohemia. They shared things among themselves, visited one another at all times of day or night, and laughed at the conventions of the indigenous population.

A Night at the Death Trap

Once some fellow students and I and our girl friends were passing a bar on Lubicz Street near the railroad station. It was a night spot known as the Death Trap, reputed to be a meeting place for underworld characters and shady ladies. Self-respecting Cracowians would not even pass in front of the Death Trap but would cross over to the other side of the street. The muscular proprietor often appeared in the door with some drunk, about to dump him unceremoniously on the sidewalk. One of us suggested that we go in for a beer, and the rest agreed. The place was a large room with tables around the walls and a simple wooden floor, waxed for dancing. In the corner a phonograph was playing a popular song. When we appeared in the doorway, everything came to a standstill: everyone in the room was staring at us over their mugs of beer. We sat down at an empty table, a long wooden affair with matching benches. The proprietor came over, took our order for beer, brought it in coarse heavy mugs, and we began to drink. The others returned to their business, ignoring us, and someone put on another record, a waltz. Two couples began to dance. We sat and watched. Suddenly a burly fellow got up, came over to our table, and with a dash of bravado asked one of the girls in our group to dance. After him came others, and before long all our girls were whirling around the room. There was nothing for us men to do but go up to the other tables and ask some girl there to dance. They didn't hesitate. After the waltzes came Polish dances like kujawiaks and krakowiaks, with lots of jumping and stomping, and the party got started. Strangers came to sit at our table, some of us joined other tables, and we stayed there until dawn. The customers kept buying us more and more beer and would not let us pay for a single round. When morning came they insisted that we be driven home in hansom cabs. We hugged our new friends warmly as we parted, promising to drop in again.

It was amusing to see the expressions of shock and disbelief on the faces of our Cracow colleagues when we told them that we had spent the entire night merrymaking at the Death Trap. Their first question was whether we had had anything stolen; they could not believe that we had not been allowed to pay for anything, and that we had even been sent home in cabs! It was really quite interesting; the two societies lived side by side in the town and didn't know anything about each other. Even the students were divided into two groups, the locals and the out-of-towners. Each lived its own life and was not interested in getting to know the other.

The Cracowians were thrifty; people from Warsaw called them tightwads. They, in turn, referred to people from Warsaw as tinhorns, trying to impress people with a cheap display. Those from Warsaw retaliated by referring to Cracowians jokingly as "Galileans" (instead of Galicians), an exaggerated reference to their provinciality.

The Cracow Cabby

Another unique local type was the Cracow cabdriver. The cabbies were distinguished by their black derby hats, which could express as many moods as there were ways of wearing them. If the cabby was in a good mood, he tapped the derby lightly onto his head and tilted it back. If he made too little on a fare, or if the tip was too small, he would angrily cram his hat down over his ears as he drove off. When he needed to give his horse a drink, he would fill this all-purpose headgear with water, take a drink from it himself, and then give it to his animal. What was left he poured over the horse's back to cool him off. When he was waiting for a fare at a cab stand, playing blackjack with the other drivers, the derby hat served as the bank; in the afternoon, when the sun burned down and no customers were in sight, he lazily stretched his legs out in front of him, covered his face with his hat, and slept the sleep of the just. In the early morning hours, when he returned home drunk from some tavern, flopping back and forth on his seat with his derby hat all askew, the horse knew that the day's work was over, and he would clip-clop gently home.

These blackjack games were a sight: great histrionic talent went into them. In the midst of the circle of players lay the derby bank holding the pot. The banker dealt a card all around; then each player had to pay to see a second card. A cabby never looked at a new card right away. He would put each one he drew in back of the others and then slowly, ever so slowly, move it aside a millimeter at a time, to see what he had: was it enough or should he take another one? If he took another card he eased it into his hand with the same intense concentration, and this ceremony was usually repeated several times until at last he announced in a wooden voice, "Stay." The entire brotherhood played the game in exactly the same way. When it came to the banker, he drew openly, and when he considered that he had enough points, or that it would be risky to take any more cards, he too would say "Stay." Whoever the banker beat would throw down his cards with an expression of complete indifference; whoever had a higher score than the banker would take one card after the other from his hand, display it in the air, and then fling it down with a flourish, triumphantly counting aloud, "Eleven! Fourteen! Sixteen! Twenty!" Then he would take the amount he had won out of the hat, his face beaming more brightly than if he had just broken the bank at Monte Carlo. I know many great cities of the world, and I can say that the Cracow cabby was a unique and inimitable type.

The Jewish Dormitory

Despite the great appeal of the city, however, I needed a roof over my head, a paying job, and a place at the university. My entire fortune consisted of my diploma from the gymnasium and my lucky five-złoty piece. I spent my first two nights on a bench in the park. It was the end of August, and the weather was still warm, or at least tolerable. I would place the little suitcase containing my few belongings on the bench under my head and cover myself up with my greatcoat. After two nights I had had enough of this, and went to the Jewish dormitory on Przemyśl Street to see how one got a room there. At the door, however, I was told it was no use. There were only ninety-three places, and these had already been taken by students who had sent their applications before the vacation. Even then, an ordinary mortal had no chance of getting accepted. There were hundreds of applicants; only those with connections had any hope of success, and I did not know anyone; besides, I had come too late.

I asked whether anyone from Przemyśl lived in the dormitory, thinking that perhaps such a person could tell me where I might find accommodations. I was given the name of one Józek Reben. He was from Przemyśl, and, as it happened, his family lived on the same street as mine. He was a tall, strong, and well-built fellow, over thirty years old; he had been a medical student for as long as anyone at the university could remember. The story was that he was so well known that whenever he stood for his medical examinations his professors no sooner saw him than they groaned, "Oh, Mr. Reben, it's *you* again," and failed him without further ado.

Actually Reben knew a lot about medicine and could find a cure for any ailment. He was also a mechanical genius; there was nothing he couldn't fix—radios, irons, hot plates, and all sorts of more complicated appliances. As an expert in all matters, he always had a kind word or piece of friendly advice for everyone. He had no official position in the Jewish dormitory, but everyone listened to him.

The dormitory administration consisted of a manager and three floor captains. Artek Hausman, also from Przemyśl, was the third-floor captain. He was a good-looking, energetic, friendly medical student. Reben went to him right away and said, "Artek, give this person a room."

Artek was astounded. "What do you mean, 'Give him a room'?" he asked.

"You figure it out," said Reben. "He's one of us, from Przemyśl. He's been sleeping in the park for the past two days."

Artek hesitated for a moment, then said, "Come with me." He took me to a room and pointed to a bed. "Take this bed," he said, "and don't worry about a thing." Then he left.

Number 41 was a tiny room for three students. There were three beds, three chairs, a small table, and a wardrobe about a yard and a half wide partitioned into three spaces. In a few minutes Artek returned with a receipt for one and one-half złotys covering three nights' lodging. At the Jewish dormitory, as long as the permanent residents had not all arrived and there were empty beds, the beds could be rented for a nominal charge of fifty groszy per night to cover the cost of laundering the sheets. Most of those taking advantage of this arrangement were students who had come to town for a few days to take make-up examinations.

After three days Artek brought me a second receipt for three more days. (I learned later that rooms could not be rented to transients for longer than three days at a time.) After a week had passed, the student whose accommodations I had been renting arrived, and all hell broke loose. Artek showed him proof that I had paid for the next three days and said that nothing could be done. After those three days were up, I could not be moved, for I had nowhere to go. The manager was furious and threatened to report me to the university, but Józek Reben, who had orchestrated the whole affair, told me calmly, "Don't worry. They never kick anyone out just because he's poor and has no place to go. The manager's business is to rant and rave; that's what he's paid for; your business is to sit tight and not to worry."

Thus it was that I came to live in the Jewish dormitory. Everything was completely different from what I was used to. Until now I had spent my time with friends with likes and dislikes similar to my own. I had been a child of nature, rising at dawn and going to bed with the hens. The students here were city folk; they rose late and went to bed late. There were students from all over Poland, with different interests, personalities, and attitudes. Almost everyone belonged to some Jewish organization or other and had gotten into the dormitory because of this affiliation. As far as the dormitory administration was concerned, I was an intruder; they looked on me as a "dangerous element"; I had no organization to stand up for me. My strange habits of getting up at dawn and going to bed early did nothing to help, and for the first several months I was something of an outcast.

Some students were lucky enough to live in two-person rooms; there were three in my room, and my two roommates were not particularly to my liking. One, like Reben, was one of those "perpetual students"; he had been at the university for years. He was a rather neurotic type; he would lie in bed all day dozing and then disappear at night—I had no idea where. This arrangement suited me, for I was out during the day and slept at night. My other roommate, however, was unbearable. After dinner he would play cards in someone else's room until two or three in the morning. When he returned he would be hungry and would turn on the light and bang around fixing himself something to eat. He was deaf to arguments and entreaties, so I decided to take direct action.

One evening before bed (the neurotic student, as always, was out), I unscrewed all the lightbulbs, first moving around all the furniture in the room. The card sharp came back late as usual and tried to turn on the light. When it didn't work, he felt his way in and crashed into a chair which I had put on its back on the floor with the legs pointed toward the door. He swayed back and forth, trying to catch himself on the table, but the table wasn't there, and he fell heavily to the floor. He tried to crawl over to his bed, but he couldn't find it in the dark and suffered more bruises for his trouble. In the morning his face was all covered with scratches. It would have been no use for him to complain because cardplaying in the dormitory was strictly forbidden, so he said nothing. The experiment was a success: from that time on, when he returned late at night he crept into bed in the dark as quiet as a mouse, without his snack.

A month or so after this incident I became embroiled, completely unnecessarily and accidentally, in a more serious quarrel, and not just with one person but with an entire group of dormitory residents. There were two Jewish fraternities at the university, Kadimah and Emunah, whose members lived in our dormitory. Fraternity members wore club caps and bright-colored scarves; they spent their evenings in taverns tippling beer from heavy mugs and lustily singing Gaudeamus Igitur. A number of them owned sabers and liked to dress up in their fraternity uniforms and preen like peacocks. They considered themselves very important people; politically they belonged to the far right.

One day during dinner in our dining hall one of the fraternity boys shoved a girl off one of the benches where the club members usually sat, simply because he disapproved of her political views. I did not care much for politics, but this action made me angry, and I told him what I thought of his behavior, adding that he had gotten away with it only because his victim was a girl. Several students sitting nearby noticed the incident; not wanting to carry the matter further, I left the dining hall.

Imagine my surprise the next day when two formally dressed individuals came around to my room and presented themselves as the "seconds" of their fraternity brother. They demanded a public apology from me; if I refused, they warned me that I must fight a duel, and must choose two seconds with whom they could meet next day in the dining hall to make the arrangements. They then laid their calling cards on my table and left.

My first impulse was to throw them out the door, but after a moment I decided to teach them a lesson. By this time I had made friends with another dormitory resident named Szymon Breit. Szymon could not stand the fraternity men. We discussed the matter and decided on the duel. (I must mention here that these fraternity saberrattlers rarely used their weapons: there was an agreement between the two Jewish fraternities that all grievances between members were to be submitted to arbitration by an inter-fraternity council; in case of a dispute with a Polish fraternity, there was no problem, as a Pole would never "give satisfaction" to a Jew in any case.) Szymon chose a friend, and the next day the two of them met the fraternity seconds at the appointed time. The fraternity men were so sure that I would back out and apologize that they gave my seconds the right to choose the weapons. The next meeting was set for the following day, at which time I was to answer regarding my choice of weapons or apologize publicly.

Next day my representative declared that I had chosen pistols; the duel was to take place the following Sunday in a wood called Wolski Lasek; I would provide both the weapons and a doctor. In the meantime

73

Szymon was busy spreading rumors—I was a veteran sharpshooter, I had won first prize during the recent trials of the National Riflemen's Union (an organization he invented for the occasion), and all sorts of other sinister details. My opponent took fright and his seconds never reappeared.

Szymon and his friend took great satisfaction in drawing up the so-called official protocol of the dispute, stating that the opposing side had withdrawn in fright, preventing the duel from taking place. The whole thing was a farce, of course; I had no pistols, was never a sharpshooter, and certainly never dreamed of turning up in Wolski Lasek, a fact which Szymon proclaimed to all who would hear. No wonder, then, that brothers living in the dormitory were not kindly disposed toward me after that.

A Hearty Welcome from the Walds

Finding a job was no easy matter. Most new students thought of giving lessons, but there were so many tutors in the city that a newcomer had no chance. I was surprised that it was so difficult to find a job. I was a good mathematician and had counted on that to earn a living. What I did not realize was that Cracow was a university town and that I would be competing for pupils with student-tutors majoring in mathematics. If someone were temporarily too busy to give lessons or had to leave town for a while, he would simply sell his students to another tutor. I began looking around for other possibilities. I worked in the dormitory cloakroom during meetings, parties, or other such functions. For ten hours of work, I could make five złotys tending coats. This was not bad, but the work was infrequent.

As I mentioned, my mother's maiden name was Katz, and her father came from a long line of rabbis and priests. Her mother's family was Wald; that family had settled in Tarnów and Cracow. Her cousin Baruch Wald, of whom she always spoke with affection, lived in Cracow. As soon as my plans for going to the university became firm, my mother made me promise to look up her cousin Baruch. If I were ever in need, he would be sure to help me, since I was the son of his closest cousin. For her sake I promised to visit him, and now I needed his help.

He lived at Rynek Podgórski. A sign above a wide entry gate proclaimed "Baruch Wald—Wholesale Wines." I passed through the gate into a cobblestone courtyard. The smell of wine filled the area. Sunning himself against the opposite wall of the building, where the sun was still shining, was an old Jew with a long beard and waistcoat. I greeted him and asked whether he might be Baruch Wald, and he nodded. When I introduced myself I could see that my name meant nothing to him, so I mentioned that I had come at the request of his cousin and my mother, Ewa Wald, and that I brought greetings from her.

"Ah, you're the son of Chawcia ['Ewa,' in Yiddish]. Where is she now? How is she?"

I answered his questions, and he said no more, having apparently exhausted his interest in conversation with me. As he sat there warming himself in the sun I felt that his silence was an attempt to get rid of me. However, I summoned my courage and told him that I had come to Cracow to study and intended to stay here. I was not looking for material assistance; I was a good mathematician, but I lacked friends who could recommend me as a teacher. From my mother I knew that he had a large family, and I wondered whether they could recommend pupils to me.

Wald listened in silence with his eyes shut. Then he opened one eye, studied me for a bit, and finally spoke a little of his family or, rather, of his two sons. One was a director in the Holzer Bank, a very busy man whom it was not worth bothering, he thought. His younger son, Janek, was an attorney. He could give me Janek's address and I could try to talk to him. I knew that other members of the Wald family included, for example, a sister, named Orenschtein, who owned the Orenschtein shopping mall on the corner of Stradom and Dietl Street, as well as many other large commercial buildings. However, since he did not mention these others, I hesitated to press him. I said goodbye and left, something less than thrilled by this "hearty welcome."

I did not visit his son the lawyer immediately but continued my search for work. However, a week later, seeing that my efforts were fruitless, I decided to pay a visit to the young Wald. His office was on Starowiślna ("Old Vistula") Street next to the Uciecha ("Delight") cinema and across the street from the municipal court. I entered and found an elegant secretary sitting behind a desk. She had fair skin, hair tinted silver (a style then in fashion), and a coiffure piled so high that it reminded me of a bundle of wheat sheaves in the field, covered with another sheaf to protect them from the rain. When I said that I would like to speak with Mr. Wald about a personal matter, she took a look at my outgrown and unfashionable clothing and decided that I was not

75

worth her attention. "He's busy at the moment," she said. "As soon as he is free I will announce you."

She returned to her occupation, that is, examining her fingernails under the lamp to see whether they were properly done. I sat down on the edge of a chair and waited. When the secretary finished her manicure, she took up a novel which had been lying open next to her on the desk. Twenty minutes or more went by. Finally she got up, entered another room, returned after a while, and announced, "Attorney Wald will see you now."

I thanked her and entered Wald's office. Wald sat behind a long desk with some documents open in front of him. "What can I do for you?" he asked.

I stood before him, since he had not invited me to take a seat, and repeated the request I had made of his father. He was not surprised; probably he had already heard of my meeting with his father and had been expecting me. Without a word he lifted the telephone receiver and dialed a number. Someone answered. "Maciek?" he asked. "You need a math teacher? Good. That's all. Goodbye." Later I learned that "Maciek," his nephew, was a student in the seventh year at the gymnasium.

"I'm sorry; I called, but my nephew does not need any help at the moment. If I hear of anything I'll let you know."

With this my audience came to an end. Of course I never told my mother of the welcome I had received from her family.

Here I must digress and leap ahead six or seven years. At this time I was trying a case in court, and my opponent was this same Wald. I had seen him frequently in the courtrooms and corridors of the courthouse, but we had never spoken. After our case was over we walked together into the counsellors' waiting room. "My dear sir," he said, "I have the impression that we have met somewhere before, but I can't remember when or where."

"Of course, we have seen each other often enough here in court and in other court buildings," I replied.

"No, I am sure that that's not it," Wald answered. "I have a good memory for faces. I must have met you somewhere else."

"That's possible," I smiled.

"That means that you know where."

"Maybe I do, but it's not worth mentioning."

"I don't understand. Why are you being so secretive?"

Chapter 6

"Mr. Wald," I replied. "I would prefer that we drop this conversation."

"No. I can't agree. I demand an explanation."

"Very well, since you insist, I have no other choice. You see, six or seven years ago a young distant relative of yours from the provinces came to your office asking not for money but for help in finding lessons. This young man was good at mathematics but was a stranger in town and had no one to turn to. You promised that if you heard of anything you would let him know. You were not interested in learning his name, where he lived, whether he had a place to live or the means to live, or how he was getting on. In any case, it seems that he did get on, for we are both discussing this subject today as attorneys."

Wald looked at me and, without a word, turned and left the waiting room. A voice behind me boomed out: "Bravo, sir! It's high time that these puffed-up types got taken down a peg or two. My sincere congratulations!" I looked around. It was Dr. Wilhelm Immerglick, whose law office was located on Sławkowski Street (he and I later became good friends). As for Wald, we nodded to each other in the courtroom after this but never again exchanged a single word.

Szymek

This was a very difficult period for me. What I did earn from occasional jobs was not enough to cover the cost of living and eating in the dormitory. Often enough I went hungry. During this period my friend Szymon ("Szymek") Breit came to the rescue again. An orphan, he received a small pension because his deceased father had been secretary of the appelate court in Tarnopol. He also received food packages each week from his older, married brother, a physician in Bielsko; because of his membership in the Zionist student organization Ha-Shomer Ha-Za'ir, he got a big discount in the dining hall. Although his situation was not luxurious, he at least was better off than I.

Szymek had a large head, wispy light blond hair, a pink complexion, and pale eyebrows. In coloring he looked like an albino, although he was not. The antithesis of an athlete, he had an odd, disjointed walk. He studied law—or perhaps I should say that he was enrolled in the first year of law school: he certainly never studied. He was destined for law school in the same way that I was destined for the Academy of Fine

Arts. On the other hand, he had a marvelous spoken command of Polish and wrote the language even more beautifully. His speech was exceptional, rich and witty and at the same time very caustic. Once one fell into his verbal clutches, it was all over. No one, least of all Szymek, knew what he was doing in law school.

From our first meeting Szymek never called me by name but always referred to me as "Fascist." I did not know why he chose this name, as I was not political at all, but I could see that it reflected no ill-will on his part, so I did not take it amiss. One day in the dining hall, instead of eating dinner, I took a glass of hot water, which cost nothing, and started upstairs with it to my room.

"Hey, Fascist! Why aren't you eating?" Szymek's voice rang out behind me. I hadn't even noticed that he was standing there. "My stomach's upset," I answered, and went on upstairs. Szymek just stood there looking after me. I returned to my room, lay down on my bed, and tried not to think about food. Suddenly Szymek rushed in with a large package. Without formalities, he plumped himself down on my bed and unwrapped his package. Lord, what wasn't in that package! Fat sausages, luscious cakes—treats I had not seen for ages. My mouth was watering at the sight.

"Listen, Fascist," Szymek said, "either you start eating right now or I'll set up a howl and say that you hit me, and then you'll get thrown out of the dormitory."

The wonders I saw in that package were too marvelous to resist, and I proceeded to dig in. When I was sufficiently sated I saw Szymek's eyes twinkling with glee, although he was trying to look serious. "You know what, Fascist?" he said. "I think I'm getting to like you!" From that day on we became fast friends. Later he was named my second in the notorious affair of the duel with the fraternity brothers, and even when I moved out of the Jewish dormitory the next year our friendship continued.

The Tourist Guide

By chance I discovered a paying job for which there was no competition. One day as I was passing Market Square I noticed a teacher and a large group of children in town for the day. They were standing in the square while the teacher held a guidebook in his hand, from which he was pompously declaiming: "On this spot stood Tadeusz Kościuszko when he swore to the nation that he would fight for freedom" (Kościuszko, the Polish national hero and military leader, led the fight for Polish independence against Russia).

The mob of children gazed at the spot with reverence. I explained discreetly to the teacher that there was a special marker commemorating the spot where Kościuszko made his vow to the people, but that it was on the other side of the square. He was embarrassed but at the same time grateful to me for whispering so as not to make him look foolish in the eyes of his pupils. He admitted that he was in the city for the first time and had not been able to follow the tour map printed in his guidebook. Also, the group could not visit every sight, and he did not know what to leave out. I offered to take them around and show them only the most interesting sights. I spent the whole afternoon with them, ate lunch at their expense, and at the end received five złotys in payment.

I was very pleased; from that day on I took my books and manuals to Market Square or to Wawel Castle and waited there for tourists to whom I could offer my services. Often there were no tourists or no one wanted a guide, but most of my income came from this new role which I had discovered and came to enjoy. I could study while sitting all day in the fresh air and earn a little cash besides. The students from my dormitory saw me leaving in the morning and returning late in the evening. No one ever saw me studying, so I was typed as another "perpetual student" who intended to spend his life at the university.

The Girl in the Butchershop

Besides my irregular income from guiding tourists, I had another piece of good luck during this first and most difficult year. Not far from the dormitory, just around the corner of Przemyśl Street, was a butchershop. I often stopped in front of it and looked in the window. There was the figure of a little pig's head with a carrot in his mouth, surrounded by various delicacies, including strings of wonderful-looking sausages, which I could almost smell through the glass. One day a young girl, about sixteen years old, came out of the butchershop wearing a white smock and started chatting with me. She said that she often saw me looking in the window and wondered why I never came in to buy anything. I replied, honestly enough, that I had no money. Thereupon she asked me inside, went behind the counter, and in a very "professional" manner explained that not everything there was expensive. She pointed to a pile of fatty trimmings, next to which was lying a pile of beautiful, evenly cut slices of ham. "You see," she said, "this whole handful of trimmings costs only five groszy. Would you like it?"

I nodded my head. The girl was alone in the butchershop—the owner was out somewhere. She put a dozen or more slices of ham on a piece of waxed paper and added a piece of hunter's sausage, two large rolls, and, on the very top, for camouflage, a few pieces of trimmings. She packed it all nicely together, put it in a neat white basket bearing the shop's name, and presented it to me solemnly.

"Five groszy please." I paid her. "Come here next Tuesday at the same time," she said. "The owner is never here then. I'm all alone, and I'll always be able to find some trimmings for you." I came regularly every week, and thanks to those trimmings I was able to make ends meet during some very difficult times. My contact with the girl ended only when I left the district.

A few years later I was living with Antoni Paczka, a well-known glass artist, on Łazarz ("Lazarus") Street. Paczka only accepted orders requiring genuine creativity and craftsmanship. He did the glasswork for the Jagellonian University library, the Mining Academy, and many other beautiful buildings in the city. He lived in a luxurious duplex apartment designed by a first-rate architect. The architect had designed elegant bachelor's quarters for himself on the first floor, but he was not able to enjoy them for long, for his work took him to Lwów, and I took over his charming apartment. It consisted of a pentagonal living room and bedroom, a luxuriously appointed bath, an entrance hall, and a tiny kitchen. To the Paczkas I became a member of the family, and I came to like them very much.

On one occasion I had a small party at my place. Among other things, I needed some cold meats, so I took a cab to my favorite butchershop. The same young girl was still at the counter. From my appearance she could tell that I had come up in the world, although she was too polite to comment on it. I had provided myself with a bouquet of tea roses and a big, expensive box of Wedel chocolates. Handing these gifts to her, I asked for a kilo of ham and three rings of hunter's sausage. Both she and her employer were amazed at my largesse, so I explained to him that I once lived not far from here and bought sausage regularly in his shop. The flowers and chocolates were an expression of gratitude for the prompt and friendly service I had always received from his assistant. The owner was delighted and began to boast that his one desire was to satisfy his customers; he was glad that a few people, at least, appreciated his efforts. I stole a glance at the shopgirl. She was blushing and staring down at her shoes.

Chapter 7

Law School

      It was no easy matter for me to gain admission to the law faculty of Jagellonian University (the official name of the university of Cracow) because I had graduated from a mathematics and natural science gynmasium, while the law school required extensive preparation in Latin. As a rule the school would accept any graduate of a humanities or classics gymnasium without question; others had to pass an examination in Latin given by the district board of education. One could lose up to a year studying for and passing this examination. As I have already mentioned, my diploma stated that I had taken Latin as an extra subject and had passed with distinction. All my life I have been an incorrigible optimist, and I felt sure I would find a way to avoid taking the district board examination. It all depended on the dean of the law school; he was the only person empowered to waive the examination.

Professor Kumaniecki

      The dean at this time (it was 1931) was Professor Kazimiez Kumaniecki, a handsome, fifty-year-old gentleman, always impeccably dressed in a dark suit, elegant tie, and silk handkerchief flowing from his breast pocket. He walked the corridors of the university with a dignified tread, extremely gacious in his dealings with others as long as they were suitably deferential in their dealings with him. A lecturer in administrative law and statistics to third-year law students, he had been Minister of Religious Faiths and Public Education for a short while in 1922. Ever since, he wished to be addressed as "Mr. Minister"—God forbid that anyone would simply call him "Sir." To do so would be taken as a personal affront, almost as serious as though the petitioner were slouching, or dressed in some color other than black. However, whoever indulged his one foible could expect to be treated with kindness and even charm, for apart from his ministerial airs he was really a very charming person.

Suitably warned, I prepared for this important interview. I borrowed a black suit and black tie; my white shirt was immaculate, my black shoes polished like mirrors. This was how I presented myself to Piotr, the law school's beadle,* who led me into the presence of "His Honor the Minister." I found him seated behind an enormous desk, and I stood before it at attention, as etiquette demanded. The professor put out his hand for my documents, which I was holding in my hand—actually, he did not exactly reach for them but rather waved his hand languidly in front of him in such a way that it was impossible to hand him the documents across the desk. If a petitioner actually dared to attempt such a faux pas and leaned his entire body forward, he would probably lose his balance and fall flat on his face on the desk.

I had been warned about this peculiarity. I was instructed to march around the right side of the desk, stiffen to attention, and wait until "His Honor" deigned to reach out his hand for the papers. When he did, I was to bend slightly forward, hand them to him deferentially, come again to attention, about face, and march back to my former place in front of the desk to await Mr. Minister's queries. I followed all these strictures to the letter, having thoroughly practiced my part of the interview. I could see that Kumaniecki was satisfied and that so far my performance had been a success.

After a brief pause he opened the conversation. "I see that the petitioner has a diploma from a mathematics and natural sciences gymnasium."

"Yes, Mr. Minister."

"But I also see that the petitioner has taken Latin as an extra subject."

---

*The beadle was a minor university functionary whose job was to conduct visitors and assist at examinations and university ceremonies.—*Tr.*

"Yes, Mr. Minister."

"Anyone who has voluntarily taken Latin and has applied himself so diligently as to pass with distinction deserves to have his examination waived in the subject."

"Thank you, Mr. Minister."

I respectfully received my documents, now with a note that my Latin examination had been waived; I bowed, marched to the door, bowed again at the door, and thanked him once again. Thus it was that I was unconditionally accepted into law school.

Scylla and Charybdis

The Jagellonian University in Cracow was the only institution of higher learning in Poland which accepted law students without restriction. Anyone with a diploma from a gymnasium and 147 złotys for tuition (or even 49 złotys for the first trimester) could enroll. As for the applicants, they were mainly rejects from other universities who had studied in Lwów, Wilno, Poznań, or Warsaw for three years without passing a single year of law and were finally dropped, so they went to Cracow. Some of them were already working in other parts of the country and were unable to devote full time to their studies, so they studied at home and came to Cracow once a year to stand for the law examinations. Then too there were a few native Cracowians at the school.

The average number of students in the first year was around thirty-five hundred to four thousand. About two or three hundred— only some 5 to 8 percent—succeeded in passing into the second year. There was a very narrow, dangerous strait through which one had to navigate to sail safely into the next year. On either side of this strait stood two monsters—Scylla and Charybdis. Scylla took the form of a tall, balding man with a drunkard's red nose and face, large eyeglasses, beady eyes, and a little turned-up mustache. He taught the history of Polish law and was named Stanisław Kutrzeba. His text, which he himself had written, was an enormous conglomeration of useless dates, facts, and information, and it was necessary to know all of it by heart and to be able to repeat it all quickly, a task almost beyond human capability. Even today, after so many years, if someone were suddenly to awaken me from a deep sleep and shout in my ears, "What was the *liberum veto*?" I would shout back automatically, "Unanimity taken to the extreme, used for the first time at the Diet of 1652 by Władysław Siciński.'' This was the way we had to learn his book. He himself was reputed to have said, ''In my course you don't have to think, just cram.'' Half the students crashed against this stony figure, burst asunder, and sank out of sight.

The second monster, Charybdis, was a short, bald man with a big head, protruding eyes, fat, puffy lips which made him look like a carp gasping for air, arms which almost reached his knees, and short bowed legs. He was always deadly serious: he was our professor of Roman law, Rafał Taubenschlag. Whoever got past Kutrzeba crashed on Taubenschlag. No one in the first year ever asked how you had done on the exams; they merely asked whether you passed. For every thirty-five to forty students who stood for examination each day, two at most, or sometimes only one, would slip through, but even then only provisionally—they would have to take make-up examinations in the summer. It was said that in the entire history of the university the largest number of students passed in a single day was five. No wonder that only two or three hundred students survived such a bloody slaughter.

Examinations

The end of my first year arrived, and I felt prepared for the examinations. It was not that I thought I would do well—I doubted that I would pass on the first try. However, I decided that there was no point in cramming any longer, for I had learned as much as I felt I could. If I were going to fail, I might as well get it over with early, rather than late, I thought, and so I did.

Examinations began at eight o'clock in the morning. Up to forty candidates were taken at a time, divided into groups of eight. Besides Scylla and Charybdis, the examiners included Professors Stanisław Estreicher, in western European law, and Jerzy Lande, in legal theory. The candidates sat at an oval table, and the professors either walked around the room or sat at the head of the table. They had the habit of firing short questions at a student in rapid succession. If a student answered one question smoothly and correctly, he would be plied with additional questions on the same or similar material until the professor was satisfied that he was well prepared; then he would go on to the next student. If a student stumbled at the outset, the professor would begin to examine him in depth, and that was usually the beginning of the end for that unfortunate. Students came to the examinations worried to death, their wits reduced to half their normal level, having forgotten, in their nervousness and excitement, most of what they had learned.

Things went smoothly for me. I felt that I answered all questions thoroughly and precisely. When everyone had been examined, our group was let out, and Piotr the beadle called out the names of the next victims. As I left the room, the students in the corridor began asking me how it had gone. I said that *I* thought I had done well, but who knew? Finally, that morning's examinations were over, and we awaited the results. At one o'clock in the afternoon the beadle solemnly asked everyone to assemble in the conference room for Dean Kumaniecki to read the results. He began reciting names, usually adding, "Failed." When he came to my name, only one person had managed to pass without conditions and one provisionally. "Mr. Minister" paused when he came to my name, and then proclaimed with great unction: "Gentlemen! I have the pleasure of announcing that today we have the first honors student of the year. Would Mr. Schatten please come forward?"

At first I did not understand what had happened. Professor Kumaniecki handed me my examination sheet, gave me his hand, and congratulated me both personally and in the name of the university. I was sure it was all a mistake, and as soon as I could get out of the room I went into a corner of the hall and examined the sheet. It was no mistake: there was my name, there was the examination seal, and under it was written the words "Passed with Distinction."

Now people began coming up to me, shaking my hand and congratulating me, asking me whether I would help them prepare for their own exams. I wanted to be alone to get over my shock, so I told them all that if they wanted to see me, they could come to the dormitory in the evening and we would talk over dinner.

My New Profession

I went back to the dormitory to return the dark suit that I had borrowed for the occasion, and along the way considered my changed situation. People wanted me to "prep" them for the exams. What was the going rate? Half a złoty per hour? Probably not enough. One złoty? That was too much; I would have to wait and see.

Chapter 7

I went down to the dining hall, feeling that I owed myself a good dinner for once. I had in reserve my entire savings, one and one-half złotys. I calmly ate my dinner and only then sat back to have a talk with my prospective pupils. There were ten of them gathered; I felt awkward and waited for someone to open the conversation. Finally one of them grew impatient; he had just arrived from Stanisławów, he said, his exams were in three days, and he proposed to pay me ten złotys per hour. I was astounded. Ten złotys per hour? Such riches were unthinkable! He misread my hesitation and in a flash increased his offer to fifteen złotys. As I stared, he declared, as his final offer, that he was prepared to pay fifty złotys for three hours of lessons. I managed to find my voice and agreed. Now that a price was established, two more joined me on the same terms and the rest withdrew. The word soon got around that I was polishing students for exams at these rates, and whoever could afford my terms applied.

In the space of a single month I earned two thousand złotys. I put most of the money in the bank; with what was left I bought camping gear and went up into the Tatra Mountains for the first time in my life. I wandered for over two months there, then traveled down the Dunajec River, dropped into Żegiestów, wandered around Szczyrk and Wisła, toured Cieszyn, and crossed into Czechoslovakia as far as Bratislava. I was sure that I had at last found a well-paying occupation; I was a crammer, an occupation *sans pareil*. Now to plan for the future. I knew that after the vacation I would earn even more money, for the post-vacation examination period lasted longer (in fact, upon my return to Cracow I made close to thirty-five hundred złotys). In addition, I took on two well-paying law tutoring jobs. The new academic year was off to a promising start.

I accepted one other job which I should mention, for there was something special about it. A young man from Pułtusk, a town near Warsaw, called on me. He explained that he and his elder brother ran the family business, a firebrick factory, in which his brother was the factory manager and he was the sales representative. He wanted to get a law degree, he said, because it would help him in his profession, but he was overburdened with work and could be absent from the business only two or three months during the year. He proposed that we take an apartment together. He would pay his full share of the rent for the entire year, even though he would be living there for no more than three months. When he came to Cracow he would take lessons from me, paying the same rate as anyone else. He felt that if he were with me constantly during his stay he would be better prepared for his examinations. I accepted his offer. Each year he took and passed his examinations and finished law school in the usual time. We became good friends then and have remained so. His name is Nathan Celnik, and he now lives in New York City, where he is a well-known philanthropist.

Having a steady monthly income and a source of additional funds before and after each examination period, I could now put my life on a solid footing and devote myself to further studies, while also assisting my parents back home in Przemyśl. I enjoyed the study of law and flew through law school without losing a single day. I received my degree in 1935. Along the way I became acquainted with the Cracow School of Political Science, which I entered while a second-year law student; I graduated with distinction in 1934. Two years after receiving my law degree I passed the candidacy examinations for the doctor of laws degree and then wrote a dissertation on problems of dissolving limited partnerships. I became a doctor of laws in June, 1938.*

Professor Krzyżanowski

Economics was taught in the second year of our law school by Professor Adam Krzyżanowski. He was over sixty years old, small and slender, with thick gray hair, a little goatee, and deep-set eyes under heavy brows. He spoke in a muffled voice, as though he had an obstruction in his nose. Altogether, he was a completely different type from Scylla and Charybdis. With him there was no studying economics without understanding it intellectually. Students who had reached the second year through blind memorization of the material had to abandon this method in Professor Krzyżanowski's classes. He did not merely "teach economics"; he tried to familiarize his students with the tools of the economist's trade, that is, with an understanding of the theoretical basis of the discipline so that the student could continue to follow developments in the field in the future. One cannot move freely among economic problems, he told his students, without

---

*In Poland the so-called master of laws degree, which Shatyn received from Jagellonian University, entitled the holder to practice in the legal profession after the apprenticeship period which is described later. The doctorate of laws described here was a purely academic degree, of use to a person who intended eventually to teach law.—*Tr.*

first learning certain recognized and irrefutable intellectual principles.

To illustrate this point, one of the basic theories in economics is the theory of complementarity, according to which there are certain goods which acquire full value only in pairs—shoes, gloves, or socks, for example. One shoe or one glove does not represent the full economic value of the good. There are certain examination questions which one forgets through nervousness, questions whose answers must be learned by heart. With these, one can sometimes remember part of the answer but not the rest. However, it is impossible to remember only part of a theoretical concept like the theory of complementarity. At one of Professor Krzyżanowski's examinations, he turned to a student and asked: "Tell me, please, what is the theory of complementarity?" Having posed the question, he began pacing back and forth about the room, muttering under his breath. The student began: "The theory of complementarity is . . . is . . . is. . . ."

The professor left off his pacing and came to a stop in front of the student. He tried to help: "Perhaps you have forgotten the expression in Latin. I'll say it in Polish: 'What kind of goods are there that are mutually fulfilling? What kind of value, for example, can a single cufflink have?' " So saying, he pulled down one of his shirtcuffs and pointed to his cufflink.

The student stared at the cufflink in horrid fascination. Finally he blurted out, "Two złotys."

Krzyżanowski lost his composure. "My dear sir! You are an imbecile! You don't even understand my question. You had best leave the room and stop bothering me." The poor unfortunate got up and slunk out.

After my own examination I went out into the corridor, where a rumor was already circulating that I had done well on Krzyżanowski's examination. I was immediately set upon by a mob of students who were either about to enter the examination room or were having their exams on a later day and were there to collect all questions which had been asked. Everyone wanted to know what kinds of questions Krzyżanowski had asked. I was telling them what I remembered when one of them pushed in front of the others. "Tell me, how much does a cufflink cost?" he asked.

I had already forgotten about the cufflink incident, so his question caught me by surprise. "That's not a logical question," I said. "It depends on what the cufflink is made of—gold, silver, or something else.

A jeweler or haberdasher could tell you, but that's not an examination question in economics.''

"But that was one of the questions Krzyżanowski asked! Someone flew out of the room saying that he had blown the exam because he couldn't remember how much a cufflink cost."

To give another example of the evils of rote learning, one day, long after my university studies were behind me, I was present at the examinations because one of my pupils was taking them. There I met an acquaintance from my days in the Jewish dormitory. He was one of the perpetual students; he had studied philosophy for several years and then switched to law. For three years he did penance in the first year of the law school; now he was marking time in the second year. He was very upset at his failure and asked me to test him on at least one question.

In order to develop his self-confidence, I chose the easiest question in economics, the law of supply and demand. Even the most illiterate stallkeeper selling fruit, flowers, or eggs in the marketplace knows that if there are more customers chasing fewer goods, prices will tend to rise, and that if there are ample goods and few buyers, prices will fall. My acquaintance thought for a long time about this question, and finally said: "If you just tell me the first word of the answer, I can finish it."

For this was the way the students studied. It was no wonder that the most unjust rumors circulated about Professor Krzyżanowski—that he gave argumentative questions and that he was only looking for an excuse to flunk students. None of this, of course, was true. His lectures, sprinkled with wit and irony, were among the most challenging and thoughtful of my university days.

Krzyżanowski represented the Neoclassical School of economics. A follower of Alfred Marshall, the Cambridge economist, he held that government ought to interfere in the monetary and economic life of a country as little as possible, giving free rein to private initiative. When lecturing about monetary policy, he used to say: "Poland is a poor, technologically backward country. We do have a state printing office for printing bills, and we even have a mint for striking coins, but in the printing office we print honorary diplomas for people in the seats of power, and at the mint we strike commemorative coins and medals. We have neither the time nor the technology to print money or to strike coins, so we have our bills engraved and printed in England. Of course, in the suburbs of Warsaw, in their basements, on hand-operated presses, counterfeiters are able to run off banknotes as good as the ones we get from England, so good that even the Polish National Bank* cannot tell the real ones from the fakes, but that is only 'private initiative.' Our government is unable to achieve the same results.'' This was the sort of argument in defense of an unregulated economy and private initiative that Krzyżanowski offered.

I did not always agree with Krzyżanowski's conclusions, but this did not affect my affection and respect for him. I saw him often after my university days were over. He was always eager to hear other opinions and to discuss them in a learned and polite way. He was an extremely well-educated liberal, a scholar through and through, and he had a decisive influence on my thinking about economic problems. While I was on the estate at Borek Szlachecki I visited him at least once a month to discuss economics. These visits represented an escape from everyday business, from the dangers surrounding me, from the constant fear that I would not live to see the morrow. I would return home strengthened in mind and spirit. We never talked of personal matters. He lived alone comfortably, with no one to take care of him besides his maid. She answered the telephone and usually disposed of the calls herself by saying that the professor was not at home.

Most of our discussions were about the pros and cons of labor unions. Economic theory holds that each finished product is the result of three essential ingredients—raw materials, capital, and labor. Krzyżanowski, a fervent believer in private initiative, thought that labor unions impeded private initiative and even harmed the workers by causing unemployment: for example, he said, if workers' demands in one area became greater and greater, this discouraged investment, and capital would be diverted to other areas of the nation or the world, leaving behind unemployed union members.

I did not agree with these arguments. It seemed to me that if workers received high enough wages, they would become consumers of the first order, ensuring capital an outlet for its goods. One of my favorite examples was the rapid development of the automobile industry in the United States. Henry Ford became convinced that if he paid his workers higher wages than usual while instituting the mass production of automobiles, his first and main customers would be his own workers, and this is exactly what happened. When he produced his famous Model T, he proclaimed that each worker he employed ought to own his own

*The Polish National Bank (Narodowy Bank Polski) was the central bank of Poland, analogous to the U.S. Federal Reserve, having the exclusive right to issue money.—*Tr.*

car. Ford could sell his automobile for three hundred dollars, a figure which the competition could not begin to match, and that famous Model T reigned supreme for the next nineteen years. The labor unions, while working for a better standard of living for their workers, at the same time were creating an internal market for their product. The worker is tied to his job; he has to fight to better it. Capital, on the other hand, is mobile; knowing neither pity nor patriotism, it moves anywhere it anticipates better profits. These discussions went on until it was time for me to leave. On my next visit we would take up where we had left off.

Krzyżanowski did not have many friends or visitors during the war, and of these there were few with whom he could discuss economics. Many of his friends were imprisoned or had already perished in the concentration camp at Oranienburg or in other camps.* For my part I had absolutely no one to talk to on these subjects. How I loved to construct arguments to use in our next discussion; talking with him provided me with a wondrous relief from my worries of the moment.

Count Rostworowski

In 1922 the League of Nations established the Permanent Court of International Justice at The Hague, with fifteen justices elected by the Council and General Assembly of the League for a nine-year term. One of the justices was a Pole, Count Michał Rostworowski, director of the School of Political Science which I had attended. The school was an institution for the study of contemporary issues in politics and economics. Diplomas were handed out in an official ceremony by Count Rostworowski himself. When I graduated in 1934, I was the only student to complete twenty-three of the twenty-four courses with distinction, and Count Rostworowski congratulated me. He added that after the ceremonies he would like to have a word with me in his office.

After the initial courtesies, and some general comments about the International Court of Justice, he came to the point. "I understand that you are presently finishing law school, with a record as outstanding as yours here. In my opinion your future field of endeavor should be with the International Tribunal in The Hague. This work would ensure an

---

*At the outset of the Nazi occupation of Cracow, a large number of professors at Jagellonian University were rounded up at a faculty meeting called by the Nazis and were taken to Oranienburg, where many of them were executed or died from hardship.—*Tr.*

excellent future for you. The tribunal needs men of your caliber. However, there is one minor obstacle whose elimination, I should think, would not be troublesome to a man as worldly as yourself. For the Polish government to send you to The Hague, you would have to alter certain personal details—in particular, your religion and nationality." (What he meant was that Poland recognized me as a Polish citizen of Jewish nationality, not as a Pole, and that if I converted to Catholicism my background and nationality would then be in order.) "I view such matters differently," he said, "but unfortunately our government's attitude at present is such that without a change in your religious affiliation I cannot recommend you for the post."

I thought this over carefully, and could not answer for several minutes. Then I was ready. "I am a liberal and attach little significance to religion, or, rather, I respect all religions equally. The opportunity to work at the Court of International Justice is dazzling, something of which I would never have dreamed. However, I am also a lawyer, a good one, and perhaps I never understood so well as I do now the principle of Roman law known as *res extra commercium*, that is, value holding outside of commerce. I am not a practicing Jew, and if the Catholic faith had any attraction for me I would convert to Catholicism without a moment's hesitation, but to traffic in one's faith for personal benefit seems to me debasing. I know that many people do this, but I cannot change my faith for reasons other than those of conviction. I would feel very uncomfortable in the role of a convert who changed his religion and nationality for the sake of his career. In such a case the work at The Hague, however attractive otherwise, would not give me pleasure. Perhaps my reasons seem petty, but this is the way I feel. I do not think I can change my mind, but I am extremely grateful to you for honoring me in this way."

The count was silent for a moment, then stood up, came around his desk, and shook my hand firmly. "I have greater respect for you than you might imagine, sir," he said. The meeting was at an end, and I, of course, did not go to The Hague.

Professor Taubenschlag

Another professor whom I came to know well was of a completely different sort—I would call him a tragic figure. This was Professor

Rafał Taubenschlag. I have described how, when I was a student in law school, I looked on him and Professor Kutrzeba rather with disgust, as did the other students. But Stanisław Kutrzeba was a distinguished scholar and president of the Polish Academy of Sciences, and Taubenschlag was one of the world's most renowned papyrologists.

I came to know Professor Taubenschlag in an odd way. He also came from Przemyśl, and his mother, by this time an old woman, still lived there. His younger brother was a professor at the Free University of Łódź; he himself had studied intensively under the professor of Roman law at that time, Stanisław Wróblewski. Wróblewski first made him his assistant and later promoted him to associate professor. Finally Taubenschlag himself became a professor of Roman law. In the course of his studies he became acquainted with papyri, the greatest collection of which was located in the Vatican Library in Rome. He was always visiting Rome, and with the help of those papyri he was able to re-create previously unknown pages from the history of Egypt, Greece, and Rome.

Pope Pius XI had a great influence on Professor Taubenschlag. The pope, an Italian named Ratti, was prefect of the Vatican Library during World War I. After seven years in that position, he became First Apostolic Emissary in Warsaw. He came to love and understand Poland and the Poles, and it was he who facilitated Taubenschlag's research in the Vatican Library. Taubenschlag came to feel perfectly at home at the Vatican; he became a frequent guest of Pius XI, who loved to hear of the discoveries he had made in the Vatican collections.

Taubenschlag learned about me from his mother after I had already received my master of laws degree. My sister had told her about me. He wrote to me saying that he would like me to visit him. I was very busy at the time and kept putting off the visit. In the beginning of 1937 I received a second letter from him asking whether I had not received his letter, so I telephoned him, and we made an appointment to meet at his home. He lived by himself in a spacious apartment (I had heard that his wife had left him, taking their only son with her).

Without losing time the professor said that when he had learned about me from his mother, he had conducted his own "investigation" and found that I was reputed to be a talented civil lawyer. He had friends who assumed that he knew everything about the law, and brought him their legal problems, though his specialty was Roman law and he was devoting all his time to the study of papyri. The people coming to him for advice were well-placed and important to him, and he found it difficult to refuse his advice and assistance. No one would imagine that there were whole areas of law where he did not feel at home.

Taubenschlag proposed that I handle the affairs of these friends of his anonymously; in return, he would pass on to me all fees collected from them. I accepted the professor's proposition but asked that we put off our cooperation for a time since I was finishing my doctoral dissertation, and there the matter stood. In July, 1937, I finished my dissertation. When I received the doctorate the following June, Rafał Taubenschlag was my guest at the graduation ceremonies.

When I began to work for him, I found that he had told me the truth: he had only the vaguest knowledge of Polish civil law. I handled all the cases he entrusted to me and received considerable fees for the work. One case was particularly fascinating. This was the dispute between the German owners of the Pszczyna properties in Silesia and the Polish government. In 1921 Silesia had been divided into Lower Silesia, which remained German, and Upper Silesia, which was assigned to Poland. The Pszczyna properties, although located in Upper Silesia, remained in the hands of German absentee landlords (Prince Pszczyński was a German citizen). In the years 1937 through 1939 the Polish government attempted to expropriate certain foreign-owned properties considered vital to the state. I represented the interests of the German magnates. Finally the case reached the Supreme Court. I prepared the arguments for the Supreme Court based on the contention that the goods produced by the Pszczyna properties could not be considered vital to the state and hence the properties could not be confiscated. I won the case and received fifteen thousand złotys, perhaps not an enormous fee in view of the value of the estate, which exceeded a million złotys, and the amount of time and effort spent on the case, but it was a substantial sum nevertheless.

At first my relations with Professor Taubenschlag were strictly formal. Often I did not even come to his apartment myself but merely telephoned to find out whether there was any urgent business. After a while our relationship warmed, and he began to tell me of his researches and discoveries in the Vatican Library. More and more frequently he would mention the fact that his discoveries had necessitated the revision of his handbook of Roman law. Revision was also needed in that part of his handbook devoted to analogies with Polish law, to reflect recent changes in our legislation. Before long he proposed that we revise his handbook together. He would do the work on Roman law from his new perspective, and I would revise the comparative chapters. I agreed, and we set to work. Each of us, working separately, kept very busy. Taubenschlag traveled to Rome for research whenever he could, while I was engaged in my own and his legal practice, as well as in preparing chapters for the new textbook.

Disaster soon struck Taubenschlag, however. As I have said, his wife and son had left him; soon afterward, in 1938, his friend and protector, Professor Stanisław Wróblewski, died. Taubenschlag, embittered by his family misfortunes and by the death of Wróblewski, decided to finish the new textbook as quickly as possible. On a recent visit to Rome, the pope had proposed that he move permanently to the Vatican, and he had accepted the invitation with gratitude. Less and less tied him to Cracow. He would publish his textbook and leave for Italy.

We were hastening work on the book when the next blow fell: the pope died. The new pope was the former Vatican undersecretary of state, Cardinal Eugenio Pacelli, who assumed the name of Pius XII. A different wind began to blow from the Vatican. Pacelli had been a papal emissary in Bavaria and, later, after World War I, an Apostolic Emissary in Berlin. He saw Poland through German eyes. Pius XI had lived in Poland, knew the country, and spoke the language. The new pope was a legalist, a lawyer, and a partisan of Germany. With the death of Pius XI, Taubenschlag's future seemed bleak.

Several months passed and World War II broke out. Taubenschlag left Poland for the United States to lecture on Roman law at Columbia University in New York. This was another atmosphere, a different sort of student, a different status for a university professor. The war was barely over when he returned to Cracow. His position at the university had been filled by someone else, so he settled in Warsaw and began teaching there. He went no more to Rome, for he could find no common ground with the reigning pope. Deprived of his home, friends, and work among his beloved papyri, he grew bitter and withdrawn and finally died—in the same year as the pope who had closed the door to his research, in 1958.

Chapter 8

Legal Practice

The situation for young lawyers starting a practice in Cracow was far from favorable, since the city had more lawyers than it needed. Most of the older lawyers had been trained under the Austro-Hungarian legal system in Austrian law and would not touch anything connected with the new legal system.* They either changed their specialty to penal law, which was relatively simple and required a knowledge of theatrical tricks more than a solid grasp of legislation and precedents, or they worked in legal areas that had not yet been altered, such as family and inheritance law. Still others remained, as it were, on the sidelines, employed in writing claims, writs, and summonses and filling out printed forms: for fifty groszy such an attorney would send a warning letter to a debtor; the price for a summons was five złotys. To be sure, there were also traditional law offices engaged in both penal and civil work, but their number was insignificant in comparison to the plethora of poor lawyers.

I had a somewhat different view of my situation as a fledgling lawyer from that of most other recent graduates of law school, mainly because I was somewhat more mature and experienced than they. I had

---

*In 1918 the Polish state was reconstituted out of portions of the old Austro-Hungarian Empire, former Imperial Russia, and Germany. At the time of the reconstitution, five different legal systems were in effect in the respective territories. These systems were gradually subsumed under a new uniform Polish legal code, but the work was still incomplete at the time of the outbreak of World War II.—*Tr.*

been making a good living for some time and had even founded a school, or rather, a course of study, and had been publishing workbooks and other study materials for students in all years of law school. Besides this, I was better prepared than the average lawyer. I passed my exams not once but dozens of times, for I "passed" each exam anew with each one of the pupils whom I prepared.

As far as my own legal practice was concerned, I had rejected the idea of taking in petty and unprofitable business and decided to devote myself to areas where competition was weakest, namely, to administrative law and tax disputes. I found an old and infirm attorney with an office in one basement room. His only equipment consisted of a decrepit old desk, two rickety chairs, and a telephone. He never went to court but spent all his time writing dunning letters. Almost no one came to his office. His clients, mostly merchants, would telephone to give him the name and address of the delinquent customer and the amount of the debt. He had ready-made form letters which he filled in by hand, since he did not possess a typewriter. At the end of the month he sent each client a list of the letters he had written together with a bill. For each letter he collected fifty groszy plus postage.

To become an independent attorney at this time one had to have practiced in an established law office for five years. Thus I came to the old man with a proposition. If he would agree to enter my name as his assistant, I would rent a large office in a fashionable part of town and furnish him with his own room, a private telephone, and the use of a secretary. I would pay for everything, and he would continue to do business as before, while I would handle my administrative and tax matters there.

He eagerly agreed to my terms, and I rented a handsome office, giving the old attorney all that I had promised. I registered as his assistant so that I could appear in court as his full legal representative. I took four friends of mine into the practice as my own assistants, all of them talented and eager for work, and hired three secretaries. These friends were divided into two teams. One group, with its own secretary, devoted itself exclusively to the study of the administrative code. The other group, also with its own secretary, was engaged in tax law. The third secretary was for general office work and could also be used by my patron.

Since there were few attorneys in the field of administrative and tax law, our business flourished from the beginning. Any taxpayer would willingly pay our fees if I could show him how to save money. Consultation on any matter in our office cost nothing, and I was free to reject a case if I considered it hopeless. Once I decided to accept it, I could count on a fee of from one-third to one-half of the amount that I was able to save. No client ever failed to come to terms. Cases sometimes dragged on for months, with my two assistants sifting through all existing regulations. We submitted requests for hearings and re-hearings; we lodged appeals with higher tribunals; in the end, if we won, our fees were very high. There were times when our joint earnings exceeded ten thousand złotys per month.* However, taking into account the considerable cost of maintaining the office and our system of dividing all our fees according to a set table, the income was not all that large. Still, it did earn us all a comfortable living.

At this time I became convinced that even the state officials who levied taxes on the citizenry were not well acquainted with all the regulations. Each official knew only a few of them, for they were not lawyers and could not make their way through the morass of the new laws, which sometimes contradicted one another, while this was our business and our forte. Our names did not appear in the newspapers, and we did not become famous; it was a matter of everyday hard work and battling with our wits. The victor was the person who knew the most about the laws and who therefore could better represent his client. I will take one case of an administrative nature as an example.

One day in the spring of 1938, the owner of a small but prosperous factory came to us for help. He employed eighty workers. Recently an inspection team from the Department of Social Welfare had visited his factory and determined that some employees were working by artificial light, which was considered unhealthy. The inspectors recommended that three windows be made along one of the long walls of the building to let daylight into the work space. He gave the factory owner one month either to put in the windows or close down the factory. On the outside of the building wall ran a strip of land one meter wide. The law stated that the owner of a building had the right to put windows in a wall if he owned at least three meters of land beyond it. If he did not have three meters, the so-called air rights could be granted by the owner of the neighboring property, and this was usually done through an easement. If the neighbor granted this right, he could not later retract it and block the new windows by building on the nearby land. Next to the

---

*At the official exchange rate, five złotys to the dollar, this amounts to around two thousand dollars. However, in terms of actual buying power in Poland, the amount was much more substantial than this sum indicates.—*Tr.*

factory building was a small empty lot, worth about twenty-five hundred to three thousand złotys. The factory owner was prepared to buy this lot in order to put windows in the wall, but he made the mistake of letting the owner know why he wanted it. When his neighbor heard that the factory was threatened with closure, he demanded twenty thousand złotys for his lot.

The factory owner was frantic, and came to us for assistance. We promised to examine the matter, and my team and I began poring over the pertinent legal regulations. Unfortunately, they were plain and unambiguous. We analyzed all possible commentaries on the law but found nothing to help our client, so we decided to resign from the case. Still, it fascinated us; we felt that there must be some way out of this dilemma, but we could not pinpoint it. I told my associates that I had decided to tell the factory owner that we could do nothing for him. That night I received a call from one of my colleagues; he had licked the problem, and he felt that we could win the case. There was a loophole in the law, and we could use it for our client. The key was that small strip of land which our client owned next to his wall. Next morning we took one of our secretaries to a notary public, and for a trifling sum the factory owner sold her the one-meter strip. According to the law, she was now his immediate neighbor. She then, of course, granted him the right to put windows in his wall. The owner of the vacant lot was no longer the "immediate neighbor" and so had no further say in the matter. The mistake in the law lay in the imprecise articulation of the principle of "immediate neighbor." The law did not forsee that someone might own a one-meter strip of land. Our client paid us our fee of five thousand złotys with great willingness.

The Cracow Jewry

As time went on, I became interested in the life of the local Jewry. I discovered that there were actually three different groups of Jews living in Cracow. One group, which had lived there for generations, were progressive citizens, Westernized, speaking perfect Polish as well as Yiddish, and resembling the rest of the population in most respects. They were doctors, lawyers, engineers; they lived in modern apartments or their own houses; they owned their own stores; and they were well established in all parts of town. They were really an organic part of the city's topography.

The second group were the Orthodox Jews, also living in the city for many generations. Their customs did not differ much from those of Orthodox Jews living in the part of Poland which had once belonged to Austria. They spoke a German-Yiddish mixture and lived in the Kazimierz district of Cracow. As a young and unknown lawyer, I was in no position to draw clients from either of these groups, for they had ample legal talent of their own.

The third group of Jews were newcomers, settlers from the eastern territories.* They lived in a network of crooked little streets—Miodowa, Boże Ciało, Józef, Ester, Rabbi Meisels, and others—in the Kazimierz district. They were also Orthodox but differed from the other Orthodox Jews in almost everything. During the week they wore short-visored caps and dressed modestly, but on the Sabbath they sallied forth in long black silk coats and *stramels*—hats of black velvet shaped like bowls, fringed with a red foxtail. They spoke a Polish-Russian-Yiddish polyglot dialect; they did not use last names (although they possessed them) but called each other by first name preceded by "Reb" as a term of respect, just as in Spanish one says Don Pedro, Don Antonio, and so on. They made fun of the "western" Jews who had been in Cracow for centuries; instead of using their last names they made up expressive and sometimes malicious nicknames, such as "De Kryme" ("The Crooked One"), "De Hojche" ("The Tall One"), "De Puritz" ("The Young Lord"), and so on.

They traded among themselves and did not mix with other Jews. Talkative, expansive, inventive, quick-tempered, they all knew how to count, whatever their degree of education, and could do so faster than any adding machine. They controlled the shoe industry, but for the most part they were wholesalers, supplying goods either to local stores or to shops in the many small towns in the countryside. They engaged trained bookkeepers to keep their books for tax purposes, but in addition they all carried in their pockets little notebooks in which their actual accounts were kept, accounts different from those found in the bookkeepers' neat ledgers. The information in those little books was entered in a Hebrew script, legible only to them.

---

*That is, from those portions of western Byelorussia and the Ukraine ceded to Poland by Russia after World War I. The interwar period saw the continual migration of Jews from these economically backward regions to the larger and more prosperous towns of central Poland.—*Tr.*

They were excellent tradesmen, and, universal opinion to the contrary notwithstanding, they never cheated or swindled, though they drove a hard bargain. Their prices were lower than those of the "western" Jews, but they made up for the smaller profit with a larger volume (this is not to say, of course, that they would pass up a bargain when they saw one). These Jews even had their own postal system, far more efficient than the official one. On every day but the Sabbath their couriers rode the trains in all directions from Cracow, as far as Kielce and Radom in the north, Wadowice and Nowy Targ in the south, Tarnów and Rzeszów in the east, and Chrzanów and Oświęcim in the west. They traveled all day on the local passenger trains which stopped at every little town. There messengers from their local branch would be waiting to pick up letters, packages, money orders, and the like, and to pass on their own mail. In the evening the same traffic would flow in the opposite direction, as the couriers returned to the city. In this way one could post a letter, a package, or a money order in the morning and have an answer or receipt by the same evening.

The Jewish Arbitration Committees

I entered this society through one of their clan. At first they did not trust me, for I looked too much like a "western" Jew, but when they saw that I neither put on airs nor called on family connections, and that I dealt honestly and fairly, their distrust evaporated. Even though I lived on Łazarz ("Lazarus") Street, in a duplex apartment with a statue of Jesus in a niche outside the gate, employed Catholics, and went around without a head covering summer and winter alike, they came to like me and opened their hearts to me. Never ones to hide their feelings, they knew how to laugh and were not ashamed to cry if the occasion warranted. They could be as pleased as children and could enjoy themselves to the utmost without holding back out of false modesty. In addition, they were very sensitive to the misfortunes of others. Once when I was in the office of one of these clients, a shopkeeper from Nowy Targ drove up in his cart to tell him that he was returning his goods; his wife had tuberculosis and because of the expenses he was unable to settle his account. On hearing this my client, who was known as a man who drove a hard bargain, rose, went to his small metal wall safe, took out the packet of promissory notes signed by his customer, tore them all in half, and said, "Don't worry about your bill; take care of your wife. Take away your goods and pay me when you can. Your wife and children are more important than anything else."

These Jews hated to go to court. They obeyed other rules, which were not always in harmony with the laws on the statute books. For them the admonitions of the Bible were all important. For example, it was considered a great crime to harm an orphan, a widow, or a pauper. If a quarrel broke out among them, it would be settled by an arbitration committee of their own. Before long I had become a regular member of one of these committees. Each side would choose its representative, and I, as an impartial observer, was the third member. My task was to examine the facts; then the other two issued the decision. There was no appeal from the committee's decree. I never heard of a case where a party failed to agree to arbitration or refused to abide by a ruling, which for them was sacred. On occasion even Poles would bring complaints against Jews to these bodies, and such cases would be examined in the same way as any others.

These committees functioned in an amazing way; their judgments showed a great deal of compassion for the poor, and they tried to help quietly, without fanfare, simply as a matter among friends. They did not care for formal organizations with presidents, secretaries, and treasurers. All their affairs were handled by word of mouth. If it were necessary to collect money for a widow or the orphans of some dead man, or if a poor girl about to get married had no dowry, two elders of the community would go from one person to the next, from shop to shop, collecting money. The two would explain the general purpose of the collection but never name the person for whom it was intended. They took only cash, never gave a receipt, never kept any record. It was not permitted to note who had given what, for that might shame some poorer person who could not give as much as others. There was no danger that the collectors would keep part of the money for themselves; on the contrary, everyone knew that they would add to it out of their own pockets. The collection finished, the money was given to the intended person, and there the matter ended. Next time someone else would do the collecting on the same basis.

The arbitration committees were guided more by sympathy for the weaker side than by which side was right. I recall one case where a tenant called his landlord before the committee. The landlord said that his tenant was three months behind in his rent and he wanted him to move out;

103

he agreed to forget about the rent he was owed. In his defense the tenant stated that he had a sick child and was without work. The committee decreed that the tenant was to remain in his apartment, rent-free, until he found suitable employment, after which he was entitled to receive from the landlord the equivalent of three months' rent in cash so that he could get back on his feet again.

In another case a merchant from Chrzanów brought before the arbitration committee a wholesaler from whom he had purchased some goods, claiming that the wholesaler had charged him more than others. The wholesaler did not deny this but maintained that his other customers were bigger and that he had done business with them longer, so they were entitled to a discount, while the man from Chrzanów was new in the business, and his credit was uncertain. The ruling was that the wholesaler was to refund to the merchant from Chrzanów the extra amount he had paid for his goods; in addition, for one year the wholesaler was to give him a discount of 10 percent less than he gave his best customer. The reasoning was that the Chrzanów merchant, as a newcomer, was financially unable to compete with the well-established businessmen who had greater resources, and that it was necessary to ease him through this difficult initial period.

Trained as I was in legal regulations, I was always amazed at the quality of justice meted out by these committees. Rarely did matters ever reach the state courts. The committees cross-examined the plaintiffs and witnesses, examined the facts, weighed the evidence, and issued their verdict. Court costs were usually paid by the wealthier of the two sides. If the quarrel was between equals, the costs were split; if malicious intent could be demonstrated, however, the loser paid. It sometimes happened that a case would not get as far as the committee; the two sides would simply present it to me to decide, and my pronouncement was respected. Even the loser never complained and would pay immediately or within twenty-four hours.

My Jewish Clients

After a year of this arbitration work, my law clientele increased, and many of my regular clients' adversaries began to come to me as well. I was now handling the affairs of people who already knew one another, and I was counselor not only to the merchants themselves but to their families as well, in purely private matters. Sometimes this work was easy, and sometimes it was impossible.

One of my clients had four children of whom the oldest, a thirteen-year-old boy, already of age according to Jewish law, was his father's pride. He dreamed of sending his son to the Talmudic academy; he was to become a great scholar instead of having to struggle as hard as his father had. One day I noticed the boy's face as he listened to his father's grand schemes for him. From his expression it was clear that the father's dreams were not his own. A little later the boy came alone to my office. He obviously felt awkward and did not know how to begin. He almost left without unburdening himself, but I chatted with him until he was comfortable enough to talk about his problem. Day after day, he said, he had to sit and study the Talmud with the sun shining brightly outside the walls of his school. He loved soccer and was a good goalie, he said, though, of course, he had never kicked a real ball, only a rag one, and even that wasn't permitted by his father. If he stole a few minutes to play soccer with the other children, he had a terrible time because of his long forelocks, which kept falling into his face. When he tried to stick them behind his ears, the others laughed at him, and he would get angry, pick up his things, and leave. He would give up several years of his life to get rid of his forelocks, he said, crying bitterly. He hated them; he hated his father's ambitions for him; he hated the whole world.

I sat down at my desk, after hearing this tale of woe, and wrote a note to my barber. I sent the boy over to him with the note. In it I told the barber what to do, and before my young client knew what had happened, the barber had trimmed off one entire forelock. The boy was white with terror at what his father would say, but the barber had my instructions to tell the father that he, the barber, had made a mistake and would take full responsibility. When the boy returned home his father was furious and the boy wept and wailed, but what could they do? He couldn't go around with just one forelock, and so the other one had to be cut off. My young friend swore to his father that he would make sure they grew back as quickly as possible. (Of course, every day thereafter he looked in the mirror to make sure that the obnoxious growths never returned.) His life now took on a brighter hue, and I willingly took this sin on my conscience.

Another of my family cases involved a so-called premarital agreement. The agreement to marry involved my client's twelve-year-old daughter and the fourteen-year-old son of a rabbi from Kielce. My client undertook to send the rabbi's son to the famous Wilno Academy for advanced Talmudic studies and to maintain him there for five years, at the end of which the boy was to marry his daughter, who by then would be seventeen. This agreement was signed by the parents without consulting the children. My client was purchasing for himself the honor of having the son of a rabbi and a rabbi-to-be for a son-in-law, while the rabbi from Kielce agreed because he lacked the means to educate his son. There was nothing unusual in any of this; it was quite common for a wealthy Jew to pay for the education of someone of higher position in the social hierarchy in order to provide his daughter with a suitable husband.

The negotiations took place in my office. The rabbi, a handsome man in the prime of life, arrived from Kielce. I begged his pardon for not speaking Yiddish well and explained that, in any case, the agreement would have to be drawn up in Polish. At that the rabbi responded in fluent Polish that he saw no reason why the entire discussion could not be conducted in that language. I was surprised that he spoke Polish so well, and he explained that he was a graduate of a Polish gymnasium in Warsaw and that he intended to study philosophy at Warsaw University if his finances ever permitted.

My client came to the meeting fortified with a long list of clauses and conditions. For fear of coming out the loser in the contract, he had foreseen every eventuality that might occur during the next five years. The expression on the rabbi's face showed that he was embarrassed by the whole proceedings. After all, he was an interested party too; his own child's future was at stake. I finally stopped the discussion and asked my client to step into another room. There I told him frankly that I was shocked at his behavior, that this was no sales agreement; nothing was being bought or sold; it was the children's lives that were at stake. Either he trusted the rabbi or he did not. If he did not, then he should take his wad of papers and leave. The merchant was clearly ashamed of himself. He threw away all his clauses and conditions and we quickly drew up the agreement. The hearty handshake of the rabbi was proof enough for me that he was grateful for being saved from a humiliating situation.

Unfortunately, there were some cases which I was unable to resolve even with my best efforts. One day the fourteen-year-old daughter of one of my clients came to my office with her boy friend. She was a petite girl with a very pleasant face and beautiful, Titian-colored hair gathered into a thick braid. The boy was a strikingly handsome sixteen-year-old blond. They held hands as they asked me for help. She was Jewish and he was Catholic. They lived next door to each other and had played together since childhood. Now they were meeting in secret because they were in love. His father hated Jews, and her parents were very conservative, religious people, so there was no hope that either side would agree to the marriage. They were too young to run away, and if they did, where would they go?

I was sorry for both of them, but did not see any practical solution to the problem. I talked with them for a long time, calmly and seriously, wanting them to understand what I had to say without having their feelings hurt. I told them that before they took any action they should understand the practicalities involved. Legally there was no way for them to get married, for they were not of age and could not marry without their parents' consent. If they ran away from home and lived together, they would have no way of supporting themselves. The boy had barely finished six years of gymnasium, and he had no trade or profession. And the girl? No one would hire her for any kind of work. Then as far as their parents were concerned, this would be a severe blow. As far as they themselves were concerned, I said that I was not certain whether their love could survive outside conventional society, without means of support, with their guilt about their treatment of their families. Not only would they probably cease to love—they might even come to hate each other. I pointed out that our society was still very backward where religion was concerned, and that the runaways would become pariahs, tolerated neither in Jewish nor in Polish society. I advised them to let time solve the problem. Perhaps they would some day decide that their love had gone. Beyond this advice I was unable to do anything for them.

That young couple provided me with an excellent example of the absurdity of religious obduracy. People had not yet come to understand that religion is a question of accident and upbringing. I was reminded of the play by the Polish writer Antoni Słonimski called *The Family*, about the families of a Jewish tenant farmer and a Polish landowner, both living in the same small town.* By coincidence a son was born to both families at the same time. The son of the landowner finished high school and went to the university. He began his studies by joining a Polish fraternity

---

*Antoni Słonimski (1895-1976) was an eminent Polish writer of both the pre- and postwar periods. Shatyn's summary of the popular play, staged first in 1933, is true to its spirit, if not in every detail.—*Tr.*

and buying a walking stick to knock out the windows of Jewish stores and to threaten passers-by who looked Jewish to him. He nurtured a great hatred for Jews and had a special reason for it, for nature had played a trick on him. His father was a blue-eyed blond, but he had a hooked nose and curly black hair. Were it not for his fraternity cap, with which he never parted for a moment, and his stick, he could easily have passed for a Jew. He particularly hated his neighbor, the tenant's son, a blond-haired youth with eyes as blue as cornflowers.

The town where the tenant and landowner lived was small, and hardly anything ever happened there. Even the death from old age of a hospital nurse was an event which attracted attention for a time. But it was only after the nurse's death that the townspeople received a real shock. When the priest came to administer the last rites, she admitted that by accident many years before, when she attended the two births, she gave the tenant's baby to the landowner and the landowner's baby to the tenant. At first she had not realized her error, as newborns are pretty much alike, but as the boys grew up it became obvious to her, and she recalled how it could have happened. Now, on her deathbed, she confessed the story to the priest, and made him swear that after her death he would reveal the secret and rectify her error.

The Jew's son, the fraternity thug, left home forever, unable to bear the discovery that his real parents were the same Jews whom he had hated for so long. The landowner's son, in spite of the pleas of his natural father and the prospect of a considerable inheritance, would not desert his true parents, the Jewish tenant farmers. He understood that love decides whose one's parents are, and upbringing determines one's religion—genetics plays no role at all.

Chapter 9

I Fall in Love

By the beginning of 1938 I was devoting less and less time to my law office. I had an experienced staff who functioned well without my supervision, and at Taubenschlag's insistence I was spending more and more time on my contribution to his handbook on Roman law, which was to be ready for the printer early in 1939. I was also preparing for my doctoral defense. By spring, however, I felt that I needed a holiday to refresh myself for the coming year. I had been working from morning to night without a break since I opened my law practice.

This time I set out for the Beskid Mountains. I visited Szczyrk, Brenna, Wisła, and Ustroń,* crossed the Czech border at Cieszyn, and then strayed as far south as Bratislava. That spring was so beautiful that, after several weeks back in Cracow, I took off once again, this time for the eastern stretches of Poland, to Jaremcze, Tatarów, and Worochta;† in Zaleszczyki I crossed the Prut River and went as far as Czerniowce‡ in Romania. On the way back I stopped in Przemyśl and took my mother to Rozłucz for a holiday. In short, I let work in the office slide and devoted more and more time to my scholarly work and to exploring southern Poland.

---

*Tourist spots in the Silesian Beskids.—*Tr.*
†The other spots mentioned now belong to the Soviet Union.—*Tr.*
‡Present-day Chernovtsy, Soviet Ukraine.—*Tr.*

The area covered by my scholarly work was rather broad. Along with my comparison of modern Polish and Roman law for Taubenschlag, I was gathering materials for a book on political science which I intended to publish early the next year. So my plans for 1938 and 1939 were made when, suddenly and unexpectedly, I fell in love.

I met my future wife, Basia (Barbara) Neulinger, one day in October, 1938, in the Artists' Café on Łobzowska Street. She lived in an attractive part of town called Nowa Wieś ("New Village"). Her family had lived in their small house on Kazimierz Wielki ("Kazimierz the Great") Street since before World War I. In this house all the children of Isaak Neulinger, Basia's father, had been born and all the daughters married.

For all his Jewishness, Mr. Neulinger was a typical Cracowian, with the conservative views I have described. Everything had its own time and place: family, neighbors, friends, colleagues, even chance acquaintances. To disturb this order was unthinkable. He had a fixed place in the social firmament and was known and respected by everyone. Basia was his youngest daughter and his favorite. Both older sisters were married, and her father had his eye on another son-in-law, a physician whose relatives and background were well known to him. He was horrified when Basia told him that she was in love with a young lawyer from a small town in an eastern county, about whom nothing was known, and about whom no one could find out anything. In short, Mr. Neulinger considered the match a misalliance.

"Authoritomania"

One thing about me that particularly annoyed Mr. Neulinger was that I recognized no established authorities but rather tried to assess people and things on the basis of their innate worth. This habit was formed in the days when I had not yet acquired any social standing myself. "Authoritomania," an exaggerated respect for authority, position, or social eminence, obsessed Mr. Neulinger and, indeed, many Poles at the time, and I had seen many students of mine come to grief because of it. I am reminded of a pupil of mine who was deputy inspector of the main police force in Warsaw. To climb higher up the administrative ladder, he needed the degree of Master of Laws. He took classes for three years at the university in Warsaw, in a dilatory way, without ever taking an examination. Finally he decided to come to Cracow and enroll at the law school there for serious study. Remember that this man was not an eighteen-year-old; he was not unaccustomed to the everyday struggle for existence; he held an important and a responsible position in society. What is more, he was a giant of a man, muscular, with a barrel chest. When he strode through the halls of the university in his elegant uniform discreetly decked with medals won at the time of the fight for independent Poland (at the age of fifteen he had fought heroically in the ranks of the Polish army*), not a single woman student failed to turn her head to stare admiringly after him. He himself was well aware of the impression he made.

But all this glamor did not serve my policeman at the university. He had been brought up to respect, and even fear, people of higher social standing than himself. He did not understand that most so-called authorities are merely clever people with good connections and that they occupy positions for which others are undoubtedly equally well suited but which they are too modest or too poorly connected to demand. Thus, at the thought that he must come before a professor of the university and recite his lessons, and that his whole administrative career depended on the opinion of this lofty personage, he would come down with a fever. For days before his examinations he would be prostrated with diarrhea, witless and incoherent.

I told him that Professor Kutrzeba was nothing but a drunken sot with a pig's nose and buttons for eyes; I told him that Professor Taubenschlag, with his goggle eyes and dangling arms, was only a fish gasping for air, or perhaps studying to become an orangoutan. Nothing helped.

"Yes, Bronek, you are absolutely right," he would say. "It makes no sense to be afraid of them." And then examination time would come and my hero would whisk himself back to Warsaw.

I Meet Basia's Family

After a six-month courtship I proposed marriage to Basia Neulinger in March, 1939, and she accepted me. First, however, I had to undergo a baptism of fire—that is, I had to pay a visit to the Neulingers

---

*With Józef Piłsudski's Polish Legions during World War I.—*Tr.*

to ask them for her hand. I agreed reluctantly; clearly there was no escape. I was invited to Kazimierz Wielki Street for Friday supper.

Since the visit was an official one, I came in a dark suit, feeling very ill at ease. Besides Basia's parents, there were her elder sister, that sister's husband and their two sons, her second sister, that sister's husband and six-year-old daughter, her brother, her brother's fiancée, and some elderly relative and his wife. The conversation was labored from the beginning. I had heard about her father's conservative views from Basia and hesitated to introduce any topic on which our opinions might differ. Soon Mrs. Neulinger, a sweet, kind, quiet woman, excused herself from the dinner table to lie on the sofa, explaining that she had back trouble. She walked with a cane inside the house and often had to rest. Without worrying about form, I got up and went to sit next to her. I could see that she wanted to encourage me and that she understood it was not pleasant to be under observation by so many pairs of eyes. She told me that she knew a lot about me already, as Basia talked about me constantly, and that she was sure we would be very happy. From that moment on I liked her very much.

On July 2, 1939, we were married and went to the small resort town of Rytro for our honeymoon. On the first day of September, Hitler invaded Poland, and World War II had begun.

Chapter 10

Flight to the East

The war broke out at dawn on Friday, September 1, 1939. I was mobilized immediately, but my mobilization point had been moved to Tarnów. On Saturday all government offices were moved, all officials left Cracow, and all trains stopped running. On Sunday the male civilian population was also in flight, as sound trucks drove about the city ordering all able-bodied men to leave immediately and head east. On Sunday I too said goodbye to Cracow. I took a streetcar but got only as far as the main post office. It was eight o'clock in the evening, and a blackout was in effect. Near the offices of the *Codzienny Kurier Ilustrowany* (*Daily Illustrated Courier*) the streets were in chaos, as countless horsecarts, trucks, and automobiles on their way out of town tried to turn onto Starowiślna ("Old Vistula") Street. The noise was deafening. People were shouting, vehicles were colliding, frightened horses were whinnying. The streets were blocked by broken-down automobiles, stalled streetcars, and throngs of people, staggering along under huge bundles, pushing and shoving their way toward the Trzeci Most ("Third Bridge")—that is, toward Podgórze, toward the east, toward anyplace else.

In spite of the present frenzy, everyone was convinced that the whole crisis would be over in a few days. England and France would show Hitler what war was like. The whole world would attack Germany, and Hitler's swaggering and plundering progress across the face of Europe would halt. The Germans had managed to do a little damage, perhaps, but in a month everything would return to normal and life would go on as before. To me, however, the commotion, uproar, screaming, and swearing up and down every street in town said something else. This was no organized withdrawal but a panicky flight. In any case I could not remain in town, so I walked to Płaszów, an eastern district of Cracow, where there were said to be trains waiting to take people east. Freight trains were standing there all right, but they weren't going east; they weren't going anywhere. There were no trainmen anywhere in sight; all was at a standstill, with swarms of disoriented people milling about the station. Without further ado, I started walking along the tracks in the direction of Tarnów.

I was lightly dressed, wearing my usual hiking outfit—heavy slacks, windbreaker, stout walking shoes, and a knapsack containing spare socks, a razor, and a supply of the bittersweet chocolate that hikers carried as a reserve. The night was cool, perfect for a march, and I tramped briskly along. Near me on the tracks others, whose faces I could not see, were also trudging. When they grew tired, weighed down by their burdens, I said goodbye and left them behind. After a while I would catch up with another group which I would also leave behind in a few minutes, for I was a good hiker and I found the slow pace of these people wearisome.

I walked on without stopping throughout the night. With the first rays of dawn I could make out the silhouettes of the people now walking alongside me. It was different than it had been that night, when one could only hear disembodied voices. What a motley throng it was—men, women, old, young, even children. Few were prepared for such an arduous march. Some had on elegant clothing and city shoes totally unsuited for walking through open fields, forests, and sand; some were wearing fur coats and dragging along suitcases, sacks, and other bundles which only held them back. They would not get much farther, I thought.

The first rays of the sun appeared on the horizon. A light blue haze hung over the fields, but the chill of the September night persisted. I did not slow my tempo but ate some of my chocolate and marched on. I wanted to be in Tarnów as quickly as possible. I passed through Bochnia; in Brzesko I would take my first rest. I knew that it was not far from there to Tarnów.*

---

*Tarnów is about ninety kilometers east of Cracow. See the map at the beginning of this book for an outline of the author's journey.—*Tr.*

The sun was high now, and I had a clear view of the stream of humanity headed east. Some were walking along the railroad line, others along the embankment beside the tracks; still others were resting or eating something by the side of the path or in the nearby fields, still wet with dew. Those who were most weary were lying next to the burdens which they had carried for so many hours; others sifted through bundles which had been abandoned, hoping to find something of use—a pair of socks or comfortable shoes. As far as the eye could see lay suitcases and bundles and swarms of refugees—from Cracow, Wieliczka, Niepołomice, and Bochnia. All along the road the farmers stared in amazement at this winding river of people, without beginning or end, this river of anguish. Here and there some youngster, caught up in the excitement, would tear away from a farmhouse and join the throng, while other marchers fell by the wayside, one night's walk having utterly exhausted them. Many had no food, and there was no place along the way to buy anything to eat. Some said that it would be better to return to the city; others simply sat down, unable to move another step. While night had concealed the hopelessness of the situation to some extent, morning drew back the blinds. Everyone was hungry, dirty, exhausted, and in despair.

All the while I steadfastly pressed on. Along the way I passed trains standing on the track without engineers, motionless specters. Many people had gotten into the cars to rest, and I entered one of them to break my march for a short while, but I left as quickly as I entered. The car was already crowded, and newcomers were not welcome. No one would make room for a new arrival if he were not a friend or traveling companion. Giving up the idea of resting in the train, I turned my thoughts to Brzesko: there I would wash, shave, rest, and relax. On to Brzesko.

The Snake

Noon arrived, and I decided to stop after all. I walked down off the railway embankment and into a little woods about a hundred meters away. I ate some more of my chocolate and then took my ease on the grass. Just as I was settling down, I heard a kind of droning above my head, barely audible, like a flying beetle. I looked up but saw nothing. After a moment the sound got louder. Now I could hear an engine.

There was a tiny airplane, without escort, not as large as those we had seen bombing the airport in Cracow on Friday. As I stared up at it through the treetops it dove, leveling off about two hundred meters above the ground. People were looking up at it; some of them were waving to the pilot. From beneath the plane they couldn't see its markings, but at my distance I saw the swastika painted on the fuselage. It was a German plane. After a moment I heard the chatter of a machine gun. The pilot was firing into the crowd of civilians walking along the tracks. The bullets dug a furrow in the dirt beside the tracks and ricocheted off the rocks of the embankment, scattering in a loop as though a large snake was dropping on the people from the sky. People fell, and the plane flew on. The whole thing lasted perhaps a minute.

I ran to the tracks: the snake's victims lay everywhere, soaked in blood. The wounded lay writhing in anguish; the dead lay still, contorted in odd positions. The living were bent over the dead, trying to bring them back to life. Belongings were scattered everywhere. Despairing cries, chaos. Then came the sound of the engine again. The plane had circled back and was diving toward the railroad tracks. The panic-stricken people ran for the fields, rolled down the embankment, threw themselves into ditches or any place on the ground. After a moment the snake dropped again along the tracks, scattering pebbles in all directions. Three or four times this machine of death returned to the slaughter. Finally, it flew away.

It was past noon. I could do nothing for the dead or wounded. There were no bandages; it was better to get to a village and bring help. I went to the nearest village, about three kilometers away, but there was no telephone. No one there knew what to do. I went back to the main road and tried to flag a passing vehicle to get help, but no driver would stop. What was the use? Everywhere it was the same—everywhere these tiny single-engine planes had terrorized the civilian population. Who could bother about a single attack on one stretch of track? There were dozens, hundreds of victims along every kilometer of the railway line east of Cracow. There was no defense against this death from the air.

I hiked on; by four o'clock I was in Brzesko, by evening in Tarnów. I had seen enough to make me want to get as far east as possible—far from the scene of these murders. First, however, I decided to look for my mobilization point. No one knew anything. I was told to go to Rzeszów to see about it. Everything was in turmoil. There were no

116

mobilization points; there was no organization at all. It seemed that everyone was on his own.

Jurek

That night I caught a freight train from Tarnów packed with people headed east. It traveled about thirty kilometers before coming to a stop. The signal was not working, and, incredible as it seems, the engineer refused to go on, saying that he was afraid he might lose his job or at least be taken to court and fined. People still believed that this turmoil would not last longer than a week or so. Off I set on foot again. In the darkness a man came up alongside me. He had a pleasant voice, somewhat mocking in tone; he moved briskly along, and I could tell that he was young and an experienced hiker. As we talked, he offered me a cigarette and lit one for himself. His name was Jerzy (Jurek) Sroczyński, he told me. He was an engineer from Lwów; he was thirty-two. Toward morning we entered a small village and found a tavern where we were able to get some breakfast and rest a bit.

Jurek recommended that we keep moving, for he was afraid of being surrounded by the Germans, so we soon set off again. We avoided large concentrations of people but did keep to the railroad line, which exposed us to attack from the air. That night we found an empty railroad car and slept there, warm and comfortable, but the thought of getting home kept running through my mind. We passed Dębica, Sędziszów, then Rzeszów, Łańcut, and, finally, Jarosław. I had friends in Jarosław and expected that they would put us up for the night, but no one was at home. The doorman of their apartment house told me that they had left for Lwów several days earlier. I told him that I was a relative of theirs from Cracow and asked whether he would let me into the apartment, for I needed to bathe and take a nap. The doorman was in no hurry to do so; I had to recite the names of my friends and of their daughters before he would consider it. Finally, he reluctantly yielded to a two-złoty tip, warning me that he did not want any trouble and that "nothing better be missing."

When we entered the apartment, we saw that my friends must have left in a great hurry because they had left almost everything behind. It was already Wednesday. How long had it been, I wondered, since I had been inside a house and had taken off my clothes? The first thing we did was to take baths. Then Jurek, who turned out to be an excellent cook, started to fix a meal from what he found in the cupboards. We relaxed; the apartment house was far from the railroad and we could not hear the bombing.

I watched Jurek as he moved about competently in the kitchen. "Why are you always so sarcastic?" I asked him unexpectedly. Jurek heard me, but did not answer. His tasty meal was soon ready, and we devoured it with relish. Then, instead of taking the empty dishes back into the kitchen, he sat there quietly at the table and looked at me. "I've just got out of jail," he told me in a low voice. "They opened the jails in Tarnów, so I left. Now you know what kind of company you are keeping."

I sat for a minute without commenting. Finally I said, "What do you expect me to do? Did you think I would run away because you have been in jail? I'm a lawyer; I'm used to such things. It doesn't bother me at all. It must have been a youthful mistake, but in any case you're a fine traveling companion, and you probably have other good points as well."

He thought for a while, and then said, "I didn't lie to you about being an engineer. I studied at the university in Lwów. I got a job there, and I had friends. They were a bad influence, I embezzled some money, and got three years. I have already served over a year."

"Jurek," I said, "that's all in the past. Forget it. Now we are at war. There are more serious things to think about. And after the war nobody will even remember all this. You'll be a different person." I could see that he was grateful. From our further conversation I learned that he had training as a pilot and was planning to get across the border to Romania or Hungary to join the resistance. His confession had brought us closer; he put aside his bitter and mocking tone.

Toward evening we left for the station, hoping to catch a train. Just as we got there an air attack began. We took cover next to the thick trunk of a tree. Jurek warned me not to run, just to hide. The first attack came, and then a second. Jurek explained the type of planes these were, for he knew something about it, and then leaned out from under our tree to get a better view. There was a hail of machine gun fire. I did as Jurek had told me, and kept the trunk of the tree between me and the airplanes. They flew on. On the other side of the tree Jurek lay on his back. I shook him, but it was clear that he was dead. The bullets had torn through his whole body. Still, I raised his head, shouted, begged him to answer. I stood there over him for a long time, not wanting to leave him but not knowing where or how to bury him. I was close to the railway station, which had been set on fire by the bombs. The bombing continued; the fire made a perfect target. The force of the next explosion hurled me to the ground, but I was uninjured. I had to get away from those flames into the darkness. I crept away, shaking, and instinctively headed toward the road leading to Przemyśl.

I walked away from the town along country roads already familiar to me. I passed Monina and Radymno at a distance, avoiding the main highways, keeping to the small villages, all the time heading east. Night fell, and I thought of Jurek, of his spirit, his new-found hopes for the future, and his body lying unburied under the tree. By morning I was in Przemyśl. My parents were at home; thank God my brother had not run away: nowhere was safe. I decided to remain in Przemyśl until the situation cleared up. Two days later the Nazi troops entered the town.

Chapter 11

Massacre

My march had given me a taste of the Nazi way of dealing with the civilian population, so until the situation became clearer I decided to find some kind of official occupation. I thought immediately of the power station. It was not functioning: the wires and utility poles were down, and there were almost no workers left. Some of them had been mobilized and others had fled to the east; even the man in charge had gone, in his official car, driven by his official chauffeur.

The day after the Germans entered Przemyśl, they demanded that the damages caused in the military operations be repaired and the power plant put back in operation. Coke was used to turn the turbines, and the nearest coke supplies were in Żurawica, a nearby town. I immediately signed up at the station as a driver, for I had a chauffeur's license entitling me to drive motorcycles, cars, trucks, and even public vehicles. I had obtained it a year earlier in Cracow, never suspecting how useful it would be. The power plant had two light panel trucks and one five-ton truck. The truck was something of an antique, a French Berliet, which rode on hard rubber tires and had drive chains on either side instead of differential gears. Its top speed was eight kilometers per hour, and when the truck was moving the engine vibrated so much that one could hardly hold on to the steering wheel. It had to be cranked to start, and it took tremendous strength to turn over the engine.

This Berliet was what I used to pick up the coke. The trip to Żurawica was all uphill, and this antique of mine barely crawled, but then it was empty. It was much worse coming back down the hill with the truck crammed with coke, for the old brakes were uncertain. I was constantly prepared to end the trip in a ditch or up against a fence. In town I used one of the light trucks to carry supplies to the workers replacing the broken electric wires. The Germans instituted a curfew; after five o'clock no one was to be on the street without a special pass. All the electrical workers had such passes because they worked both day and night, trying to get the street lights in order. I felt safe in my uniform behind the wheel of a city vehicle, complete with my pass. In this guise I was free to observe what was going on about me without exposing myself to danger.

Several days after the arrival of the Germans I was driving along Mickiewicz Street, one of the main thoroughfares in Przemyśl, when I saw a ragged line of people running down the middle of the street, all with their hands clasped behind their necks. I pulled over to one side and stopped my truck. Around a hundred people ran past, and as they did I saw that they were Jews. They were half naked and crying out as they ran, "Juden sind Schweine" ("Jews are swine"). Along the line, revolvers in hand, German soldiers were running, young boys about eighteen years old, dressed in dark uniforms with swastikas on the sleeves, with light blond hair and rosy faces. When someone fell behind or broke pace, they beat the victim with the butts of their revolvers or with whips, or simply kicked him. Poles gathered on the sidewalks, incredulous, some crossing themselves at this monstrous sight. The faces of the old Jews were contorted with pain, and the young boys were crying, but the Germans ran along the street almost joyfully, drunk with power. As I later found out, the soldiers had fallen on the Jewish section of town that morning and had driven all the men and boys out of their houses with blows and kicks. They made them do calisthenics for several hours in the street, and now they were driving them toward the railway station and on, until they crossed the city limits.

I returned home, shaken. Only in the afternoon, when I had calmed down somewhat, did I go out again to return my truck to the power station. Now a new horror met my eyes: distraught, weeping women were running toward the cemetery, for they had heard that all the Jews taken in the morning had been shot in Pikulice, the first village outside town. I put a load of these wailing women in my truck and headed for Pikulice. Right at the edge of the village, beside a small hill, a swarm of people had gathered. I drove up and stopped. What I saw

121

surpassed all belief; it was a scene out of Dante's hell. All the men driven through the streets in the morning lay there dead. Some men from the nearby houses told me what had happened. The Jews had been driven up to the side of the hill and ordered to turn around. A truck was already standing there. A canvas had been lifted off a heavy machine gun, and several bursts of fire rang out, sweeping back and forth. Then a few more shots were fired into the few bodies that were still writhing. All was still. The soldiers climbed into the truck, and drove away.

I went quietly up to the little hill. The corpses were lying on their backs or sides in the most contorted positions, some on top of others, with their arms outstretched, their heads shattered by the bullets. Here were pools of blood; there the earth was rust-colored with blood; the grass glistened with blood; blood was drying on the corpses. Women with bloodied hands were hunting through the pile of bodies for their fathers, husbands, sons. A sickish sweet smell pervaded the air.

I felt something inside me die, as though my heart had turned to stone. I was choking from the smell, from the sight, from the cries filling the air. I saw everything, but I could not grasp what I saw. Before my eyes I had an image of the laughing young Germans, the proud representatives of Hitler's New Order. It seemed that everything that had occurred in my life up to now—my struggle to earn a living, my studies, my success at the law and hopes for the future—had been meaningless. What I had witnessed in the last few minutes destroyed my vision of the world as a place in which there was a thing called justice. I had seen people die of natural causes, and I had seen ordinary people killed and wounded during the German strafing on the railway, but I had never seen anything like this outrage.

In that moment by the hillside all my thinking changed. I now understood that the war was not going to be over in a couple of days, and that we Jews were condemned to extinction at the hands of these monsters. I realized that I too must surely die—but not like this. No one would drive me through the streets and make me cry "Juden sind Schweine." No one would mock and debase me, only to kill me a little later. I would fight for my life to the end. It would not be an armed struggle, for in that I was no match for them. My weapons would be my wits and whatever experience I had gained in my twenty-eight years. I was not going to wait until they came for me; I was going to take preventive action immediately. As long as there was one German in the country, I was not going to be a Jew. I would obtain false papers. My appearance and my pure, unaccented Polish speech would make it possible. Nothing in my way of living distinguished me from the Poles around me. I would find a peaceful haven somewhere where no one knew my face or name.

I took the truck back to the garage and returned home, saying nothing to anyone. Tomorrow they would hear about the massacre from others.

Hoodwinking the Germans

Several days later in my truck I was flagged down by a German soldier asking for a lift. As we drove along, he asked whether I intended to stay on this side of the San River when the Russians took over the town. (The town itself was on the east side of the river; its suburb, Zasanie, was on the other side.) I said that I had heard nothing about the Russians. The agreement between the Nazis and the Soviet government, he told me, was that the Russians would occupy the city of Przemyśl, while Zasanie would remain in German hands. The soldiers had been ordered to transfer their operations to the other side of the river by next Wednesday. He thought it was a shame for a useful man like me, who could drive a truck and speak good German, to be left on the Russian side. He was also surprised that the plant management had not told us about the partition. I mumbled something to the effect that perhaps a notice about it was posted at the plant and that I had not seen it because I was always out on the truck. I added that I would certainly transfer to the German side because I had no taste for living under the Communists.

I dropped him at his destination, and he marched off with no inkling of the tremendous shock his words had had. My thoughts were in a whirl: today was Wednesday—I still had seven days. How was I to go to Cracow for my wife and bring her back to Przemyśl, with no trains running? I drove along sunk in thought. Who could help me get to Cracow? Only the Nazis; they controlled all transport.

I sat up late that night. Every scheme I devised was more fantastic than the next; none led anywhere. I kept arriving at the same conclusion: I had to find some way to get orders to Cracow. I took out my permit to move about town after curfew and studied it carefully. Suddenly a thought struck me: only the commander-in-chief of Przemyśl could issue such an order. How could I get him to do it? Once again I read my pass.

In the plant office passes already typed in German and signed by the deputy directors were kept. They indicated that the bearer was a worker in the power plant and was permitted to be on the streets after curfew to repair the electrical system. I myself was entrusted with entering the names of the workers, the number of the pass, and the date, and taking them to army headquarters for the signature of the commander-in-chief. The Germans always respected these passes on the streets of the town.

The next day, Thursday, in the afternoon, when no one was in the plant office, I went in and ripped a handful of blank pass forms from a pad. Then I sat down at the office typewriter and on one form typed a few lines that I had composed during the night, instructing me to go to Cracow immediately to get my wife. I included a sentence requesting authorities, government offices, and military units to provide me with all necessary assistance. I had carefully chosen the wording and the length of the lines so that superficially this pass would look like any other. When I got home with the forms I entered the fictitious name of Engineer Wladimir Hajduk. I always wrote the names in by hand, so the writing on this pass was the same as usual.

I tossed and turned in bed all Thursday night, as I thought over my plan. I had also written out a number of passes for non-existent persons; I wanted to have a whole stack of them with me when I went to the office so that mine would not be conspicuous. What would come of it all was hard to guess, but the penalty for failure was death. The Nazis were methodical and brutal, but I thought that they would not be prepared for a frontal assault on their own fortress, staff headquarters.

The office was busiest around ten o'clock in the morning, so this was the time I chose. The adjutant knew me; I always came on the same errand. I had sensed a kind of sympathy between the two of us. We were the same age and both wore uniforms. To be sure, he wore an officer's uniform, while I wore the garb of the power plant, but Germans respect all uniforms, no matter what they represent. We were both working "for the good of the Reich," and then too, we could converse in German, which also created a bond. Perhaps each of these factors was insignificant in itself, but all together they might give me an advantage.

Chapter 11

On Friday morning at my parents' home I announced that I had to leave on business and did not know when I would be back—perhaps in a week, perhaps less. My parents did not know, of course, that the Russians were to occupy Przemyśl the next Wednesday. My reasoning was simple: if my plan failed and I perished, it was best for them not to know anything about it. After the Russians arrived, my parents would conclude that I had not been able to get back in time and was still on the German side of the river. I do not suggest that I expected death rather than success—actually, I rather believed that my plan would work—but I used this tactic just in case of an accident.

And so on Friday, September 22, at ten o'clock sharp, I reported to German army headquarters with my bundle of passes. As I expected, a large number of officers were already waiting to see the general. I approached my friend the adjutant and asked him for a favor. My truck was parked outside, loaded with valuable equipment and supplies. The truck platform was uncovered, and he knew how it was—I was afraid that something might disappear. I wondered whether he could make an exception and take care of my business out of turn.

He looked at my papers, at the officers waiting for an audience, looked back at my papers, then opened the drawer of his desk and took out a red stamp pad and two stamps—one round, with a swastika and eagle and the insignia "Militärkommando Przemyśl," the other oblong, with the name and rank of the commandant. He quickly began stamping all the passes, the rook on the left side, the general on the right. In a minute he had finished, put the papers in a special briefcase, and went with it into the commandant's office. I waited; it was taking too long, or perhaps it only seemed that way, for my nerves were stretched to the limit. Then he came back, and handed me the signed passes. I thanked him and headed for the door. I knew that I had made it; on the steps I glanced through the passes. Engineer Wladimir Hajduk was there among them. I was elated: I had struck the first blow, and at the very highest level!

The Nazis had a standard image of how a Jew should behave. A Jew should hide himself in a hole in order to be invisible. To enter the office of the commander-in-chief and induce him to sign false orders? That was a joke. Jews don't lead the Nazis around by the nose! During my brief experience with the Nazis I had learned what tactics to employ with them. Germans form their impressions of a person on the basis of

125

his external appearance, his speech, and his way of treating others. My uniform did not reveal my position; my boastful way of speaking might indicate that I was a German; and the fact that I had direct access to the leader of the military unit proved that I was undoubtedly an official of some importance. If I treated them with lofty self-assurance, I should not run into any difficulties, I decided.

Traveling on the General's Papers

And so I set off for Cracow. I drove my truck to the pontoon bridge across the San to Zasanie. I had to wait in line, for vehicles could travel in one direction only. The Germans let vehicles pass for ten minutes in each direction. There were no vehicles other than military ones, for the Poles had no cars. The peasants forded the river in their wagons, and other people crossed in rowboats. The bridge was only for Germans and official vehicles like mine.

While waiting in the line to cross the river I was thinking that I had left Cracow barely nineteen days ago. In three weeks I had seen such things as I had never before imagined, and I had discovered a taste for playing with danger that I had never suspected in myself. Suddenly I remembered that today, in the evening, in every synagogue in the world, the song of woe, the Kol Nidre, would be sung, for tomorrow was Yom Kippur, the Day of Atonement, the most solemn day of the year. Until the stars appeared at night, strict fasting would be observed. I thought grimly that I would not sing the Kol Nidre tonight, but I would certainly fast, for I had nothing with me to eat.

Slowly I moved over the planks of the pontoon bridge, turning on the other side toward the main road leading to Cracow. I parked the truck by the roadside with the keys on the seat and shut the door. Then I stood on the road and tried to flag a car headed west toward the city. I had been waiting for an hour or more when a passenger car finally drove by, and I flagged it down. In it five German officers were seated. I showed them my travel orders and asked for a lift. They replied that they were not going far, only to Próchnik, some thirteen kilometers away, so they could only take me to the turnoff. That was all right with me. There was no room inside, so the Germans rolled down the front window, and I stood on the running board and held on to the window frame. The ride lasted only twenty minutes or so, after which I was back on the main

Chapter 11

road, waiting for another ride. Half an hour went by; I spotted a cloud of dust coming in my direction. I stood in the middle of the road and waved. It was a motorcycle and sidecar. The driver was an SS man; his passenger was an SS officer. I handed the driver my travel orders and repeated the same story as before. He read the orders and passed the paper to the officer, who read it very slowly and carefully. He must have read my documents from beginning to end at least twice; finally he looked up and asked, "How did you get this paper?"

Without batting an eye I replied calmly that I had been told that the future border between Russia and Germany would be the San River, and that the Russians were to enter Przemyśl as early as next Wednesday to occupy the town. I was a Ukrainian, the chief engineer of the power plant, and the German authorities had put me in charge of seeing that there was no interruption in electrical service to the other side of the San. Because my wife was in Cracow, I had obtained permission to get there by whatever means and bring her back to Przemyśl before Wednesday. The permit was issued by the military commander under whose authority I was to work in the future, although I would be living among the Russians, in Przemyśl.

The officer handed me back my permit without comment and pointed to the seat behind the driver on the motorcycle. We rode off through the mountains as far as Rzeszów. There they stopped, telling me to go to the train station, for the line had been repaired and there was a chance that a military transport would come through. If not, then something else might turn up. I thanked them for the lift and set off toward the station.

The building was partly in ruins, and there was no sign of life. I approached the office of the traffic controller, located in a part that was still standing. I showed my orders to the official in charge and said that I wanted to go on to Cracow. He said that there were no trains going as far as Cracow, but that a military transport to Tarnów was being made up on a siding; I might have a talk with the officer in charge. I went off to the siding. There were about twenty cars of the "C" (covered) freight type, with a passenger car in front, one in the middle, and another at the rear. The freight cars were filled with Polish prisoners of war. The guard directed me to the officer in charge, who was sitting in the first car. They were waiting for a locomotive to take them to Tarnów; he had no idea when it would arrive. I could wait if I wanted, but he could not guarantee anything. I sat down in the car and tried to be patient.

127

Time flew by; it was now afternoon. After another couple of hours an old locomotive was located in a nearby town and hooked to the train. It was already evening. Little by little we pulled away from the station.

It would be an exaggeration to call this part of the trip "traveling." It was more like crawling. The train stopped every minute or two so that the state of the rails in front of the train could be checked. The tracks were being repaired by German sappers with the help of civilian conscripts from the neighborhood. We stopped at one place for around two hours. When the Germans got out of our car, I followed them. I did not dare go near the freight cars; the prisoners were closely guarded by soldiers with machine guns at the ready. Instead I walked up to the locomotive, where the workers were toiling over a crater in the ground. They did not even bother to fill in the hole but merely laid down the cross-tie, put the rail on top, and fastened it down. After two hours we were allowed to proceed. We crept along at the rate of one meter per minute—one meter and stop, one meter and stop. In this manner we inched along until we were safely over the unfilled crater.

We arrived in Tarnów the next day, Saturday, at four o'clock in the afternoon. The train station had been demolished; we came to a stop on a siding, and the soldiers began to unload the prisoners. I could not find out where they were being taken. I found the traffic controller's office, showed my pass, and asked about the chances for a ride into Cracow. The man on duty said that two transports had just arrived from Cracow and that if he received orders to return the locomotives I could ride back on one of them.

Evening arrived, and it began drizzling. I had had nothing to eat since Friday morning, when I began my trip. In my light denim uniform I was cold as well as hungry, but I had no alternative but to wait. Around eight o'clock in the evening the traffic controller said that one of the locomotives was being sent back to Cracow. I talked to the engineer, who already knew about my travel permit, and he let me up the steep iron steps to the cabin. Besides the engineer there was the fireman; both men were Germans. We set off, just as slowly as before. It was dangerous to ride at night because the tracks were laid only temporarily. Every so often we would come to a stop while the engineer climbed down from the cabin and talked with the men working on the tracks. They would direct us past the obstacle. There were no signals; we rode completely in the dark.

Chapter 11

At one point, the fireman, who was by then utterly exhausted, asked me to take his place for a while. I agreed, and he collapsed in a corner and immediately fell asleep. I took up his huge coal scoop and began to heave coal into the boiler, seething with heat, light, smoke, and soot. The shovel was so heavy that I could hardly lift it when it was full. I worked like an automaton the whole night through. My uniform became soaked with sweat. I was dirty and exhausted; my hands were swollen and covered with blisters. In the morning the fireman awoke and took over.

It was eight o'clock Sunday morning by the time we arrived at the Cracow-Płaszów station. As I walked out onto the street, a trolley came up and I stepped onto the rear platform. The conductor, a Pole, came up to me and then hesitated, not knowing whether I was Polish or German. "Do you need a transfer?" he finally asked in Polish.

"I have no money," I croaked.

He looked me over from top to bottom and calmly asked once more: "Do you need a transfer?"

I nodded, and he went away. In a minute he was back and handed me a transfer stub. I do not know whether it was the ticket of a passenger who had gotten off or whether he had bought it himself. With difficulty I grasped that precious slip of paper between one blistered thumb and forefinger.

I rode past my apartment house but did not get out, for Basia would not stay there by herself. She was sure to be at her parents on Kazimierz Wielki Street. It was nine o'clock by the time I arrived. I rang the bell, and Basia opened the door. Crying, she threw herself on my neck and kissed me. "I knew you would be back today," she kept repeating.

I dragged myself in, black as coal except for my eyes, which were burning from lack of sleep, for I had not slept since Thursday. I had last eaten two days ago. Everyone was excited and was showering me with questions until my mother-in-law took things in hand. She ran me a bath, brought me water to drink, and prepared a light breakfast. I had trouble swallowing the food and could not finish. I lay down on the couch and fell asleep.

I slept until afternoon. Even after I awakened I was still only half conscious except for the pain in my hands, but I wanted to start making our plans right away. I told the family that I had come for Basia and would be ready to leave for Przemyśl next morning at the latest. The town would be in Russian hands on Wednesday, and I intended to live there. My father-in-law could not believe his ears. I emphasized that I did not want to live with murderers; I had witnessed the butchery of defenseless civilians. He argued that there would always be victims in wartime but that the Germans had been in power for more than twenty days now, and all was quiet. They were not killing anyone. He had no way of knowing that I was older in experience now, not just by twenty days but by entire centuries. I was no longer the man he knew when I left Cracow. "I have come for my wife," I said calmly. "It is up to her. If she agrees, we will leave tomorrow; if not, I will go alone."

My father-in-law kept arguing, but I had stopped listening to him. He called in a family counselor, a relative by the name of Apek Rosenzweig, the official in the Holzer Bank whom I have already mentioned, for advice. I briefly described to Rosenzweig the events in Przemyśl, omitting many details out of delicacy. He asked me how I planned to leave, with all the roads closed. I said that I would return the same way I had come, and showed him the travel order signed by the German general. He doubted that such an order would be adequate, and so the arguments dragged on.

I realized that it would be no easy matter to convince Basia to travel with me into the unknown. Our personalities and upbringing had been completely different. I left home at the age of fourteen to make my own way. I was used to hardships and sudden changes in fortune. Basia was brought up in a loving family, surrounded by friends. She loved and respected her parents; she had been born in the same house in which she was married. We had lived together not quite two months when Germany invaded Poland, and I had left her two days later. After eighteen days I was back, and the family was at first overjoyed—I was the first man they knew who had come back from the trek east, and my reappearance had kindled everyone's hopes that the other men who had gone east were also safe and would return. Now Basia was faced with the fact that I had come back only to ask her to leave her family and follow me into the unknown, to Russian territory.

I expected even more opposition from my father-in-law, and so it turned out. He had taken me for a good-for-nothing from the start, but now I terrified him. What did I mean by saying that I had come to get Basia and intended to "travel" back to Przemyśl with her? How? There were no trains. Surely I did not intend that she stoke boilers with me or ride on the back of an SS motorcycle, if my story was not a dream and I

130

had really reached Cracow as I had said. And where did I want to escape to? Russia! A crazy plan. Who had been filling my head with nonsense that the Germans were murdering innocent people?

Then he begged me—which was not at all his custom—not to take his daughter from him. "Bronek," he said, "come to your senses. You're not a child any longer. You must start thinking and acting sensibly. Look at yourself. You've been gone for barely three weeks and you return a wreck—dirty, half-starved, in greasy overalls like some laborer. This is what you want to take Basia away to? What sort of fantastic tales are you telling about murders? If what you are telling us is really true, why are you the only one who knows about it? No, this is simply your way of frightening my daughter into going away with you. How far will you get? To the train station? What then? Jews are not allowed on the trains, even if they were running. You must be delirious."

Despondent, he was quiet for a moment, and then started up again. "Are you really so cruel as to take my daughter away to certain death? Do you suppose that you are smarter than everyone else? I know a thing or two myself. Think of where you're running to—Przemyśl! Who told you that the border will run through Przemyśl? Why is it that you are the only one who knows about this? And what do you know about Russia? Why this sudden affection for the Communists?"

Finally, he made one last appeal: "Please, I beg of you, do whatever you want with your own life, but don't endanger the life of my child. Don't take advantage of her willingness to do whatever you say. She is young and inexperienced and does not see the dangers that I do. I ask you one more time—leave my child, don't take her away to a life of misery."

I heard my father-in-law out. I saw that I had three people to convince, and that Basia would be the easiest, but I didn't want to leave my father-in-law and his friend with the impression that I had done them an injury. I would try to explain to them, although I was sure that nothing I could say would change their minds. Basia's father and his friend were decent and respected people, born and raised in a secure world. They could not see that we were now living in a time of violence, sadism, and murder.

"If I may say a few words," I began, "I would not like us to part with anger and misunderstandings. I know, Mr. Rosenzweig, that you hold an important post in the Holzer Bank, earned by your hard work and honesty, and that you, Father, have also struggled hard to achieve your present position. I admire both of you for this, but you must not forget that you belong to an older generation and think along different lines. You both went through the last great war, and there were civilian casualties then too, but military actions were not directed against the civilian population. Then armies fought against armies. It is difficult for you to understand the times in which we live today. You, Father, do not take my warnings seriously because our views are so different on all subjects. But please remember that I am not without achievements myself. You are both Cracowians; you have friends here, relatives, associates. Neither of you has ever slept in the park for want of a roof over your heads; neither of you has ever gone hungry. If I managed to attain the position I had in Cracow before the outbreak of the war in spite of overwhelming odds, that fact should speak for itself.

"I did not lie about anything I have seen," I continued, "and I am not trying to frighten any of you; in fact, I have not even told you the whole truth because the details are too horrible to repeat. There were pogroms in Russia in the past, but they were instigated by individuals, as you know, and the crowds joined in only later. Today's Nazis are not like the Russians; what I am describing is not a pogrom but a deliberate state policy of cold-blooded mass murder, executed with true German precision. These Germans are planning genocide. The Nazis are going to murder all the Jews. It is only a matter of time and capability. And no one will help us; there is not one government, large or small, which will stand up in our defense. For myself, I am not going to be slaughtered like a sheep without a struggle. I am going to fight to my last drop of blood. Listen to what I say: if you expect to survive to the end of the war by prayers and groveling to the Nazis, you are deceiving yourselves. You'd better organize and fight. This is my final advice to you."

Then I turned to my wife. "Basia, it would have been easy for me to get from Przemyśl to Romania alone, and from there to safety. I exposed myself to death many times over to come here for you, to save you. I know that you are accustomed to your life here, that you love and respect your parents, and that I can't promise you much. There is no telling what may befall us among the Russians. You won't have the comforts you have at home, but how long can you count on the Nazis leaving you in peace here in Cracow? If you decide to stay with your parents, I will understand. It's your life, your future, and only you can decide."

132

I looked at her, waiting for an answer. "I'm going with Bronek," she proclaimed, and burst out crying.

Her father still would not give up. He kept arguing, trying to convince us that my plan was impractical, that we would get no farther than the train station, that no one could get through. Basia began packing. Not knowing anything about what Przemyśl would be like under the Russians, we did not know what to take, and I wanted to travel light because I still did not have a plan worked out for the return trip. I only knew that I had to cross the San River by Wednesday noon at the latest. There was not much time.

We hardly slept the whole night. Basia's father would not admit defeat. He was not accustomed to having someone else decide the fate of his child, even if that someone were her husband, and he was absolutely convinced that I was taking his child away to a life of suffering, perhaps even death. He thought that my warnings about the Nazis were sheer fantasy. He knew better; there had never been and never would be a people on earth who would exterminate another people. He knew it would be difficult during the occupation, for the Nazis detested the Jews and had issued many anti-Jewish ordinances, but it was ridiculous to think that they would murder them without cause.

I should say that Mr. Neulinger was not alone in his opinion. All the educated Jews of Cracow felt the same way. Throughout their long history the Jewish people had undergone many such trials and had survived, and in the present instance, they knew, we were dealing not with barbarians but with a civilized European nation.

Back to Przemyśl

On Monday Basia and I left the family nest. I stopped a cab, and we were off. The family maid came with us to the station. There she unhooked a golden chain with a medallion of the Madonna which she wore around her neck and, as she kissed Basia goodbye, hung it around hers, for protection.

The main train station, or at least the terminal building, was not damaged, but the entrance was locked. The square in front was blocked by rolls of barbed wire, with a gap for vehicles and pedestrians to enter. A German guard was checking everyone's passes. Just as we arrived, a group of wounded Polish soldiers in tattered uniforms was being led off one of the platforms. Some were missing legs and supported themselves on crutches; others were being helped along by their comrades; still others had head wounds bandaged with dirty rags. The most seriously injured were carried on stretchers by able-bodied soldiers. Seeing this tragic procession and the guarded entrance to the station, Basia lost heart. "Maybe we had better turn back," she whispered. "We always have time for that," I replied.

This was not the station where I had arrived the day before, so what I saw here was unexpected, but I quickly resolved to find some way through—if not here, then at the suburban station in Cracow-Płaszów. Not far from the main entrance on the left stood the railway post office building, now deserted. My power plant uniform was the same color as the one worn by the postal employees, and so I boldly approached the building, telling Basia to wait quietly with the luggage, that I would be right back. I went straight through the hall of the post office and out onto the train platform. The approach, it appeared, was not guarded at all. I had my plan ready. I have mentioned that my experiences in the company of Germans for the past several days had convinced me that the way to deal with them was to shout. Walking briskly, and holding my permit from Przemyśl in my hand like something immeasurably valuable that would protect me from arrest, I came to the traffic controller's office.

I didn't walk in but rather burst through the door, shouting, "Es ist eine Schweinerei! Es ist eine Schweinerei!" ("This is an outrage!").

The head traffic controller heard the ruckus and rushed up to me. "Was ist los?" ("What is wrong?"), he asked.

I just kept bellowing, "Es ist eine Schweinerei!" and pushed my travel orders under his nose. Finally I let myself be calmed down enough to tell him that I was under military orders to return to Przemyśl as quickly as possible, that there was some sort of guard out there who did not want to let me in, and so my wife had been forced to wait out on the street with her bags. He didn't see much of my paper, for I kept tight hold of it while I was waving it in his face. In any case, he could see the Militärkommando Przemyśl and German eagle and swastika stamps and me, and I was swearing fluently in German and wearing some sort of uniform.

Unbelievable as it seems, what happened at this point was that he turned to a master sergeant who was standing there and barked out, "Na es *ist* ja eine Schweinerei!'' ("Well it certainly *is* an outrage!''). He thereupon began to upbraid the sergeant for not letting me and my wife onto the platform.

The sergeant saluted, nodded to two soldiers, and the three of them set off at a trot in the direction of the main hall of the station, with me panting along behind them. The sergeant pushed aside both guards at the gate and asked where my baggage was. I nodded toward Basia and her maid. He ran over to her with the soldiers, picked up two suitcases himself, each of the other soldiers took one apiece, and they all galloped back to the main entrance. Basia's eyes grew round, and the maid was no less astounded. I waved a hasty goodbye to her, grabbed Basia's hand, and we rushed after the Germans carrying our things. Both guards stepped aside from the gate respectfully, and with a calm and dignified air we now proceeded toward the platform. The soldiers put down our suitcases, saluted us, and left, and the sergeant hurried toward the controller's office, evidently to report that he had carried out his orders.

Soon the controller himself appeared and respectfully offered the information that there was no passenger traffic at all, only irregular freight shipments and military transports. The military transports kept to no regular schedule, and he himself did not know when the next train would be through. He was informed of the traffic, train by train, over the telephone. Of course, as soon as some transport arrived headed east, he would see to it that we got places. I nodded my head that I understood and would wait.

We strolled up and down the platform until four o'clock in the afternoon, when a shipment of tanker cars arrived on the way east. Right behind the locomotive was a solitary passenger car occupied by guards and German railway personnel being sent to their posts. The traffic controller must have whispered to them that I was somebody important, for they emptied one whole compartment for our exclusive use, an elegant first-class compartment which converted into comfortable double sleeping quarters at night. The train soon got under way. It was close to evening: we had not quite two days left to get to Przemyśl.

We got only as far as Bochnia before stopping for the night. In the morning we pressed on. At every station there were field kitchens set up serving hot meals, and our fellow passengers brought us food in mess kits. I ate heartily, for I was ravenous, but Basia could not eat a bite. All Tuesday we traveled slowly east, arriving in Łańcut by evening. This was the end of the line. Where the station, now in ruins, had stood, a line of tank trucks was waiting to take the gasoline from the train. There was also a military headquarters with a large sign over the entrance reading "Juden und Hunden Eintritt Verboten" ("Jews and Dogs Not Permitted Inside"). I entered, introduced myself as usual, and asked for transport to Przemyśl. The commandant explained that he had no vehicles at his disposal, but he would see to it that one of the gasoline trucks picked us up. I agreed, and at ten o'clock we were in Jarosław, only thirty-two kilometers from Przemyśl, but that was as far as the truck was going.

I asked the driver to take us up to the highway leading to Przemyśl and leave us and our baggage there. We waited on the road for an hour, but nothing was moving in the direction of the San. It was already eleven o'clock in the morning, and I knew that the pontoon bridge would be rolled up at noon. Finally, a military truck with trailer, both covered with a tarp, came in sight. I flagged it down and explained my situation. I was in luck: the driver was headed for a spot not far from Przemyśl. He and the soldier riding with him lifted the tarp, threw our suitcases in the trailer, and put us up in front with them. When I told them that I was the German representative on the Russian side and showed my document with the seal of the local military headquarters, they decided, after only a moment's hesitation, to take us all the way to Przemyśl. We drove into Zasanie and right down to the edge of the river.

We were half an hour too late. The sappers, directed by an elderly major, were dismantling the pontoon bridge. In the distance flames were shooting high into the sky. The Nazis were throwing incendiary bombs into the Jewish temples before leaving Przemyśl. The beautiful modern temple and the historic old synagogue in the Jewish quarter were burned to the ground that day, I later learned. I went up to the major supervising the dismantling of the bridge and told him that he had to get us to the other side of the San. Unfortunately, he had not noticed us driving up in the military truck. "What?" he said to me in a sarcastic voice. "You want to get to the other side of the San? Swim, Jew! Swim across the river! Get out of here before I shoot you on the spot!"

I shouted back at him in such a loud and furious voice that the soldiers nearby stopped their work to stare at us: "Sind sie verrückt? ['Are you crazy?'] When did you see a Jew being chauffeured by the army? I'm going over to the other side on orders of military headquarters. What is your name and regiment? I'm going to report this to the general as soon as I get to headquarters!" (I was so near my goal that I felt I had no choice but to plunge ahead.)

Chapter 11

The old soldier paled and snapped to attention, clicking his heels. He reported that he was major such and such, from such and such sapper battalion, and began to apologize for his behavior. I would not be mollified and kept sputtering with rage and threatening to report him. The despairing major ran up to Basia and began kissing her hand. "Gnädige Frau, bitte um Verzeihung! Gnädige Frau, bitte um Verzeihung!" ("Dear lady, I beg you to forgive me!"), he cried to her. He had seen a lot of Jews going across the river, he explained to us, but that was none of his business. His business was to take apart the bridge. He was not paying attention when we arrived, and that was why he had made such a dreadful mistake. He assured us that he would never forgive himself as long as he lived. After a good deal more of this, I allowed myself to be soothed. Some soldiers carried our baggage from the truck to a pontoon boat, and Basia and I got in. The major stood there on the shore at attention, saluting us, while four soldiers rowed us to the other side.

In ten minutes we were in Przemyśl, with the Germans behind us. Across the river the sappers were bustling around. At this distance they looked like toy soldiers. I took out the general's travel orders to Cracow, now crumpled and grimy, and looked at the swastika on the slip of paper. So this was the symbol of the nation of writers, scholars, and musicians, I thought to myself. What a country. With a little screaming and a scrap of paper you can lead these supermen around by the nose. No wonder Hitler had such an easy time with them. I crumpled the pass and tossed it in the river. It would be of no use to me in Russia.

I stopped the first horse cart passing by for a lift, piled on our suitcases, and we rode to my parents' house. I had kept my word. I was back by Wednesday. The date was September 27, 1939, and it marked the beginning of a new stage in my life.

Chapter 12

Przemyśl under the Russians

Przemyśl was a small town of around fifty thousand inhabitants. Before World War I it had been an important military outpost. After the war traces of the military establishment remained, in the form of a significant number of barracks and other installations. This, no doubt, was the reason why a large part of the Polish army, including the headquarters of the Tenth Division, was stationed there. The troops and especially the officers set the tone for the entire town.

It was a town of both Polish and Ukrainian influences. The surrounding villages were mostly Ukrainian; the townspeople were a mixture of Ukrainians, Jews, and Poles, the Poles employed primarily in government offices. The Ukrainians considered Przemyśl their last western bastion and tried to maintain influence in the town by any means at their disposal. They had their own gymnasium, several teachers' colleges, strong agricultural cooperatives, a credit union, physicians, engineers, and lawyers, and many religious institutions, including seminaries and a bishopric. One could sense the struggle for cultural and economical domination over the town, the Poles wanting to Polonize the city and the Ukrainians doing whatever they could to combat this. Between hammer and anvil, as it were, were the Jews. Each of these groups represented approximately one third of the population.

This picture changed drastically after the outbreak of the war. The army withdrew; most of the Polish men had been mobilized and withdrawn to the east. When the Nazis arrived in the city, the Ukrainian group came to power. After two weeks, in accordance with the Russo-German agreement mentioned earlier, the Nazis yielded the town to the Soviets and retained the suburb of Zasanie. Almost all of the Ukrainian middle class, which was concentrated in the town, fled across the river to the Nazi side. As a consequence, Przemyśl was stripped of both its Ukrainian and its Polish intelligentsia. Only the Jews, who had nowhere to flee, and the poor, irrespective of nationality, remained.

Swelling the group of poor people of the town were Jewish refugees from the western part of the country who had crossed the San River to escape the Nazis; Polish refugees who had fled east to get away from the bombings and who were now trying desperately to return to the west; and, finally, former soldiers of the disintegrated Polish army, who were pouring into the town in increasing numbers, convinced that the Nazis would open the borders and let them return to their families. In short, Przemyśl was crammed with poor, starving, and homeless people, all awaiting some kind of salvation.

Everything in Przemyśl was in short supply. During the mobilization and then the abandonment of the town by the army, the soldiers had commandeered much of the available food. Then the Nazis came, methodically stripping the city of anything of value that was left and taking it across the river. After them came the Russians—the border patrol, the regular army, and the civil administration—all of which had their own food supply but no provisions for the local population. The residents had to wait until the new administrative organs began to function.

Before the war the surrounding villages had provided the town with all necessary commodities. Now, however, the farmers in one month had seen three different currencies in circulation—Polish, German, and now Russian. When the Nazis entered, złotys were abandoned, and they introduced the German mark. Now the Russians had come, the mark was worthless, and the farmers were offered rubles, for which nothing could be purchased. As a result, farmers stopped selling food to the town entirely, and people returned to the archaic barter system. The whole town turned into one enormous marketplace, with people carrying all manner of goods in their arms or on their backs offering to trade them for what they needed. There were few takers, for most people had nothing at all, and the number of the poor increased daily.

Clever people who knew how to negotiate and bargain could get everything they needed, but people with no connections or special talent for trade either had to rely on food distribution centers or face starvation. Under the Russians there were no private shops, only the distribution centers, which were state-owned and state-run. In order to obtain bread, salt, sugar, soap, and other essential items, you had to get in line shortly after midnight. Often when the weary customer was finally near the door a sign would be posted announcing that everything had been sold, and the center would close. If one were lucky enough to get inside the door, one found only the worst grade of produce for sale. All the better items had long since slipped out the side entrance to be sold on the black market.

Winter came earlier than usual in 1939. Those who had expected the war to be over in a few days and who, therefore, did not have proper clothes or who had bartered their heavy clothing for food were caught unprepared. As long as the weather held, people could camp out on a park bench or find some kind of shelter, but when the early winter came, one needed to be indoors. However, no housing was available. Many buildings had been destroyed in the fighting, especially in the old section of the town, which was now in the Russian zone. The new residential part of the city was on the other side of the river. On the Russian side one was lucky to find any sort of shelter at all.

Eventually, the Nazis sent in a commission to screen refugees who wished to return to the western sector of occupied Poland, but it worked slowly and with the greatest possible bureaucratic malice. It demanded personal identification cards, certificates of birth and religion, and a host of other documents. No one had taken any of these papers with them when they fled for their lives or entered the army. Accordingly, only a small number of people were allowed to cross the border for home. However, word spread in the area that in Przemyśl there was a German commission processing refugees back home to the west, and more and more "escapees" crowded into town. The Nazi commission operated for a short time, then disbanded, leaving many refugees with no hope of returning home legally.

The Soviet authorities attacked the housing crisis by removing certain "undesirable elements" from town. They declared that Przemyśl was a border city and that only trustworthy Soviet citizens could live and work there. They began "passporting" everyone; that is, they issued identity cards which they called passports and which automatically conferred Soviet citizenship on the segment of the local population which would be permitted to remain. Those lucky enough to be issued a passport and a work permit stayed; the rest, the "undesirables," were removed from the town and deported far to the east.* However, this approach solved little, for new unfortunates poured into the city to take their place—either Jews fleeing from the Nazis or people trying to go west to the German side, either for political reasons or to return home.

The Russians also began making innovations in the economic sector. They tried to persuade small tradesmen to combine and form cooperatives. The government promised to provide these cooperatives with the necessary raw materials. Cooperatives of shoemakers, tailors, glaziers, and bakers arose, at first in small numbers, since people were not yet used to the Soviet way of doing things. Belonging to a cooperative had its positive side, since the participants paid themselves in their own products, which they could then use themselves or trade for other commodities. Both barter and black-market trade flourished, and almost nothing of quality found its way into the government centers. Of course, some people who wanted a certificate proving membership in a cooperative bought their way in and then engaged in black-market profiteering.

My parents' apartment was too small for all of us. After much effort I managed to find a single room—a passageway, really—in a broken-down building on Smolna Street. In one of its walls there was a hole left by an artillery shell. As long as it was warm, we had plenty of fresh air through our hole, but once the temperature fell, the cold was biting.

Because I was from Przemyśl my wife and I both got Russian passports giving us the right to live in the town and to obtain work permits. Basia got a job in the newspaper department of the local post office. Her work consisted of selling, at a tiny newsstand in the hall of the railroad station, such Russian papers as *Pravda*, *Izvestia*, *Krokodil*, and *Ogonyok* (the last two were humor magazines), as well as the Ukrainian *Visti* and other Ukrainian papers from Kiev, Lwów, and the newly created Drohobycz district, and the Przemyśl papers. Basia, who was now expecting a child, worked until six weeks before it was due. She obtained a doctor's permit for a maternity leave; after that, because she had to take care of the baby, she obtained a final release from the job.

I took a job at the railroad station at 150 rubles a month, not realizing that these wages were not adequate to support my family. My task was to list the freight cars standing at the station, dividing them into

*The Russian passports contained a place indicating nationality, and Jews were listed there as such. However, Jews in Russia were not discriminated against, at least not openly, and could obtain work permits on the same basis as other Soviet citizens.—*Tr.*

loaded or unloaded, to note down the number of each car and its type—boxcar, coal car, tanker, or flatcar—and to relay my tally by telephone each evening to the district railway office in Lwów.

After nine months I began to look for another job. By chance I learned the name of the city engineer, and applied to him. I was perfectly frank, telling him that I was looking for any sort of job at a wage that would feed my newborn child, my wife, and me. He was sympathetic and offered me the job of head warehouseman in the local building supply yard. I accepted the job with thanks without knowing what the work consisted of. I soon learned that this was the local supply depot for all construction materials; from it all the housing authorities under city jurisdiction drew their allocations.

The Warehouse

The warehouse was located on Kopernik ("Copernicus") Street. I knew the address, for on that site there had been a small house with a large garden belonging to an old bachelor named Michał Kruk. As a small boy I used to visit him. He was already quite old when I was a boy, his beardless face a mass of wrinkles. Very tall and thin, he stalked along with long strides, reminding me of a heron moving through shallow water. He liked children, and I was fascinated by his talents. He was completely self-sufficient, growing all his food in his own garden and making his own shoes, clothing, and household furniture. He taught me how to shape boards, sole shoes, and fix locks, but his specialty was firearms. He earned his living by repairing weapons and by making beautiful hand-tooled leather saddles.

I reported to the depot the next day. The little house in which Michał Kruk once lived was gone, and in its place were the warehouse offices. Where Kruk's beautiful big garden had been there was now a cluster of workshops and storage areas. I found my "staff" waiting for me in the office. They were a close-knit band of Przemyśl boys, and I could see that my arrival was not to their liking. There were four of them: my assistant, about thirty years old, a bookkeeper, and two men who received and dispensed the materials stored there. Around nine other men were about in the yard, sorting and piling material.

I introduced myself, but I need not have bothered. They already knew that a lawyer, a Cracowian to boot—in short, a foreigner—had been hired to supervise them. In order to familiarize myself with the operation, I asked the accountant to show me his record sheets. I could see that they were carefully kept. Then I looked through the orders for the receipt and issue of goods, the daily and monthly ledgers, and the inventory of materials on hand. I asked few questions, for the men gave stupid, nonsensical answers to those I did ask. Either they did not understand me or they did not want to give me the information—in short, they were playing dumb. They didn't like me, that much was clear, and would do whatever they could to smoke me out of there.

After my examination of the accounts and inventories, I expressed a desire to see the stores. My assistant accompanied me on my tour. I was amazed to see large quantities of building materials lying around the yard. I had thought that everything was in short supply, but in the storeroom for cement, in the very center, a veritable mountain of the precious stuff was piled; the remainder was stacked up along the walls in the original fifty-kilogram sacks in which it had been shipped. A similar sight greeted me in the storeroom for lime and plaster. In the ironware shop various lengths and sizes of water piping lay all mixed together; the situation was the same with the sewer pipes, pipe joints, gratings, and nails of various lengths and gauges. New and old door locks were jumbled together, broken and bent window frames were thrown among new ones, and so on.

Out in the yard next to a stable there were several horse carts and a carriage. In the stable were several horses, including two carriage horses (not the sort used for drawing heavy loads). Huge amounts of oats, hay, and straw were stored next to the horses. A mountain of top-grade shiny black Donbass coal* was piled in the back of the yard next to a stack of boards of various lengths and sizes and a woodpile of logs cut and ready for use as fuel. The coal was sitting in a big pool of water. At this moment the yardmen were filling an order. They were shoveling up the coal—from the bottom of the pile, of course, mixed with wet coal dust, mud, water, and other additives—and putting it into bags to be weighed. Orders for firewood were by the cubic meter. Four thick stakes had been driven into the ground to the height of a meter, forming a one-meter square. Logs were then piled in this box to the height of the stakes, but I could see that the logs were cleverly arranged so that they were not

---

*Donbass, the most important coal-producing region in the European part of the Soviet Union, in the Don River basin, was known for its high-grade coal.—*Tr.*

lying alongside one another but had huge gaps between them, leaving at least a quarter of a cubic meter shortfall in each batch.

I had seen enough. I returned to my office and again went through the inventory lists. There was no mention of fodder or straw for the horses; in fact, there was no mention of horses at all, much less carriages or carts. There was no point in probing any deeper, for I now understood why the men had looked at me askance. I said goodbye and went home thinking about all that I had seen. It was clear that the main business of these workers was common theft and that in order to prevent anyone from checking up on them they probably destroyed more than they stole. For example, cement should be kept in closed sacks because it deteriorates in the air. But sacks are easy to count, so the warehousemen tore them apart and piled up the cement, not caring that before long it would be useless. The heaps of lime and plaster would deteriorate in the same way. They poured water over the coal, supposedly so that it would not catch fire. The real reason, of course, was that they could swindle people by giving them a load of coal dust with a little bit of mud and water thrown in. I have noted the trickery with the firewood; and the lumber was rotting in the open yard. As I said, they ended up destroying more than they actually took. No wonder that this tightly knit bunch of black marketeers wanted to get rid of me. I decided to act right away. I could not correct the evil, for it was everywhere, but at least those men would know that here was one city slicker who was not fooled by a bunch of local operators.

When I got to the yard the next day, I called my assistant and got down to business. "I know why you are trying to make life difficult for me," I began, "but you are wrong if you think it will be easy. I did not come here as a spy or an informer. I have a wife and child and took this job in order to make a living, so get the idea out of your mind once and for all that you can chase me away or sabotage my management. You can get along with me, or we can declare open war: I am used to hard times, and I can be much tougher than you, so you had better think it over before you act hastily."

It seems that this declaration helped, for I had no more trouble. Everyone knew where I stood and what I thought; the men may well have decided that they were better off having me for a superior than an unknown who might give them trouble. After a while I think they even came to be fond of me, for they began helping me in little ways. I don't know how they happened to find out about the shell hole in one of the

144

walls in our rooms, but they did. Not only was the hole plastered over but the entire room was also repainted. I had received an allottment of half a ton of coal for the winter. One day I came home to find the whole cellar of our building filled with Donbass coal. These crooks swore that it was only half a ton, but I was sure that there was at least three times as much. They told me that they had gotten the yard horses free—that they had been abandoned by their owners. That might even have been true! I never did learn where they got the fodder for them. One gray winter dawn, when I was going out to work, I found the yard's carriage waiting for me outside my house. The drivers said that they had to exercise the horses from time to time and so had come to pick me up so I wouldn't have to walk to the yard through the wet snow. I found that almost every one of the bunch had a relative in the country who brought him milk, eggs, and first-rate sausages and meat. They even had more than they needed, and they would not dream of selling it, they told me piously—they were not profiteers! They preferred to share their treasure with me.

So my situation had taken a decided turn for the better. Basia and I did not go hungry, we had more than enough coal to keep us warm, and the unpleasantness at work disappeared. My conscience often bothered me, but what was I to do? Graft was everywhere; everyone in town was involved. Instead of battling windmills, causing unpleasantness, and losing my job, I preferred to accept not luxuries but the basic necessities of life. The standing in long food lines through the night was over. I was no angel, and the welfare of my family took precedence over all else.

Przemyśl Friends

I cannot conclude my description of my stay in Przemyśl without saying a few words about my friends. First there were Józek Moskalewski and his wife. Before the war he had worked as an inspector in the Lwów office of the railroad. During the war he did not do anything in particular, but this idleness of his was infinitely more profitable than any ordinary job could have been. Józek was a tall blond with a large, perpetually smiling countenance and a manner which inspired trust. Officially unemployed, he had plunged into the barter economy with enthusiasm. He knew all the local farmers—what they needed, what they had to sell, where one could sell it, and what one could get for it. He was an entrepreneurial genius in this area, and it is no wonder that nothing was lacking in his home for himself and his friends. His wife, a powerful woman no less congenial than he, was a wonderful housewife.

The Moskalewskis gathered us in like their own brood, looked after us, and made sure we had enough to eat. They even took under their wings a good friend of mine from Cracow, Mietek Misiolek, with whom I had gone to law school. At the beginning of the war Mietek had been mobilized. When his regiment fell apart, everyone in it was trying to get home on his own. At that time I was still working at the railroad station, and as luck would have it I ran into Mietek hanging about the station trying to find out when, if ever, the trains would begin running again. I took him home with me, and we shared whatever food we had— precious little, but it lifted our spirits to be together. After a while, in the period when the Germans were letting some refugees across the border, as described earlier, Mietek left for Cracow.

Another good friend at this time was a Ukrainian, Professor Mylanko. While Basia was still selling newspapers at the train station, a nattily dressed, pleasant-looking elderly gentleman came by her stand almost every day and read the headlines. Basia correctly guessed that he had no money to buy the papers and so limited his reading to the headlines. She suggested that he stand there and read whatever papers interested him; she would put them back in place after he was through with them. The old man was delighted and from then on came almost every day. He introduced himself to her as a professor emeritus from the Ukrainian gymnasium in town. Basia in turn volunteered that she was from Cracow and was the wife of a Cracow attorney. When he heard my last name, Mylanko remembered that he once had a student by that name whom he had liked very much. When Basia told him that her husband came from the town and had attended the Ukrainian gymnasium, the professor became eager to see whether I was really the person he had in mind. I came that evening for Basia and of course immediately recognized Professor Mylanko, whom I had respected tremendously in school. We embraced warmly, and from that time on became the best of friends. He visited Basia daily at her stall, and on occasion even relieved her and sold the newspapers himself.

These two wonderful people, Mylanko and Moskalewski, never deserted me even in the days after the occupation of the town by the Germans. They eventually helped us escape, as I will explain later. I had other friends, but none so warm and close as these two.

The Germans Invade Russia

Before the war three bridges joined the two parts of Przemyśl. The main bridge, built of reinforced concrete, the Piłsudski bridge, was for motorized, pedestrian, and horse traffic. An iron bridge, for railroad traffic, was part of the Cracow-Lwów line. The third or "old bridge," made of wood, had been in use since the days of the Austro-Hungarian Empire. In September, 1939, the retreating Polish army demolished all three. While Przemyśl was occupied by the Nazis, they erected a wooden pontoon bridge, which they dismantled upon leaving, as described earlier. A year later the Germans and Russians rebuilt the railroad bridge. The main railroad station was in Przemyśl, two or three hundred meters from the bridge. The freight depot was two kilometers away from the town in Bakończyce. When the Germans occupied Zasanie, they expanded a nearby station, in Żurawica, and made it a main transfer point for all German-Soviet freight. Goods from the Soviet Union arrived on the Russian wide-gauge rails and in Żurawica were loaded into standard European-gauge railroad cars by the Germans for shipment west.*

Despite the fact that the boundary between the two countries was a river, goods and news from "the other side"—that is, from Germany—arrived in Przemyśl regularly. Nominally Germany and Russia remained allies. Throughout June, 1941, however, we talked of little else but the impending German assault on Russia. The Germans had assembled a massive attack force on the other side of the river. Day and night tanks, artillery, trucks loaded with military equipment, armored personnel carriers, and countless military divisions moved toward the border. No one doubted that the attack would begin soon, but no one knew exactly when.

The behavior of the Russians was incomprehensible. Life in Przemyśl went on as usual. Soviet trains arrived from the east to be shunted across the bridge to Żurawica and returned with shipments from Germany. There was no increase in military activity on our side of the river. No new army divisions arrived, nor was there any buildup in military equipment. Przemyśl continued to be a sleepy border town. Everyone speculated, but no one could find a reasonable explanation. The

---

*The Russians maintain a different gauge of railroad track from the rest of Europe for purposes of military defense. They laid wide-gauge rails in Przemyśl when they took over.—*Tr.*

massing of armies on the other side of the San was hardly secret: the river was only one hundred and fifty or two hundred meters across at its widest point. Was this pretending-not-to-see some new tactic? Perhaps Russia simply wanted to draw the enemy deeper into its territory before striking back?

Then came June 22, 1941. Before describing the events of this day I should explain the manner in which Soviet and German rail shipments were handled. Each transport coming from the east was thoroughly inspected and shunted across the bridge to the Germans. The locomotive was detached, sent to the roundhouse, and readied for its return trip with a shipment from the other side. A Przemyśl locomotive manned by Poles was attached at the rear of the train, at which time the traffic controller in Przemyśl would telephone the station in Żurawica to tell the German controller what sort of shipment was about to cross the border. As soon as the German side gave the signal to go, the engineer of the Polish locomotive was ordered to start pushing the train over the bridge. When the front of the train reached the middle of the bridge the train would stop. Several Russian border guards, the conductor, and a customs official would climb out. A locomotive would arrive from the other side, carrying the German officials empowered to receive the shipment— the Nazi border guards and customs official. The Soviet conductor would hand over the freight shipment to the German conductor, the German locomotive was hooked up, and the train would continue across the bridge. The Przemyśl locomotive, with the Soviet conductor, customs official, and border guards, would return to the roundhouse. Transports from the German side were handled in the same way, in the reverse order. The shunting back and forth took place only in the daytime.

On June 22, at four o'clock in the morning,* the German station in Żurawica telephoned that thirty freight cars were ready for shipment across the border. As usual, a locomotive was sent out from the roundhouse at the Przemyśl station with two border guards and one customs official. They rode to the center of the bridge and waited. After several minutes a train arrived from Żurawica, pushed from behind by a locomotive. Some Nazi soldiers alighted from the train and approached the Soviet officials, but instead of giving them the freight documents they drew their pistols, placed them to the heads of the unsuspecting

---

*June 22, the longest day of the year, marks the beginning of summer. In the days before daylight saving time, by four A.M. it would have been broad daylight.—*Tr.*

Russians, disarmed them, and led them back to the cars in which they had come. Leaving them there under guard, they went to the locomotive, ordered the engineer and fireman out at gunpoint, and took them back to the same car, guarded by a dozen heavily armed soldiers. Two Nazis now alighted from the train, this time dressed in the uniform of the Polish railway. They hooked up the Przemyśl locomotive to the train and calmly chugged off the bridge and into the Przemyśl station. Armed German soldiers poured out of the cars. Some took control of the station; others occupied the railway machine shop and the freight depot in Bakończyce. Still others secured the bridge against sabotage.

Everyone was completely taken by surprise. Not a single shot was fired. At this hour there were only a few workers in the station, the machine shop, and Bakończyce, none of them armed or able to resist. In the meantime trainloads of German soldiers were pouring across the bridge. Fully armed detachments stepped off the flatcars. Small tanks, light armored cars, and motorcycles with sidecars were unloaded and headed toward the town. By six o'clock that morning Przemyśl was in the hands of the Nazis. All morning long trains loaded with soldiers headed for Lwów and Drohobycz rumbled across the bridge.

I know the events of that day so well because several days later I talked with the engineer and fireman of the commandeered Polish locomotive, who were both acquaintances of mine. When the train was captured, they were led off along with the two Russian border guards and the Russian customs officer. At Żurawica they were separated from the Russians and did not know what became of them. They themselves, as Polish employees of the Przemyśl station, were kept for a day and then released with instructions to return to work, as indeed they did.

The Russians in Przemyśl had nowhere to run. To take the road east was the logical choice, but there they met the German army. They had no way of knowing that the Germans had broken through the border in numerous places and were already everywhere. Some larger units tried to break through the German lines, but they were either cut down by German fire or taken prisoner. Others, caught in bed, ran out of their billets, rifles in hand, defended themselves to the last bullet, and died in the streets. Almost none of the Russian garrison survived. The Nazi civil authorities let the corpses lie in the streets for two days before having them removed. Many Poles were also caught by surprise on the streets and killed in the crossfire. Terror reigned for two days. No one dared go out of doors.

Przemyśl under the Germans

On the third day the representatives of the military occupation force began to appear—the gendarmerie, the local military command from Zasanie, uniformed SS men, the Gestapo, and the rest of the occupation authorities. The police force, made up of Nazis and local Ukrainians, took for their quarters the city hall. The Gestapo chose a handsome modern building which they immediately surrounded with barbed wire and closed the street on which it stood. The Nazi civil administration took up residence in the former Przemyśl district office building.

For two days the Nazis had shot at everything that moved. Now the fighting columns moved on, and murder began to be organized according to the principle of selection. The SS and Gestapo had lists of names and addresses, and with them in hand they proceeded to apartments and dragged the occupants away. None of those taken ever returned; they disappeared without a trace. The main charge against the victims was "cooperation with the enemy." But everyone had "cooperated" with the Russians to one degree or another, since there had been no private enterprise at all in the town while they occupied it. Anyone able to work had been employed in one Russian office or factory or another. On this basis the Nazis could actually have exterminated the entire population. People tried to escape by hiding with friends, to no avail. They would be picked up somewhere else, as soon as it turned out from their documents that they did not live at the address where they were found. Arrests assumed massive proportions, and perhaps even more inhabitants perished during the days following the invasion than in the early days of random fighting.

Before a week had passed, the local authorities issued their first decrees, which they posted on the sides of buildings. The Nazi military commander ordered everyone to surrender any weapons they possessed; the penalty for disobeying was death. A curfew was instituted from five o'clock in the afternoon to five o'clock in the morning; anyone found on the street without a pass during the curfew hours was to be shot on the spot. The shops were ordered to open, although there was nothing to sell, and everyone was instructed to return to work.

After several days, these regulations were relaxed somewhat, but in their place new proclamations appeared. Jews were permitted on the streets only between the hours of two and four in the afternoon unless

150

they had papers to show that they were employed. They were required to wear armbands indicating their nationality, and they were to register immediately with the Arbeitsamt for mandatory labor. They were forbidden to be near the railroad station, the post office, or any other government offices; they were not allowed to buy anything from anyone in town or in the countryside, nor could they possess any of the German occupation marks which had become the official currency. Many other proclamations were issued aimed at beating down the Jewish population and reducing it to starvation.

I was most affected, obviously, by the prohibition regarding the purchase of food by Jews. Our family had no reserves. I had to concern myself with obtaining food right away without regard to the danger. From time to time farmers would bring some kind of produce into town. As I have explained, barter was the only means of exchange they recognized. They demanded the most valuable goods and, of course, got them, for all over town people were dying of hunger, but because of the regulations the farmers would not sell anything to the Jews.

I decided to take action before our family was among the numbers of the starving. One morning I took off my armband and headed out of town toward the nearest village. German soldiers were stationed on almost every road leading into town, looking into the market-women's baskets of food and taking whatever struck their fancy, despite loud complaints and protestations. In exchange they would toss them fifty or sixty pfennigs to dry their tears.

I stopped on the road, some distance away from one group of these soldiers, and, imitating their gutteral shouts, I began to call out "Mashlo! Yoyka!" ("Butter! Eggs!"). Looking into the women's bags, I picked out whatever I wanted, paying no more attention to their lamentations than the Germans did. In this way I "purchased" a pat of butter, a heart-shaped cottage cheese, and two dozen eggs, paying with Russian kopecks, for as a Jew I had no German money. I was so delighted with the success of my ruse that I completely forgot the danger.

Our three-story apartment building had two apartments on each floor. The staircase leading to each floor had sixteen steps—first eight steps, then a sharp turn, then eight more to a small landing. We lived on the top floor on the left. As I was returning home from this adventure I met Basia in front of the house. She was not wearing her armband and had come downstairs with our daughter, Elusia, to get a breath of fresh air. Neither of us knew that the German police were at that moment

151

searching every apartment in our building. I do not know what they were looking for, but all the tenants were Jews. Rushing up the stairs several steps at a time, I reached the top floor and ran right into them. The door to our apartment was open, and in it stood the frightened child of the widow with whom we shared the apartment. (We lived in a two-room apartment, of which we occupied one room; another family, a widow and two daughters, lived in the other.) The child who opened the door to the police was now staring at them in terror. The police heard a noise on the stairs, looked around, and saw me without an armband and with food in my arms.

"Do you live here?" asked one of them in German. I pretended not to understand him.

"Do you live here?" he asked me again. There was no point in delaying any longer. Pointing to the food I was carrying, I said in broken German, "Verkaufen" ("Selling").

The German was not particularly satisfied with my answer. "Does he live here?" he asked the little girl. She began to cry.

I knew that it was all over for me, that nothing could save me. Anyone caught violating the Germans' regulations was shot on the spot. One way or another, I was a dead man. Both men momentarily turned their backs on me, one to question the little girl and the other to listen. Bracing myself against the wall of the corridor and letting the food fall, I gathered all my strength and hurled both men through the door into the apartment. In one bound I flew down all eight steps, richocheted off the wall at the turn, and with a second mad leap flew down the remaining eight steps to the second floor landing, out of pistol range. I ran down the second flight and leaped out into the street where Basia and our child were still standing. Basia later told me that I looked like a ghost. I gasped out only a couple of words: "Don't go in—police in the house"—and I ran on.

It made no sense to run along the sidewalk, where the police could have a clear shot at me, so I ran into the nearest building and up the stairs to the second floor. I banged at the door of the nearest apartment; it was locked. On the other side of the hall the door was also locked, but at the end of the corridor I saw a door opening and an old Jewish woman about to come out. Leaping inside her door, I cried out a single word: "Police!" She immediately understood. She ran into the bedroom, opened the bed, drew back a thick feather quilt and bedspread, and told me to lie down. Then she covered up the bed, smoothed the quilts over my head, and quickly left. She locked the door from the outside with her house key and went calmly down the stairs. She later told me that the policemen were standing outside with their uniforms all smeared with egg, looking up and down the street, cursing. Naturally, I never returned to our apartment again.

Chapter 13

Moving Back to Cracow

When the Nazis entered Przemyśl, the temporary feeling of security I had had under the Russians vanished in a flash. After my adventure with the police, described in the preceding chapter, I decided to leave the town for good and move back to Cracow. Of course, it was easier to make this decision than to carry it out. First of all I would have to get back across the San River; then I would have to get to Cracow to have a look around and lay the groundwork for our move. People from Przemyśl were not yet permitted to travel to Zasanie: the only link between the two places was the iron railroad bridge, which was in the hands of the army, and only authorized persons had the right to use it. I told Basia that I was headed for Cracow and that if I failed to return home before curfew, that meant I was already across the river.

When I got to the river, I sat down on the bank to consider my next move. I had no idea how to get across. After a few minutes I noticed a small rowboat headed in my direction from the other side of the river. In it were four German officers. As they approached the place where I was sitting, I could hear their conversation. They wanted to have a look around Przemyśl but were afraid to leave the boat without a guard, so they discussed leaving one of them by the boat while the other three went into town. They were talking it over without paying the slightest attention to me, but finally one of them was struck by an idea.

154

He came over to me and asked, "Verstehst du deutsch?" ("Do you understand German?").

I looked at him with an idiotic expression, and he repeated the question. At last I sullenly answered, "Nicht verstehen" ("No understand").

They could see that this approach was no good, so one of them took out a packet of cigarettes and gave some of them to me. Of course, I understood this gesture and eagerly grabbed for them. At this the German indicated in sign language that I was to climb into the boat and look after it while they went into town. I nodded that I understood. Still speaking in signs, they promised that when they returned I could get the rest of the cigarettes in the pack. They then set off for town; I climbed into the boat.

In fifteen minutes or so, after making sure that they were safely out of sight, I untied the boat, picked up the oars, and rowed across to the other side of the San. I got out and shoved the boat back into the water so that the current would take it down the river, then headed to the railroad station in Żurawica. The train to Cracow was not due for several hours, and I spent the time examining the tremendously expanded station. I bought my ticket with some German occupation marks which Professor Mylanko had provided. By early next morning I was in Cracow. It was the end of June, 1941. The morning papers at the station boastfully related the German triumphs on the Eastern Front. They were advancing even more rapidly than they had anticipated, taking so many prisoners that it was impossible to count them. The newspapers claimed that the entire Russian army was in disarray; the road to Moscow lay open; the German army would be in the capital before the month was up.

I took a trolley to see some friends of mine living on Zwierzyniecka Street, Paweł and Zofia Kroczewski. We had known one another since our university days, and I had attended their wedding before the war. Paweł was an assistant notary public; Zosia worked for a private company. I told them where I had come from, and Paweł filled me in on the local situation in the city. People in Cracow were elated, believing that the invasion of Russia spelled the beginning of the end for the Nazis. Evidently Hitler had not studied Napoleon's campaign. Otherwise he would never have tried to attack Russia, and especially not as late as the end of June. No one in Cracow doubted that the Nazis would lose; it was merely a matter of time.

Obtaining False Papers

The Kroczewskis offered to put me up for a while, and we quickly got down to my personal business. I confided to them that I wanted to obtain "Aryan" papers, and that as soon as I had that arranged, I would return to Przemyśl for my wife and daughter. We determined that we needed the following documents: a marriage certificate, proof of residence in Cracow, personal identification papers, and a work certificate. As far as the marriage certificate was concerned, Paweł had connections and could see to that. As to the rest, we would worry about that later.

In fact, the very next day, through his underground contacts, Paweł succeeded in obtaining two birth certificates; however, he was unable to get blank marriage certificates. No matter; for the moment we had to be satisfied with what we could get. Both blank birth certificates were from the Cracow parish and bore its official seal. We filled them out carefully and signed them with the name of an imaginary priest. I decided that I would use my own name with a slight change in spelling, from "Schatten" to "Szatyn." After all, in Cracow I was fairly well known. If I ran into some friend, a change in name could only arouse suspicion. Many of my acquaintances did not know that I was a Jew, so there was less danger on that account. Next I had to obtain copies of the false birth certificates on which I had entered my name and Basia's and then to destroy the originals. The copies would be entered in the parish register with official stamps and signatures, and would therefore become "genuine." At this point in the occupation every Pole was obtaining the documents necessary to show to the Germans when obtaining a *Kennkarte* (identity card), so that there would be nothing suspicious in my going to a parish church with a request for a copy of my and Basia's birth certificates. We filled out both certificates with the same last name so that no one would know from Basia's identification papers whether she had a husband or not.

Early next morning I set out on this mission. First I went to the parish office in St. Mary's Church. Behind the desk sat an elderly priest, to whom I handed my papers and waited. The priest looked carefully at the "originals," read them through, looked at the signatures, then went back again to review the information. Finally, he looked up and fixed me with a stern gaze. "Son," he said, "I have been a priest in this parish for years, and I can assure you that there never was a priest by this name either in this or in any other Cracow parish."

I was not surprised, because I had already realized from his expression that something was not right. I mumbled something and, before he was able to react, I plucked the two certificates out of his hand and found myself on the other side of the door.

Richer now by this experience, I decided to try my luck in a parish with a young priest who would not ask so many questions. I went to a number of different churches, but found that their priests were well along in years, so I left without a word. Finally, after a number of unsuccessful visits, I spotted a youngster at one church, a rosy-cheeked lad who looked just out of the seminary. I boldly entered his office, all the while on the alert, and asked for two copies of my birth certificate, explaining that I needed one for my *Kennkarte* and the other at home "for an emergency." He took all this in stride, opened a large registry book, entered all the information from my "original," and then made out two copies of each certificate, which he also duly registered. I paid one złoty for each copy.

Next day another friend of mine stole two identification cards for me. Fortunately I had Basia's photograph with me as well as my own. The identity cards were authentic, issued by the Cracow City Office, District Eight. They stated that we lived in Cracow in the Prądnik Czerwony District, at the aptly named 53 Wolność ("Freedom") Street. These identity cards were necessary, together with the birth certificates, to obtain our *Kennkarten*. On the basis of these other documents I also obtained a registry certificate stating that I lived at 53 Wolnościgasse (as the Germans had renamed Wolność Street). The upshot of all this was that I now had birth certificates, registry attestations, and identity cards for myself and Basia, all of them now originals, entered in the official registry books. In addition, Paweł provided me with a false work permit stating that I was employed as a bookkeeper in a business office.

One final matter remained before returning to Przemyśl for Basia and our daughter. I had to rent an apartment and to move there from my official "former place of residence," that is, from the Prądnik Czerwony address listed on the identity cards, so that there would be no reason for suspicion. It was then necessary to transport to this new apartment, for appearances' sake, all my "belongings"—furniture, kitchen implements, dishes, and other household equipment. This would be no easy task, for I had to get hold of it all somewhere, but first I had to look around Cracow for an apartment.

I set aside the third day of my stay in town for this purpose. My first move was to visit several friends. The first I saw was Edward Garbarz, the son of a railway worker from Przemyśl who worked as a cashier at the Cracow-Płaszów station. Unfortunately, although he would have been glad to do anything he could for me, he was unable to be of much help: he was a bachelor and shared a rented room with another man. We simply arranged that we would keep in touch and that in case of need I could find shelter with him.

I then visited a second friend, Mieczysław ("Mietek") Misiołek. This was the same Mietek whom in the autumn of 1939 I took home with me to the Moskalewskis' apartment in Przemyśl. At present he was living with his wife, daughter, and parents-in-law in a little house in Borek Fałęcki near Cracow, close to the Cracow-Swoszowice train station. Mietek's father-in-law, Tuncio, a retired high school teacher, was an idealistic and gentle soul. His mother-in-law, Simusia, was a grade school teacher and president of the local teachers' union. Tiny and nimble as a squirrel, she struck one as a wise and sensitive woman. She was in charge of the entire house and everyone in it, including Basia, me, and our daughter when we moved into a house not far from them. Nothing happened without Simusia; nothing escaped her attention. She knew everything and had her finger in every pie; for everyone she had an open heart and a piece of friendly advice—in short, a golden personality. I have not met many such persons in my life. My friend Mietek was a tall, very good-looking blond fellow, well-bred, well-mannered, and eventempered. Since leaving Przemyśl in 1939 he had had no news of me and was happy to see me again. Borek Fałęcki suited me perfectly; the protection of people who had lived there for a long time and who were well known in the area was very important, and so I decided to look for a place to live not far from Mietek.

Into the Cracow Ghetto

Now I had to obtain some furnishings. I had no idea where my prewar belongings were. When I left Cracow in the first days of the war, my father-in-law had volunteered to store my things. I had to find out what had become of them and whether I could get any of them back, so I decided to visit Basia's parents. In March, 1941, the occupation force created a ghetto on the left side of the river in the Podgórze District, and my parents-in-law were forced to move there from their neat, comfortable little house in the Nowa Wieś District. I knew nothing of the ghetto, at this time, but now I was to become acquainted with it.

On the fourth day of my stay in Cracow, I took a trolley in the direction of the ghetto, located immediately beyond the Vistula River, on the other side of the so-called Third Bridge at the end of Starowiślna ("Old Vistula") Street. I rode through the ghetto on the trolley, which did not stop at any point along the route. At the entrance gate in the wall surrounding the ghetto, a Blue Police officer stepped onto the running board of the trolley and stood there until the car passed through the ghetto and out the other gate. He would come back in the opposite direction on another trolley in the same way. Both gates were guarded by Blue Police officers and German guards. The Jews all wore armbands, and when they entered the gate or left for the "Aryan" side, they had to show special passes indicating that they had permission. The Germans could drive through the ghetto in official automobiles, but Poles had to bypass the area on the side streets, either on foot or in horse carts (private automobile traffic was nonexistent). I noted with amazement, however, that some large furniture vans, for example, those of the Hartwig Company, were permitted to drive through the streets of the ghetto, for they could not navigate the narrow side streets around it. On entering the walls, the driver would receive a pass, which he would return as he drove out on the other side. I noticed that within the ghetto itself some furniture vans were carrying people's belongings from one building to another.

Standing near the gate, I waited for a chance to pass a note to one of the Jews entering the ghetto, which informed Basia's family that I was on the other side wanting to get inside. In an hour or so my brother-in-law appeared outside the walls. He greeted me, told me to wait, and then went back inside. After about fifteen minutes he returned, bringing me an armband and some identification paper. I entered with him as a Jew and made my way to my wife's parents. The meeting was very moving. It was the first news they had had of us since the day of our memorable departure from Cracow, nearly two years ago. I assured them that their daughter and granddaughter were well, that they had remained in Przemyśl with friends, and that I had come only in order to lay the groundwork for our move to Cracow. They were amazed when I told them that I was not planning to move to the ghetto but would live on the outside on false papers. They argued against the idea, saying that if I were caught it meant certain death but that if I lived in the ghetto I still might survive somehow. I explained that my decision was final and irrevocable; in any case, it was our decision—their daughter's and mine. We preferred to perish in freedom rather than to suffer a kind of captivity for which we were not suited. They finally understood that it was pointless to discuss the matter further with me.

Before the war I had lived in a large modern apartment. Now I learned that some of my belongings had been entrusted by my parents-in-law to some non-Jewish friends of theirs for safekeeping. The remainder had been taken into the ghetto and placed in storage. I decided to retrieve this furniture from the ghetto—exactly how, I had no idea as yet. In the meanwhile, I had a look around the living quarters of my parents-in-law. Nine people were living in two rooms. God only knows how they all managed to fit. They were not even real rooms, but more like little cubbyholes. Both my parents-in-law looked emaciated; the signs of much suffering were evident. I asked them to show me where my things were being stored, though I was afraid to tell them that I intended to take the furniture out of the ghetto: I did not want to alarm them because it really was an insane idea. People themselves couldn't go beyond the walls without special permits; removing furniture was simply out of the question. My father-in-law took me to the storage room, and I asked him to give me the key, as I preferred to keep it. Then I bade all of them a warm farewell, promising that as soon as Basia and our daughter reached Cracow we would come to see them. I assured them that they need not worry about our safety, for I was traveling on legitimate papers. Then I left the apartment and the ghetto, thoroughly depressed at the sight of this tragic scene.

The next day I visited my friend Mietek. He had good news: his mother-in-law Simusia had found us an apartment only a few hundred meters from theirs. A certain Mrs. Proszkowski, a widow, had a nice two-family house. She occupied one apartment herself and had agreed to rent the second one to us. I put down a deposit, promising to move there in a few days. (I told her that my wife was presently staying at a summer resort, and that I would go there and bring her back immediately). Right now, I told her, we were living in Prądnik Czerwony (as entered on our false identification cards), but I considered her apartment much more comfortable and would be glad to move to Borek Fałęcki, all the more so because the resort town of Swoszowice was close by, where I would be able to take mineral baths.

Rescuing My Furniture

I spent that evening working out a plan for getting my furniture out of the ghetto. I decided to go to the Hartwig Company, whose vans I had seen there, and have a talk with one of the drivers. I told him that I bought some furniture for next to nothing from some Jews in the ghetto, and that I would pay him well if he would help me get it out. I knew that he had the right to travel through the ghetto. He would get a pass at the entrance, drive in to meet me, and we would quickly load the furniture and drive out through the other gate, so that it would look as though he were simply transporting the furniture through the ghetto. The man considered my proposition for a long time. On the one hand, he was tempted by the idea of making some money on the side; on the other hand, he was afraid to take the risk. He said finally that he would like to think about it overnight. In the end, however, he agreed. The next morning he had a job which would take him through the ghetto into the Rynek Podgórski ("Podgórze Market") area, he said, and, since he would be returning with an empty van over the same route, he could easily pick up my furniture. I assured him that there was nothing to fear; it would be standing out on the sidewalk. If anyone should ask questions, he and I would simply say that we were headed for another street within the walls. No one would suspect anything, and I would be riding in the van with him in any case. I gave the driver the address together with a down payment, and we agreed that I would wait for him next day at eleven o'clock in the morning. He would get the rest of the payment after the furniture reached its destination.

The next morning I got back into the ghetto with the help of my brother-in-law and hired some Jewish workers to help me take my furniture from the storage room to the street. I told them that I was moving into an apartment in another part of the ghetto and that a furniture van would arrive any minute to move my possessions. If they would wait around and help me load quickly, they would get a large tip. At the appointed hour, the van drove up from the direction of Rynek Podgórski. The furniture was loaded quickly and efficiently, I paid the workers, and we drove off through the nearest street, turning immediately out onto the main exit route. In a few minutes we were out and driving down Starowiślna Street. I gave the driver an address, Number 6 Cracow Street, in the city. I knew that building, and knew that it had a wide gateway. In the very middle of the gate the two of us unloaded the furniture. I paid the driver the rest of the sum agreed upon, adding that I had already engaged some workers to help me carry the furniture upstairs to my apartment. He drove off, and I breathed a sigh of relief. Then I telephoned another moving company and asked for a small furniture van with two helpers to come right away, for my things had already been removed from my apartment and were waiting to be loaded. For immediate service they demanded additional payment, and I agreed. Soon the van arrived, and we loaded my belongings and set off for my new apartment in Borek Fałęcki.

Again Przemyśl

At last everything was taken care of, and in only eight days! Now, fortified with valid documents stating that I lived in Cracow, I set out for Przemyśl to fetch Basia and Elusia. My next task was to erase all traces of us in Przemyśl—but to do it in such a way that our disappearance would not look like an escape, for then the Germans could take revenge on my parents. I did not doubt that I would be able to manage. Barring unforeseen circumstances, in seven to ten days my family and I ought to be safely back in Cracow.

Although I tried not to think about unpleasant matters, my meeting with Basia's parents, brother, and sisters was constantly on my mind. Though they did not say so directly, I knew that they continued to believe that I was an impetuous person who, sooner or later, would be taken and shot. Many wise and upright people were living in the ghetto, none of them thinking about risking their lives by adopting false papers. According to them, the idea was simply madness. How did I propose to fight the entire German occupation apparatus? These were the sorts of questions which they no doubt were asking one another.

I approached matters differently, believing that each person was responsible for his own happiness. At this point in my life I thought that it was impossible to be guided by past principles or to behave as had once been normal and customary. What was happening now had never happened before in the history of the world. Self-defense was a highly individual matter. I was determined not to settle down in the ghetto and wait calmly until someone decided to put me out of the way. I considered the Nazis murderers and equated staying in the ghetto with a death sentence. My wife's parents could not believe the Nazis would dare commit mass murder. They, like many other Jews, thought that by living in the ghetto and obeying the German regulations to the letter so as not to give any trouble, they had a chance to survive the war. On the other hand, open opposition to Nazi regulations—in my case, living outside the ghetto on Aryan papers—was punishable by sure and certain death. Knowing the perfection of the German administrative machinery, people thought that any "wise guy" would be caught and punished. We were never able to agree on the matter.

During my eight days in Cracow train service had been restored from Żurawica to Przemyśl. On the following day service was to be extended as far as Lwów. As I rode into the Przemyśl station I studied with curiosity the new official German notices hanging on the walls, particularly those concerning the Jews. The restrictions were increasingly severe. When I came into our flat, Basia threw herself on me with joyful tears. This had been our longest separation so far, and she had not known whether I was dead or alive. I calmed her by saying that all our affairs were in fine shape: I had been to Cracow, seen her parents, they sent their greetings and congratulated her on the baby, and so on. I tried to present things to her in bright colors, having decided that I was going to say as little as possible about future unpleasantness. She had not been through the same hard school as I, and for our mutual peace of mind it was necessary that she remain calm. I knew that hard times were coming for her and that in the future she would need a large reserve of spiritual strength. I warned her not to let slip to anyone outside our family the fact that I had been to Cracow and that we would soon leave Przemyśl behind.

Chapter 14

Wrapping Up Business at the Supply Yard

Upon returning to Przemyśl I learned that my assistants in the warehouse had been looking for me in connection with some urgent business, so early next morning I went to the supply yard on Kopernik Street. As I have already mentioned, three clerks and about a dozen workers were employed at the supply yard during the Russian occupation. Now more than two hundred Jews, allotted to us by the Arbeitsamt, were engaged in pulling down buildings partially destroyed by the bombings, cleaning up salvagable materials, and putting them in storage. There was now a German director in the county construction department, under whose authority our yard operated. This man had already learned my identity, for the workers had simply told him my name. Since the new German authorities had instructed each person to return to his former place of work, my assistants advised me to register with the county construction department as soon as possible; otherwise, I could be imprisoned. I followed their advice and went there immediately, wearing the Jewish armband which went with my Przemyśl identity.

When I announced myself in the main office of the construction department, a man wearing an armband indicating that he was Ukrainian looked up and immediately began shouting: "What's a Jew looking for here? Don't you know that Jews are not permitted to enter these offices?" He was speaking, or rather shouting, in Ukrainian. I answered, in Polish, that I had come because I had been called, and told him who I was. It turned out that, in fact, it was he who had been to the supply

164

yard and had reported my absence from work. Now my fate was in the hands of his superior.

The secretary entered the director's office and closed the door behind him. I looked at the nameplate on the door: Dr. Heinrich Schmidt. In a minute he came out and told me to go in. He followed after. A man in his forties wearing a brown, semi-military uniform was sitting behind a large desk.

"Your name!" Schmidt said curtly in German.

The secretary translated this into Ukrainian. He either did not want to or was unable to speak Polish. I gave my name.

"Where have you been all this time?" was his next question.

The secretary wanted to translate this into Ukrainian, but before he could do so I began answering in German, explaining that the outbreak of the Russo-German war had caught me in Lwów, where I had been on business, and that the trains from Lwów had begun running to Przemyśl only yesterday. I had caught the first train I could, arrived yesterday, and reported for work immediately.

"You speak German."

I could not tell whether this was a question or a statement, so I did not reply. The director indicated to the Ukrainian that he did not need him any longer, and he left.

"How long have you been working in the supply yard?"

"Nine months," I answered.

"And before that?"

"At the train station."

The director asked a number of other minor questions and then finally said, "You may return to your work as warehouse manager, but should you leave work a second time without authorization, I will have to report you to the proper authorities."

When I left, the secretary in the outer office showed his disappointment; I suppose he had expected that the director would call the Gestapo to take me away. When I told him that I was to return to my work, he ordered me to wait and went into the director's office to hear this for himself. After a moment he returned with an annoyed expression and, with evident distaste, wrote a letter to the Arbeitsamt stating that I was employed with the construction office. I was satisfied with the outcome and left. It never entered my mind to report to the Arbeitsamt. What for? In order to appear in one more list of names? My present goal was to disappear from every list in existence.

On my way back from this interview I dropped in to see Professor Mylanko to thank him for watching over Basia. While I was away he had obtained food for my family by walking the streets of the town bartering our personal belongings either for food or for German marks with which food could be purchased. I confided to him that I intended to leave Przemyśl, and he promised to help. I also told Józek Moskalewski, my other good friend in Przemyśl, about my planned departure three days later and asked him to see to certain details.

Next day I went to the supply yard. There had been many changes. Next to it the huge base camp of the Soviet border forces had been located. I had never before been on these grounds, for the roads leading into the base had been barred to civilians. Now the gate stood open, the Soviet administration having fled. Because our yard was the nearest operational storage facility, the Germans had placed the base under our administration. Along with the two hundred Jews working in our yard there were about eight hundred working at the former Russian base. Perhaps such a large force was not needed, but the Judenrat (the Jewish administration set up by the Nazi authorities to "represent the interests of the Jews," as they put it) pressed as many people into work as possible so that, as workers, they could be issued food coupons. The Jews themselves asked to be assigned here, for the work was not difficult and was almost unsupervised. Most important, the job allowed them to move about town from five in the morning until five in the afternoon, so that they could obtain food without danger of being caught in a roundup and assigned to much more arduous labor.

I went on a tour of the former Soviet army base. Despite the enormous amounts of materiel that had been pilfered over the last few days, the quantities remaining were still substantial—tons of cement, gypsum, plaster, brassware, ironware, and lumber—all of it for construction, and undoubtedly worth millions. There were also a number of buildings on the grounds of whose very existence I had been unaware. I selected twenty Jews as accountants and appointed others as temporary managers of each subsection of the base; for the most part these people were already experienced in the construction industry. I made the most competent accountant my second-in-command and ordered the entry gates repaired immediately so that everything would be made secure. Then I placed a freeze on the receipt or shipment of materiel from the base and instructed the other accountants to begin to take as accurate an inventory as possible. I ordered that in future everything entering the base was to pass through my yard. The workers were to sort through the existing materiel as quickly as possible and give the tally to the accountants. Goods on hand were to be listed twice—one copy for the base from which it came and one for my use. A new location for the central administration was to be found, and the entire administrative operation, including my own depot, was to be transferred there.

I realized that the warehouses were not going to exist in their present form for long, as they would no doubt be absorbed by some private German company, but for the time being the district administration was concerned only with securing the property left behind by the Russians. Although I realized that my orders were of a provisional nature only, I did not want to expose either myself or those I left behind to the complaint that we were trying to sabotage the work.

Dr. Schmidt

The following afternoon Dr. Schmidt, director of the county construction office, paid an unexpected visit to the yard. Before coming to see me, he had been to all the bases, inspected the work, and heard about my orders. When he came to my area, the same work was in progress as on the other bases, but we already had our materiel inventoried, while the inventory on the other bases was just beginning. I began to describe what I was doing, but he interrupted me, saying that it was unnecessary—that he had just returned from the other bases and could see that my orders were correct. We went into the yard to inspect the work at close hand. He looked on in silence as the workers sorted, stacked, and recorded the goods on hand. I too stood by in silence. Then Dr. Schmidt asked me what my real profession was. The question so surprised me that I did not know what to say for a moment, but finally I decided that there was no need to lie, and told him the truth.

He made no reply, as though either forgetting about what he had asked or thinking about something else. He spoke again after a few moments. "You know, sir, that's really interesting—I myself am in the law, but not an attorney. I worked all my life as a state counselor. I come from around Flensburg in Schleswig-Holstein, near the Danish border."

For the second time in this conversation I was caught by surprise, not only by his confidence, but also by the fact that in speaking with me, a Jew, he had addressed me as "Sir." I said nothing, however, and we proceeded on our tour. Before completing the inspection, at the very end of the square, when we found ourselves alone, Dr. Schmidt stopped and looked me straight in the eye. "Sie sind nicht ein Jude" ("You are no Jew"), he said.

I paused for a moment. "How am I to take that?" I asked.

"Sie brauchen nicht als solcher bleiben" ("You don't need to remain one"), he replied.

A lump formed in my throat. Here he was thinking along the same lines as I! Was this German a mind-reader? It was simply astounding! As he climbed into his car, he added these parting words: "If you have any further business with me, please see me in person." Then he drove off.

I understood what he meant. I had noticed at his office that he did not get along well with his Ukrainian secretary, and no wonder. The man was an unpleasant, scrawny sort of a fellow with a small head, dark, slicked-down hair, and a sharp nose on the end of which he wore pince-nez glasses with thick lenses. He was always in motion, continually waving his arms about, chattering in his squeaky voice. One could see that these mannerisms got on the nerves of the serious, calm, and reticent Dr. Schmidt. Still, I was amazed at this conversation. Here I had been racking my brains for days trying to figure out how to disappear from the warehouse in such a way as not to expose those close to me to any danger. Now a German, a man who did not even know me, had let me know that I should drop out of sight as a Jew, and had almost offered to help me do so. It was unbelievable. This conversation took place on Wednesday, and I set Friday as the day of my departure.

Last-Minute Preparations

I began making preparations to leave. On Thursday Moskalewski went to the train station and bought us two tickets to Cracow (I was afraid I would be recognized at the station), while Professor Mylanko dug up a two-wheeled cart from somewhere. He and Moskalewski wheeled our belongings to the station, and Moskalewski then forwarded our baggage to Cracow. I said goodbye to my parents, after arranging to keep in touch and promising not to abandon them. I was to send for

Chapter 14

them just as soon as I got set up in Cracow, and they were to be ready to leave at a moment's notice.

Finally, the big day arrived. The train was to leave at noon. Moskalewski accompanied Elusia and Basia, who was not wearing her armband, of course, to the station. He led her out onto the platform by the side entrance used by station employees, and waited for me. In the meantime I went to the county office building to see Dr. Schmidt. His secretary had evidently received prior instructions, for he admitted me immediately. Without the usual preliminaries, I told Dr. Schmidt that I was requesting a release from my job, for I was leaving Przemyśl. To his question as to where I was going, I replied that I was going to Lwów. He seemed to take both my arrival and my request in stride; he rather seemed to expect it. He told me that he had some friends in Lwów and that he could give me some letters of introduction to them if I liked. I merely smiled and shook my head. "Unfortunately, even the best letters will not be of much use to me now," I answered.

He understood what I meant and did not insist but rose from his chair, came around to the other side of the desk, and stretched out his hand. "Herr Doktor, Ich wünsche Ihnen viel Glück. Sie werden es brauchen" ("Doctor, I wish you much luck. You will need it"), he said, pressing my hand.

I prepared to leave, but he kept me a moment longer. He asked whether I had any money, and I told him honestly that I didn't have a penny. (I should note that the money for the train tickets to Cracow was a gift from Professor Mylanko and that, while in Cracow, I was at first subsidized by my friend Paweł Kroczewski.) At this Dr. Schmidt rang for his secretary, the obnoxious Ukrainian. "Mr. Schatten is being henceforth released from his position at the supply yard," he told him. "Please make out a voucher for three months' wages and go to the cashier to get it for him."

His secretary began to protest that he hadn't filled out the necessary forms, that he did not have a letter in his files releasing me from work, and other such nonsense, but Dr. Schmidt fixed on him a gaze so full of malice that the secretary immediately disappeared out the door. He returned after a short while with the money and receipt, laid it all down on the desk, and scuttled away. I signed the receipt and put away the money, much amazed by this turn of events. I had not expected such an outcome, and certainly not the money. Dr. Schmidt saw my amazement; he said nothing, but there was a smile at the corner of his mouth. I went up to him, shook his hand firmly, and left.

I never heard of Dr. Schmidt again; after the war, in Germany, I tried to trace him but was unable to. He proved to me by his conduct that one must never judge a people as a whole; in particular, one must never confuse a people with the government in power. Governments can be good or bad, cruel or bloodthirsty, but their people must be judged individually.

From Dr. Schmidt's office I went straight to the railroad station, pausing only to duck into a doorway to remove my armband, which I had worn throughout my interview with Dr. Schmidt. I already had my ticket. In order to get onto the platform I had to go through a gate where an acquaintance of mine from my railroad days was standing punching tickets. He did not say a word to me as I passed by. Next to him stood a black-uniformed Ukrainian with a rifle, a member of the new railroad police, the so-called Bahnschutzpolizei. Basia, our child, and Moskalewski were off in the distance. Soon the train arrived, filled to bursting with passengers. Moskalewski said something to the conductor, who went back into the car and opened a window in the corridor. Moskalewski shoved Basia up to him through the window, then Elusia. It was the only way of getting them onto the train. The conductor also helped them find a place in the compartment. After shoving through the crowd and embracing Moskalewski, I too somehow forced my way into the train. It gave a start, and we were off for Cracow.

All in all, I was satisfied. I had disappeared in such a way that no one would look for me, and without exposing anyone I left behind to danger on my account. Even had someone wanted to look for me, he would not know where to begin.

Getting Established in Cracow

We went straight to our new apartment in Borek Fałęcki. It was a peaceful place on the outskirts of Cracow, among the fields and meadows. We had quarters in a neat little house that faced Zakopane Street. In the back there were fields of grain running right up to the Cracow-Swoszowice train station. There, on Swoszowice Street (now called Kolejowa, or "Railroad Street"), perhaps three hundred meters from us, lived the Misiołeks. We could walk there along a well-trodden path through the fields.

I started looking for a job. I didn't want to work within the city of Cracow proper; that would be dangerous, as too many people knew me there. Mietek Misiołek found out by chance that not far from us, right outside the small town of Skawina, close to Oświęcim (Auschwitz), the leaseholder of an estate was looking for a helper. I went there at once. The estate was called Borek Szlachecki. The estate tenant, by profession an agronomist, was struggling with the paperwork. He had to supervise production and had neither the time nor the ability to handle the administrative side of things. Because of the war, the bureaucracy was enormous. The tenant had to run from one office to another, filling out forms, applications, and reports, and constantly talking to the authorities.

I told him that I would gladly take over the administration of the estate: I spoke German, I knew how to deal with the authorities, and I knew how to farm. My own requirements were modest, I said. I wanted to work in the country because in these dangerous times I thought that it was not advisable to live in the larger cities. Regarding references, he could talk to Professor Adam Krzyżanowski or to my friend Mietek Misiołek. Within three days the tenant sent me a message to come to Borek Szlachecki for an interview. There we agreed on compensation, and I started to work at once.

My job required me to be at the estate from Monday through Saturday. On Sundays I would return home by bicycle or train. It was not far, barely thirteen kilometers. The estate had been in the hands of tenants for many years. The actual owner leased the estate not, as was customary in Poland at the time, for a long period or even for a tenant's lifetime, but on a short-term basis. Because of this, the leaseholders were not interested in improving the land but only in yearly profits. The land was barren, the buildings and equipment were in disrepair, and the estate was going from bad to worse. Even in normal times, without substantial capital investment the farm would not have produced an income, and the situation was even more acute during the war. The present leaseholder had labored from morning to night, but in vain. He was unable to meet the demands placed on the estate by the German authorities. As a result, they informed him that they were going to remove him from his job.

At this point the owner started looking for a buyer. He found one in the person of Count Antoni Potocki from Cracow. Potocki agreed to take over the estate with its entire stock. Potocki's manager from his estate at Cracow-Olsza was in charge of the transaction, and I was there to represent the interests of the present tenant, for whom I had worked for only a short while. The agreement was concluded. The tenant moved off the estate and left me to complete the agreement and to introduce the new owner to its affairs.

Count Antoni's son Jerzy was put in charge of the estate by the old count. I started going over the inventory with Count Jerzy and introducing him slowly to the mysteries of farm administration. According to our agreement, I was to stay for a month. During that month, Jerzy came to see that I knew my job, that I had good business connections, and that I was fair and honest. The month passed, and after talking it over with his father, Jerzy asked me to stay. I agreed. My duties were identical to my previous ones; Jerzy took charge of production and I remained in charge of administration.

Thus, thanks to the financial help of Professor Mylanko, the three months' pay from Dr. Schmidt, and the generosity of Paweł and Zosia Kroczewski, I survived the first and the hardest period of my adventure. Before long I was earning enough on the estate to support my needs and those of my family.

The Germans had chosen to remove the former tenant at Borek Szlachecki during the fall of 1941, when most of the season's work was over. By the time Count Antoni had assumed control over the estate, and the young Potockis had taken up residence there, it was early in 1942.

PART III

Fight for Survival, 1942-45

Chapter 15

My Decision

I awoke at the foot of the haystack in the morning. The sky was beginning to pale; a thin mist covered the meadows. Here and there a star shone, but they appeared dim, small, weak. Tiny clouds appeared in the east, changing color by the minute, from dark gray to yellow, and then, catching the first rays of the sun still hidden beyond the horizon, lightening and turning bright gold. In another moment the sun appeared, first its crimson aureole, then the rim of its large bronze shield, until soon it was blazing in all its glory. It seemed to grow smaller and, at the same moment, brighter. As its rays warmed the air, the mist fell to earth as dew. Skylarks began their morning songs; it promised to be a beautiful day. It was late September, 1942, three years into the war and the day after my confrontation with Count Jerzy. I still had not decided what to do.

I was chilled as I walked through the fields toward the village, avoiding the manor. I did not want to meet our people on their way to work and have them wonder what I was doing abroad so early. From a distance I could see the reapers already at work cutting the wheat. They moved forward slowly, inexorably, and evenly, marking a semicircular swath with their scythes from right to left. This rhythmical motion was repeated again and again; they would turn slightly to the right, bend over, and, with one fluid movement, cut the stalks at the ground. They would then straighten, turn, bend down again, and once more put the scythes in motion. From time to time a reaper paused to draw his whetstone from his belt to sharpen his blade. A wide swath of fallen grain showed how much they had already accomplished.

The women were working in another part of the field, cutting grain with sickles where the ground was uneven and the use of a scythe was inconvenient or dangerous. The sickle, shaped like a new moon, has not changed in centuries, and the reaper's motions are equally unchanged: the same graceful semicircular body motion used with the scythe, but with the body more bent; the same rhythmical repetition, unerring, economical, the result of years of experience. As the workers cut the grain, they laid the stalks evenly on a binding cord on the ground. As soon as enough was cut, the workers gathered it into bundles, drew it together with the cord, and tied it. Kneeling on the bundle, they drew a peg from their belt, tightened the cord a second time with the peg, tied it once more, and tucked the ends of the cord into the side of the sheaf.

As I gazed over the fields, I continued to think over my situation. Until now I had divided my friends, acquaintances, and relatives into various categories of confidence. First came my own and Basia's family. For their own safety, I had not told them what my new name was nor where we were living. They knew only that we were somewhere in the vicinity of Cracow. As a means of communication I gave them the address of someone who himself did not know my whereabouts and whom I contacted for messages at irregular intervals. Professor Mylanko and Józek Moskalewski belonged to this group as well. The second group was composed of such friends as Edek Garbarz and the Kroczewskis, both in Cracow. They knew my old name, Schatten, and my new name, Szatyn, but that was about all they did know. They did not know what I did or where I worked. They could not get in touch with me directly; I had to contact them. Then there was a third group, consisting of the friends and acquaintances I had made since going "underground." They all knew me as Szatyn; they knew where I worked; they even looked on me as something of an old-timer, since I had worked at Borek Szlachecki even before the Potocki family took over the estate. Some of them also knew where I lived in Cracow.

The Misiołek family was a category unto itself. They knew my former and present names; they knew where I lived and worked—in short, they knew all about me, but safety lay in the fact that no one had any idea that we were such close friends. To the outside world we were simply neighbors, no different from any others, so I thought it improbable that the Misiołeks would come under pressure from anyone to reveal my secret.

I had not realized that one cannot plan every action rationally, that when emotions come into play, anything can happen. It was one thing to hear that people were being murdered, but quite another to see one's near and dear being led to the slaughter. My emotions had conquered my caution when I rescued Maria Friede. By so doing, I created yet another category of people such as the Potockis, the Kraszewskis, and Miss Liebeskind, a group more dangerous than the others because these people knew both my past and present, where I was living, and where to find me. If any of them were ever arrested and interrogated, they might well confess all they knew about me. Well, I said to myself, this new danger was just one more I would have to live with. For now, I had to return to the manor. I could not delay my answer to the Potockis any longer.

I decided to stay on at the estate, even though I realized my relationship with the Potockis would no longer be the same. Truly, I had no other choice. The machinery had been set in motion; there was no way to stop it now. Part of my family would soon be in Skawina, and the rest would follow shortly. I was also working on a scheme to get Basia's family out of the ghetto. I could not just forget about all these plans; it was necessary to be on the spot to see that they were carried through successfully.

Accordingly, after breakfast I went to the Potockis and told them that I was retracting my previous decision. They said that they were delighted to hear it. The countess again asked my forgiveness for having been meddlesome; they both understood, she said, that they had behaved wrongly. On the other hand, she continued, they now understood why I had always tried to avoid the Jewish workers. Perhaps, I thought, in a way it was best that they knew the truth. I would not have to pretend in front of them, and they might be able to help us in the future. The countess promised to explain the situation to her family that very week and to make sure that they too would keep my secret.

Though I expressed my gratitude to them, I could not respond with the same degree of candor. After all, I could hardly tell them that there were more of us to come, my entire family, in fact, and that another Jew was working on the estate as well. (Not long before this I had received word that one of Basia's distant relatives had escaped from the Cracow ghetto and was living on false papers. He was unemployed, and I had hired him as a night watchman on the estate.) The Potockis had no idea what they were getting themselves into, and fortunately they never found out. Although they themselves were not Jewish, for harboring Jews the penalty was death, as I have said, and even the family name would have been of no help.

Replacing the Steward

As if these problems were not enough, a new one now cropped up: I had to find a replacement for our steward. He was a young unmarried man, in his twenties, who had finished agricultural school and actually knew his trade quite well, but the problem was that his training had not prepared him to operate in time of war. During the war the welfare of an estate did not depend so much on administrative know-how as on the ability to get along with the occupation authorities—more simply, on the ability to sail close to the wind and to avoid filling military requisitions whenever possible. Without this ability, even the most efficiently run estate would fail. Our steward was not smart enough to see that these were not ordinary times and that it was necessary to employ extraordinary methods. Besides this, he had an overdeveloped sense of his own importance and was hostile to any attempt to modify his way of running things.

Count Antoni had hired this man before Count Jerzy and his wife settled permanently on the estate. The steward, who had apparently heard something about the cool relationship between father and son, chose to recognize only the authority of the old count and to treat young Jerzy as a picturesque resident who had no right to meddle in established routine. I presented something of an anomaly to him. He saw me merely as a bookkeeper, a person who should spend the entire day in his office writing reports, making payments, keeping Count Antoni in Cracow apprised of what was happening, and receiving his instructions. Such matters as where we were supposed to get the money to pay our workers, how we were to evade military levies so that we could provide our people with better food allotments than the German regulations allowed, how we were to wring the necessary number of workers out of the Arbeitsamt—none of this interested him. Those were the bookkeeper's problems, not his.

He was displeased when young Potocki, who had a degree in

agronomy, was not content to remain picturesque but took an active part in the administration of the estate. He could not abide the young countess, who, in his opinion, often meddled in matters which were none of her affair. His tack with me was simply to ignore me, believing that I was engaged in everything except what a bookkeeper should be doing. My constant trips, telephone calls, meetings, my use of the manor carriage, and my frequent private conversations with the Potockis were more than he could fathom.

I paid no attention to this young man's attitude, as I understood that when he reached what he considered to be the lofty position of steward for Count Potocki, he had become obsessed with his own importance. The young countess, however, was constantly annoyed by the steward's undermining of her plans, and he, for his part, did not understand that it was she above all who was able to make her way through the labyrinth of German orders, decrees, and prohibitions, and was thus largely responsible for keeping the estate afloat. In a modern enterprise one might call her the business manager, her husband the production manager, and me the public relations man who keeps in touch with the authorities and represents the enterprise to the outside world. Together we formed a smoothly running team.

It was hard enough to alter the meticulously detailed orders of the old count to adapt them to our constantly changing circumstances without having a steward around who made life even more difficult with his dull-witted inflexibility. The countess was all for firing him immediately, but the count preferred to wait. For my part, I wanted no changes, fearing that they could only hurt us. However, the tension was getting worse daily, and I realized that sooner or later things would come to a head.

Several days following a discussion with the count and countess on the subject of the steward, the chambermaid knocked on my office door with a message from the count. He asked what plans I had for the morning. I replied that in all probability I would be riding into the fields in about an hour. The maid returned shortly to say that he would accompany me.

After inspecting the work going on in the fields, we lay down to rest next to some recently harvested sheaves of wheat. Without any prelude, the count said: "I talked to my father yesterday and told him about the troubles we were having with the steward. He said that it was up to me. If I did not like him, then why didn't I replace him? So I told him I would." He thought for a few minutes, then went on: "But I don't want to talk with that character myself. Why don't you tell him for me that I am letting him go and that I would appreciate his leaving the estate as soon as possible? Tell him that we will pay him for the rest of the season, even though it is far from over."

I lay there chewing on a straw, thinking this over, while the count waited. Finally, I gave my opinion. "As I see it, the steward isn't a bad sort of fellow. He's simply in his job at the wrong time. He learned farm management during peacetime. No one taught him how to run an estate in a war. The three of us don't talk things over with him much, so it's understandable that he misunderstands us and constantly feels ill at ease and irritated. Then too, he takes me for nothing more than the estate pen-pusher and would be most humiliated to hear from me that he is being released. He really doesn't deserve that. I feel that you yourself ought to give him his notice in private, and as gently as you can." After a moment's consideration the count came around to my way of thinking and said that he would talk with the steward that very day. Two weeks later the steward left the manor.

The New Steward

I put an announcement in a Cracow newspaper and interviewed various candidates for the steward's job. This gave me the opportunity to test myself as a judge of human nature. I did not pay as much attention to what the job applicants said as to how they said it. All of them were trying to present themselves in the most favorable possible light, and it was their manner of doing so that weighed most heavily with me. After interviewing about twenty people I was still undecided. Four days after the advertisement was printed, a man of around thirty came to my office. He had a drawn face, large, kind eyes, and clothing which had seen better days (his boots in particular being in urgent need of a cobbler). He was from Wolyń and spoke with a singsong eastern Polish accent. For the last four years, he told me, he had managed an estate much larger than ours east of Tarnopol. It was easy to foresee that the Soviet-German front might well fall back onto this territory, so one day, fearing to be caught a second time in the line of fire, he hitched two horses to a wagon, gathered up his six children and his wife, and set off for parts unknown. He headed west and had been on the road for three weeks, arriving in Cracow a few days ago. He said that he had looked for work in several places, but as soon as people learned that he had six children they turned him away. He assured me that his requirements were modest because they could not be otherwise, and that he would gladly work for bread and water, so to speak, just to put an end to his family's wanderings.

He did not volunteer all this information: I had to extract it from him bit by bit. He impressed me as expert in his trade, and I liked him as a person. The main problem was those six children of his. I had been clearly instructed to hire either a bachelor or a married man with two children at most; six was out of the question. Where would we put them all? The workers on the estate slept in bunks, four to a room. Married grooms, if they lived on the estate, were entitled to a room to themselves, and the steward was allotted two adjoining rooms, but eight persons in those tiny rooms would be impossible. Besides, think of the extra food! The longer I thought about it, the more obvious it became that I could not hire this man. I was about to tell him so when I looked again at his emaciated face and kind eyes. Instead, I said, "You're hired." I don't know which of us was the more surprised, he or I. I quickly added, "Why don't you return to Cracow right away and bring back your wife and both children? We'll find a place for you in one of our bunkhouses." At the words "both children," the man from Wołyn opened his mouth to correct me, but before he could do so I told him firmly that I had heard everything that I needed to hear and that any further explanations were unnecessary. Evidently he detected my meaning in my face and fell silent, then whispered, "Thank you."

The interview was at an end. He would go straight to Cracow and would be back ready for work first thing the next morning. That was fine with me. I added that I was on my way into town now and that it would be a good chance for him to meet our miller, with whom he would be dealing in the future. So I took him to meet the miller and afterwards recommended that he look in on the miller again on the way back from Cracow to see whether there was anything to be sent to the estate. He promised he would stop at the mill, and set off happily for his family. When he left, I told the miller to issue the new steward, on our account, fifty kilograms of rye flour and ten kilograms each of pearl barley, buckwheat groats, and flour; I told him to be sure to make it clear that this was not for the manor but for the new steward himself, and that he was to mention it to no one, not even to me.

When I returned home, I gave instructions for a double apartment in the bunkhouse, consisting of four rooms, to be cleaned and all the mattresses stuffed with fresh straw. I told the stable girl that we had a new steward and that for the time being she was to issue his family a double ration of milk, four liters instead of two, since he and his family looked as though they hadn't had a meal for weeks. I went into the manor house feeling strangely satisfied and light-hearted. I knew that I would get into trouble, but I already had so many worries that one more didn't seem to make much difference.

Next day after breakfast I told Count Jerzy that I had hired a new steward who seemed to know his business and appeared to be a decent sort of person—in fact, he had already been at work since early morning. He had a wife and two children, and I had put them in one of the bunkhouses. The count rode out into the fields, eager to meet the new man, and within the hour returned, congratulating me on my choice. It was plain to see that he knew his business, the count thought: he was just the sort of person the estate needed.

Several days later, however, the day of reckoning came. The count burst into my office like a whirlwind. "Our steward has *six* children, not two!" he shouted.

I feigned immense surprise.

"Could he have lied to you?" the count inquired.

"I doubt it," I answered. "He struck me as an honest man. Rather . . . well, yes . . . it must have been I who made the mistake. I don't think that it really matters, though; there is room enough in the bunkhouses, and he doesn't need our food; he brought his own with him. All he requires is a little milk. You know, count, to tell you the truth, I would rather have him with all his children, than our other steward with neither wife nor youngsters."

The count said he supposed that I was right. "I'm certainly not going to take the food out of the children's mouths," he added. "I am just concerned about one thing. My father ordered me not to hire a steward with more than two children, and I know my father. He does not like it when someone changes his orders without his permission." He was somewhat troubled over this situation, and in the end decided that it would be best not to raise the subject with the old count at all. If we had to, we would tell him that the steward had only two children.

The new steward was a godsend. He arrived at the estate in a wagon drawn by two scrawny nags, but no sooner had these nags had a few weeks of rest and good pasture than they were transformed into a pair of excellent and sturdy farm animals, which we were delighted to put to work. As for his family, our people vied with one another for the privilege of looking after the children. The chief rivals were the head cook, who had at her disposal the entire pantry with all its delicacies; the gardener, who had field vegetables and fruits and forced fruit from the greenhouse to offer; and the stable girls, who plied the children with milk from their cows. Under this care the ragged brood took on new life, and the steward and his wife gained weight as well. No one would have suspected that only a few weeks earlier they had been in the depths of despair and near starvation.

Chapter 16

Moving My Family from Przemyśl

At the end of August, 1942, following the Ska-
wina massacre described in Chapter 4, I told my family in Przemyśl
about the impending deportation of all Polish Jews and asked them to
prepare for escape. They were to come to Cracow first and eventually
settle in Skawina, where I had begun planning for their arrival. The first
to come to Cracow would be my brother-in-law, Józef Krulig. He had
arrived in the Przemyśl ghetto not long ago from Lwów, and thus his
disappearance would not attract attention. Next would be his wife, my
sister Krystyna, with their child and our father. Last to arrive would
be my brother Emil and our mother. For the time being they would
stay with our sister Helena in Lwów and follow after the others were
safely settled.

My first job was to obtain false papers for all six of them. I had
as many blank birth certificates as I needed. As I mentioned in Chapter
2, I often dropped in at the parish priest's office in Skawina to gossip, so
I knew where the forms were kept. They were already stamped and ready
to use because the priest issued them almost every day to persons who
needed them to obtain *Kennkarten*. During one of these visits the priest
was called out of the office, and I took the opportunity to grab a handful of these precious documents. (I am ashamed of the theft to this day,
although I think that God will surely forgive me for my transgression
because it was to save the lives of others.) My friend Kroczewski arranged
for false *Kennkarten*. I registered my family as having just arrived from

Lwów (this was true as far as it went). In addition, I arranged for a work permit for my brother-in-law through the local Arbeitsamt. I then passed on the documents to my family in Przemyśl.

My brother-in-law, having acquired the papers and name of a certain Józef Górnik, arrived first. I had never met him before, for Krystyna married him while Lwów was under Russian control. I only knew that his father had owned a publishing house in Lwów, that he himself was a talented musician, and that after finishing his musical training at the Academy of Music in Vienna he had studied medicine in Berlin. His parents and only sister had perished in one of the Nazi pogroms in Lwów. Józek was short, had light blond hair and blue eyes, and spoke flawless Polish. The only clue to his Jewish origin was a slightly large nose and a certain nervousness, a by-product of ghetto life. On the whole, however, he made quite a plausible Pole, and I was certain that once he put behind him the memories and fears of the ghetto, he would not be suspected. At first he lived with our family at Borek Fałęcki, for it was necessary that he re-learn how to behave like a free man.

Soon afterwards my sister Krystyna arrived from Przemyśl with her infant and our father. Krystyna had been a beautiful child, blond, with a wonderfully clear complexion, a classic figure, and charming manners. Nothing about her had changed, and I had no doubt about her ability to adapt to her new situation. In Chapter 5 I have described my father, a typical small landholder from the east, full of life and vigor. For some time now, he had been going by the fictitious name of Jan Nowak* and felt as comfortable in his new Polish role and name as though it were his own. He took an immediate liking to Cracow and visited it whenever he could. In short, I felt that the ghetto really had not left a permanent stamp on any of these people, and that they would be able to adapt to their changed environment with little difficulty.

The situation for Jews like us hiding on "Aryan" papers was really extremely difficult. The reader must remember that Jewish and Polish society seldom intermingled. Mixed marriages were a rarity; even if a young couple did have enough strength of character and determination to get married, they would be thenceforth excluded from both societies. Because of this isolation, when the war came, few Jews could

---

*The name Jan Nowak is about as common in Polish as John Brown is in English. Interestingly, this same pseudonym was adopted by a later famous courier for the Polish underground (see Jan Nowak, *Courier from Warsaw* [Detroit: Wayne State University Press, 1982]).

pretend successfully to be Polish, nor were Poles overly eager to conceal a Jew: hiding a Jew had been made a capital offense by the Germans.

I did not really think that any of our old friends would betray us, but I kept in mind the power of human stupidity and the inability to keep a secret or to be consistently discreet. I acted on the principle that even the Gestapo could not extract information that people did not possess. This fear of human stupidity and thoughtlessness undermined the willingness of even the bravest to obtain Aryan papers and live on the outside as I did. One needed a "good," i.e., passably Aryan, appearance, sincere and sometimes courageous friends, and an occupation suited to the wartime situation—in short, one needed extraordinary good luck in order not to become the subject of speculation and gossip, with inevitably fatal results. (It should be noted that I am not talking here about the scum of society, the sort of person who, discovering that someone was a Jew, blackmailed the victim to his last penny and then, when he was penniless, denounced the unfortunate to the police, in full confidence that he would be eliminated and, with him, all evidence of the informer's crime.)

I soon told the family what I did and where I worked; I also rehearsed them in how to behave if they ran into someone they had known in the old days, as was likely enough to happen. In principle, I told them, such meetings were to be avoided, but in case of a chance encounter one must never mention one's new name nor place of residence or work and must use any pretext to get away from the old friend at the first opportunity. These were new times, I warned them, and even an honest person might blurt out everything he knew under torture. Most important, other Jews should be avoided. By this time all Jews had been officially relegated to ghettos or concentration camps. Those we saw on the outside either were living on false papers like us—and so would also try to avoid running into friends from the past—or were working for the Gestapo as informers on other Jews. It was fairly easy to recognize the latter, for a Jew hiding on false papers would turn and walk the other way at the glimpse of a former acquaintance, while an informer would rush forward to engage him in conversation and try to pry as much information out of him as possible. Such people were not necessarily cold-blooded assassins; often enough they were merely weak individuals who had broken down under the pressure of circumstances and were serving the Nazis in exchange for their own safety or in the belief that they could protect their families in this way.

According to our original plan, the rest of my family were to stay in Lwów for a year, after which they were to join us in Cracow. However, Lwów was clearly becoming unsafe, so we decided to bring them out earlier. First my brother Emil and our mother arrived. My brother, like everyone on my side of the family, had a "perfect Polish appearance," and I felt there would be no trouble with him. My mother had changed tremendously since I had last seen her; she had gotten much smaller and thinner; her skin was yellowish; she spoke almost in a whisper. She could no longer get around easily, and it was quite clear that her life was slipping away.

My sister Helena said that she would not come because she could not leave her dog behind with no one to care for it. That was the last any of us heard of her; she disappeared without a trace. Another member of the family, our cousin Ernestyna Schwartz, was saved by a miracle. She was away visiting my sister Helena when the Nazis broke into her home and took away her father and mother. Both parents died after enduring terrible suffering as the Nazis tried to force the whereabouts of their three children out of them. There were two sons—one a medical student and the other a law student—and Ernestyna, a girl just out of high school. The brothers had fled the city with the retreating Soviet army in June, 1941, while Ernestyna stayed in Lwów with her parents. On the way back from her visit to my sister, the neighbors warned her that the Gestapo was waiting for her at home, and so she was saved. She lived a hand-to-mouth existence in Lwów for a year after that before managing to get to us through contacting my sister.

Ernestyna lost all trace of her brothers during the war. One day after the war she was in a movie theater watching a newsreel. To her great amazement, she spotted both her brothers on the screen marching in a detachment of Soviet soldiers. She rushed to the projection booth and told the operator what she had seen. Without wasting a minute, the operator picked out the footage on the film which showed her brothers, clipped out the bit of film, and gave it to her. With this photographic evidence, she began a search which included a protracted correspondence with all levels of the Soviet bureaucracy and which lasted several years. Eventually her persistence was rewarded: she obtained the address of her elder brother, now a doctor, who was working in a clinic in Lwów, now under Soviet control. Later he moved permanently to Brzuchowice, near Lwów, where he practices medicine to this day. From him Ernestyna (now going by the name Ala) obtained the address of her younger brother, a lawyer in Równe. He later emigrated from the Soviet Union and presently lives with his family in Israel.

My Brother-in-Law, Chief of the Arbeitsamt

, I rented an apartment for the "Górniks" (that is, my brother-in-law Józek and my sister Krystyna) and their child in Skawina. It consisted of two small rooms. Later, when my mother arrived, she also lived there. My next problem was to find work for Józek. I counted heavily on the help of my friend Tadek Słomka in the Skawina Arbeitsamt. There was no sense in hiding from Tadek the fact that Józek was a Jew; I had to tell the truth, or at least part of it, so I told him that in September, 1939, when the Polish army was breaking up in the east, I arrived in Lwów without a penny in my pocket or a roof over my head, and that if it hadn't been for my friend Józek, a Jew, I would never have survived. Józek, I told him, was now living on Aryan papers and had come to me for help. I had rented an apartment for him here in the town and needed Tadek's help in finding a suitable job for him.

At first Tadek was frightened, but he knew me well enough to realize that if I were asking for a favor of this magnitude it must mean a lot to me. My relationship with him by this time was so close and cordial that it would have been difficult for him to refuse to help me, and in the end he said to send Józek to see him at the Arbeitsamt. In the meantime he would think about what he could do for him. Tadek kept his word: he found Józek a job in the Skawina city hall as a night watchman.

After a week I stopped by to see Józek and asked him how his work was going. "To tell you the truth, I'm afraid of that job," he admitted. "These people are not fools, and everyone can see that I look and speak differently from the local crowd, and in any case I don't seem like a night watchman. I can see trouble brewing." There was truth in what he said and something had to be done, so I went to the Arbeitsamt and had another talk with Tadek, telling about Józek's fears. Tadek promised to find him something more suitable.

Chapter 16

I should note here that the Arbeitsamt's central office, or Haupt-stelle, was in Cracow. There were a number of branch offices, or Neben-stellen, one of which was in Skawina. The Nebenstellen in turn had their own subdivisions located in different towns, called Hilfstellen. Among other things, the Nebenstelle in which Tadek worked was constantly busy relaying the contents of various memoranda, written in German, of course, from the Hauptstelle in Cracow to the branch offices. Joachim Mann, the director of the Arbeitsamt in Skawina, a German, was in charge of this work, primarily because nobody else there spoke German. However, he was often out of the office. Memoranda would arrive stamped "important" or "urgent," and when Mann was gone, Tadek Słomka could not deal with them and became very upset.

At just such a moment Józek reported for his interview. When Tadek explained his plight, Józek offered to help. He knew German, could easily transcribe the memoranda, compose appropriate messages for the branch offices, and type them out on a typewriter. Słomka could hardly believe his ears. "You can do all that? Well here, help yourself!" Józek quickly glanced through the papers, sat down to the typewriter, and typed whatever was needed in German. Tadek was enthralled. "God in heaven! Here I have been looking for a job for you, and it turns out that you are what we need right here in this office. Wait a moment; I have an idea."

He ran into the next room and brought back one of his fellow workers. He introduced him to my brother-in-law and told him of Józek's valuable skills. Józek made such a good impression that the colleague agreed that they could use him in the office. They needed only to obtain the permission of their superior, Herr Mann, but that should be no problem since they were receiving more and more German correspon-dence and Mann was increasingly absent from the office.

Several days later Józek had an interview with the director, whom he impressed with his perfect command of German, and was hired. In this miraculous manner Górnik was transformed from a night watchman into an office worker in the Skawina Arbeitsamt. He had found his hid-ing place in a German government department. Not only was this work a perfect cover, but it also provided a salary which allowed a modest degree of comfort.

I breathed a sigh of relief. I had not dreamed of such a successful solution to Józek's dilemma. What was even better, I was confident that

189

with his help I would now be able to find jobs for the other members of the family. In fact, Józek later found a job for my own brother Emil, now going by the name of Kazimierz Zdżałka,* as a game warden in the German District Forestry Office. He gladly donned a green uniform and went off to live in a forester's cottage in the woods. The relative of Basia who had first worked for me as a night watchman (see Chapter 15) also obtained work through Józek as a game warden. In their German government forestry uniforms, they both could live relatively free of suspicion.

The Skawina Arbeitsamt had under its administration a Hilfstelle in the nearby town of Kalwaria Zebrzydowska, but they had no one there to run it who knew German. Mann decided to send my brother-in-law to them as its manager. Józek was worried and came to me for advice. I suggested that he had no choice but to agree; evasion would only arouse suspicion, and suspicion for him meant death for all of us. Thus Józek became chief of the Arbeitsamt in Kalwaria Zebrzydowska. At first he commuted to work but later moved to Kalwaria with his entire family and with our mother, who was now to be known as Ewa Nowak, the mother of Mrs. Górnik. There he often transacted business with the higher authorities in the course of his work and almost forgot that only half a year earlier he had been in the ghetto and had had to be taught how to act like a free man.

Toward the end of November, 1942, Ala, our cousin, arrived from Lwów. My sister Krystyna was determined that no matter what, Ala would live with them, but it was necessary to arrange this in a legal way to avoid arousing suspicion. Józek came up with a good plan. The wife of the mayor of the city was renowned for being a terror to her household help. No maid had been able to stand working for her more than one or two weeks. The girls kept leaving, and she kept telephoning to the Arbeitsamt and making a nuisance of herself until they found her a replacement. Józek decided to place the new arrival with the mayor's wife; after fourteen days she, like all the others, would quit and he would take her into his own household. In this way everyone in the

---

*The names Józef Górnik and Kazimierz Zdżałka, adopted by the author's brother-in-law and brother, were legitimate names appearing on the birth certificates and other documents these men were able to obtain. Since many men of their age had been killed or had fled the country, it was fairly easy to find papers of people falling into their age group. For older people, the situation was more difficult, hence the adoption by Shatyn's father of the name Jan Nowak. It was for the older members of his family that Mr. Shatyn primarily needed the stolen birth certificates.—*Tr.*

neighborhood would know that Krystyna had hired a girl who had worked in the mayor's home. The plan worked perfectly, and after a brief "internship" in the mayor's house, Ala was hired by the Górniks as a maid.

This city girl, a high-school graduate, managed to transform herself so effectively that whenever I saw her I was startled. She dressed just like the village girls, and braided her beautiful light blond hair just as they did, sometimes in one braid, sometimes in two, and tied them up with bright-colored ribbons. She made friends with the daughters of the local villagers, and went with them to all the local parties, on dates, to market, and to church. Whispering and giggling, they would confide to one another their special secrets. She ate and slept in the Górniks' kitchen and did all their washing, cleaning, and cooking. She always addressed my sister as "Ma'am" and got so used to this expression that even after the war she would catch herself using it to Krystyna from time to time. I greatly admired her in this role, though I reached the point at which I was finding it difficult to believe that the girl in the kitchen was really our cousin from the big city. The kitchen became her kingdom. She rarely left it and never entered into our conversations, but retained her grace and charm of movement through it all.

With my own family taken care of, and not at all badly, I thought, I now decided to occupy myself with the fate of Basia's family, still living in the Cracow ghetto.

Chapter 17

My Last Meeting with Basia's Family

I entered the Cracow ghetto and made my way to my wife's parents. There I found the entire family waiting for me. They knew that I was coming, for I had asked them earlier to obtain a falsified pass for me. They were no longer in the quarters I had seen on my previous visit but were living in worse and even more crowded circumstances. Three years had passed since that memorable Friday when I visited my father-in-law's house to ask for Basia's hand in marriage. The same gathering was here today, and their eyes were riveted on me just as before.

I thought of them as I had seen them that first time. Basia's sister Rózia had been a tall, very good-looking blond, thirty-six years old, in the full bloom of womanhood, with a lively and provocative glance, conscious of the impression she made and enjoying every minute of it. Her husband, Samuel, about two years older than she, had struck me as a quiet, reserved man with elegant manners. He worked as a cashier in the Holzer Bank in Sukiennice Square. Their son Zygmunt had been a dreamy-eyed sixteen-year-old in the seventh grade of the gymnasium. Adam, their other son, was now six and much too serious for his age.

That had been only three years ago. Now they all sat before me, thin, wan, looking much older and unkempt, their eyes filled with a hopeless sadness. Perhaps only little Ritulka, Basia's charming and lively blond-haired, blue-eyed niece, now eight, reminded me of the child I had seen that other time. Then I looked at my father-in-law. At first I

192

didn't recognize him, he had changed so much since our first meeting. After spending so many years of his life in his own house in the Nowa Wieś District, surrounded and respected by family and friends, to have his orderly world collapse completely had been catastrophic. Conservative in his customs, as I have often mentioned, he had taken me at first for a foolhardy soul who, as soon as the war broke out, had spirited away his youngest daughter to Russia. He couldn't understand any of this; he and his entire family and all his friends, together with all the level-headed members of Jewish society, had stayed where they were, hoping that they would somehow survive this difficult period with the Nazis. Two years had passed and again I appeared before them, but not to join them in the ghetto where life was difficult but at least relatively safe, but to take his daughter along the dangerous path of living on "Aryan papers," a life fraught with danger and the constant threat of death. By now, however, all his firm convictions had come unstuck; I was no longer the reckless spirit he had once thought. Even he had to admit he had been mistaken, that all those who had voluntarily entered the ghetto had judged wrong, that I had been the only one who fully understood the situation from the beginning. The dangerous path I had chosen was today the only hope of salvation. He could see that the question was no longer one of which was more dangerous, life inside the ghetto or life outside on false papers: the question now was whether one's escape from the ghetto might endanger relatives and friends already living in some security on the outside.

I did not want to worry them, but I did not want to raise false hopes either, so I described the situation as I saw it. "Almost my entire family," I told them, "are registered and living near here, and by taking the proper security measures, and given a little luck, they will probably be as likely to survive as any other Polish family. Basia and I sincerely believe that you should leave the ghetto. I can arrange for false papers and can even find work for the younger members of the family." And speaking to my parents-in-law directly, I said, "You can live in my house as my parents."

Everyone listened intently, but no one wished to be the first to respond. Finally my father-in-law broke the silence. "I can speak only for my wife and myself. My children are all adults and have to decide things for themselves. I see now that everything I believed in was a sham, but I'm not sure that I would be able to live on false papers, to live a lie. What could I say if I ran into an old friend? That I'm not the same

Neulinger they think I am? And even if I got by the first or second time, what about the third? But even putting all that aside, I know I shall never leave the ghetto walls as long as my wife or a single one of my children remains inside. As for my wife, I can see that it would be a good thing for her to go to live with her daughter, but that's up to her. I can't make up her mind for her.''

In the silence that followed, I turned first to Rózia's husband. I had come to know him fairly well during the memorable days of September, 1939, when all the men in Cracow fled east. Samuel made it as far as Lwów, but when he heard that Basia and I were living in Przemyśl, he stayed with us briefly before returning to Cracow. He seemed to me an intelligent, forthright, and worthy individual. He was not talkative, but when he spoke, he was concise and to the point. "What will you do?" I asked him.

I could see from his face that, as usual, he was considering how best to put it. Finally he said: "I saw Apek Rozenzweig the other day, and he told me that three months ago you visited him at the bank and warned him that the Nazis intended to exterminate all of us, that the ghetto was to be liquidated, and that the so-called deportation to the former Soviet territories in the east was a hoax. He didn't believe it, and I don't blame him; I wouldn't have believed it myself. We worked together for twenty years in that bank. We were an international institution; we knew and respected the German bankers. Who could believe that these proper, upright, hard-working people would commit mass murder? Even now, when we know that it is true, we still can't get used to the idea. But even if Apek had taken you seriously, what difference would it have made? We are still not prepared either physically or mentally to defend ourselves against this genocide.''

I thought that he had finished, but after a moment he said in his quiet way, "You, Bronek, are made of different stuff. I got to know you better in Przemyśl. People who don't know you might take you for a dreamer, but I believe that you are simply putting your wits to work at the job of getting through the war. You may be sure that we all wish you the best, but at the same time, you should try to see our side; you should try to understand that we can't come with you. I was born into a Jewish family and I have been a Jew all my life. Even if I wanted to, I couldn't act like a Gentile. I wouldn't get through a single day. Not only would we perish, but we would also drag you and all those you are protecting down with us. No, this step is just not for us.

"We knew why you were coming to see us today, and Rózia and I have been up half the night discussing it. Father is right; we are adults and have to decide for ourselves, and I say that escape is not the way for us; each person has to find his own way. You know, there are people in the ghetto who are now in the Gestapo's service; they go out into the town every day and look for Jews hiding on false papers because they think that they will save their own skins that way. Even one of my colleagues at the bank, a man I have worked with for many years, broke down and now works for the Gestapo. He turns in *everyone*, even members of his own family. Not long ago he whispered to me that he knew that Basia was living on false papers somewhere in the vicinity of Cracow. He doesn't know you personally, and doesn't know your name or where you live, but he is looking for you and is convinced that sooner or later he will find you. When he does, he will turn you in. I had always thought him a man of honor, but the times have changed. Without sitting in judgment over anyone, I have to say that what's going on now around us is utter madness—it's insane."

He fell silent, but was only pausing for breath. "You can be sure that we want to live. There are four of us in my own family. I wonder whether some miracle will occur to save us. I don't really believe in miracles, but it's hard to believe that England, America, and the other civilized nations will just stand by and watch us be slaughtered. Maybe they'll be able to stop it. I'd like to believe in anything that sounds like a chance for us. I'm not a coward, and I'd do anything to save myself and my family if I knew what it was. In any case, Bronek, we are all inexpressibly grateful to you for your good intentions and for the chance you took in coming here." He had made his decision. Neither my other brother-in-law nor Basia's brother Leon had anything to say.

Basia's Mother Leaves the Ghetto

My mother-in-law was lying in bed listening to all of this. I knew perfectly well that neither her husband nor her children would abandon her. If I were to save them, I must persuade her to leave. I went over to her and began telling her how much we wanted her to come to stay with us. We would all be there together, I told her, and her granddaughter, whom she hadn't even seen, was also waiting to meet her.

195

She thought for a while and finally spoke with the same sweet, gentle voice I remembered: "I can't be of any use to anyone here; in fact, I am the one who needs the looking after. I'm willing to come to you and Basia." Her husband, in a trembling voice, whispered that perhaps a gracious God would let them see the end of the war and live many happy years together again in peace. With this the discussion ended. I had achieved all I could for the moment, and in any case I was not prepared to rescue several persons at once. One or two at a time were the most I could manage.

I stayed in the apartment for the night, beginning to formulate a plan. I discovered, for example, that my mother-in-law was permitted to visit a specialist in town once every two months. She was taken to the doctor and returned by a specially hired horse-drawn cab. Her next visit was scheduled for some time in the second half of November, which gave me plenty of time. I was certain that the trip to the doctor would be the key to my mother-in-law's escape.

Over the next several days I busied myself with details that had to be taken care of no matter what my actual escape plan looked like. I let slip to Mrs. Proszkowski, my landlady, the news that I was expecting my mother to arrive soon from Tarnów, where she had been living with my brother. We felt it was time for her to stay with us for a while, I said, and our larder was full, so the extra food would not be a problem. Our worthy landlady took all this in stride. I secured the necessary false *Kennkarte*; all that remained was to get her out of the ghetto and to erase all traces behind her. I considered all possible schemes until I had a plan I thought could succeed. Sometime in the second half of November, 1942, my mother-in-law set out as usual for her doctor on Wielopole Street. Her appointment was for four o'clock, but she arrived quite early, sent the cab away, and went upstairs to wait in the reception room. Some time later Basia arrived and went up to the receptionist's window to inquire about the doctor's office hours. At the same moment my mother-in-law arose, went to the window, and excused herself to the receptionist, saying that she felt very weak and would not be able to wait any longer for her appointment. She would return for her usual visit in January. Basia in the meantime had received the information she had requested and graciously offered to help the unknown old lady with the cane down the stairs. They went out together. On the street a cab was waiting, they got in and drove off, and that was the last anyone knew of Mrs. Neulinger.

I felt that smuggling my mother-in-law out of the ghetto would be a great psychological victory, that with her out it would be easier for me to convince the others to leave. I began with Basia's brother Leon and his wife Sara, and there I met with success. Three weeks after my coup they too decided to escape, and I had my hands full making preparations for receiving them.

The SS Man and the Little Girl

I learned from Leon that the Nazis were issuing new identification cards to those inhabitants of the ghetto who were still fit for work. I wondered what this meant, and concluded that in all probability the Nazis intended to eliminate all those unfit for work now, leaving the rest for the time being as a reserve labor supply. Two days later, during one of my business trips to Cracow, I learned how accurate my forecast had been.

I usually rode into town through Rynek Podgórski. Circling the ghetto, I would arrive at the so-called Third Bridge; across the Vistula River was Starowiślna Street, my destination. As I was driving past one wall of the ghetto I saw two SS men coming toward me, engrossed in conversation. One of them must have told a joke, for they were both laughing heartily. Suddenly a child was thrown over the wall—undoubtedly some frantic parents inside had done this in the desperate hope that some kind soul outside would find her, take pity on the innocent child, and raise her as his own. She was a beautiful little girl, about six years old, with dark hair in a long braid. She fell right between the SS men and my carriage. As I stared, she scrambled up. The SS man who had been telling the story walked over to her. She looked up at him for a moment as if in a trance, paralyzed with fear, while he drew his pistol, placed it to her head, and fired. I never heard the shot because of what I saw. The girl's head literally burst apart. The back of her skull with its long braid flew up in the air like a rocket as the front exploded into several fragments and flew off in different directions. Now instead of the child's head all that remained was a stump, the end of her spinal column. What gushed forth was not even blood but some sort of yellowish red gelatinous substance. The body stood upright for a moment, its arms still raised for balance, then toppled to the ground and lay twitching convulsively. The SS man returned his pistol to its holster, carefully checked his polished boots to make sure that they had not been dirtied, and sauntered back to his friend to continue their conversation.

I could not go on to the office where I had business that day, and turned the carriage into Zwierzyniecki Street and the Kroczewskis. They saw immediately that I was almost in a state of shock and pressed a glass of brandy on me to loosen the enormous lump in my throat and bring me back to my senses.

This story is only one example of how thousands of children died. Although in general I have avoided descriptions of the Nazi terror, I decided to describe the death of one child which I saw with my own eyes.

Ritulka

To my wife's niece Ritulka I can devote only a few lines. After witnessing the death of the unknown child, I decided to save Ritulka next, for I felt that she, a child and hence of no value as a worker, was in the greatest danger. Her parents, the Steins, had good contacts in the ghetto and would be able to get her beyond the walls safely. Thanks to Leon I was able to get in touch with them, and they agreed to entrust Ritulka to me. We had set the day and time. I waited outside the ghetto walls until midnight, but no one brought her. At the last minute, her parents decided that this evening was not safe and that they would put it off until another time.

But there was not another night. The next day the Nazis began their planned campaign (signaled to me by the new passes) against children and the infirm. Among the first to perish were Ritulka and my father-in-law, at the age of fifty-eight. They deported Ritulka's mother, a year older than Basia, to a work camp in Tarnów and later to Ravensbrück in Germany. Her husband was sent to Oświęcim.

Thus ended the history of the Neulinger family of Cracow. The life of the family advisor, Apek Rosenzweig, ended no less tragically. He, his wife, and their only daughter, Stella, my wife's best friend, all perished.

Chapter 18

Leon and Sara

My friends the Misiołeks knew all about my activities, as I have said. Mietek helped me find work in Borek Szlachecki. They knew that my family had arrived from Przemyśl and that my brother-in-law Józek was working in the Skawina Arbeitsamt. They had met my mother-in-law, now known as "Maria Szatyn," and they knew that Basia's brother Leon and his wife were about to escape from the ghetto as well. Leon was blond and spoke perfect Polish; I had no fears on his account. His wife was a different proposition, however. She was born in Berlin, where her parents immigrated before the war. In 1938 the Nazi government deported all Jews of Polish descent, including Sara and her parents. She was dark with a typical Jewish appearance; worst of all, she spoke only broken Polish with a heavy German accent. I couldn't imagine what to do with her. We had only a kitchen and one other room, and there were four of us living there already. My father, who actually had no permanent place of residence, stayed with us most of the time.* I could find a job and a place to live for Leon, but Sara posed a serious problem.

Mietek's mother-in-law, the energetic Simusia, could see that I was troubled, and I did not conceal the reason from her. Before the war Simusia had been president of the local teachers' union, which had

---

*As an older person (sixty-eight at the time), the elder Schatten would naturally have had less trouble with the German authorities.—*Tr.*

denied membership to Jews. The Union of Polish Teachers had considered Jews a foreign and undesirable element and favored limiting their rights, and these had been Simusia's sentiments too. She did not know any Jews, had never lived near any, and did not care to have anything to do with them. Now, through me, she had come to know Jews as friends for the first time in her life. She looked after Basia and the baby as though they were her own, and through me she learned of the tragic circumstances in which the Jews were now living. It was none other than Simusia who now declared that as long as Sara was unsafe anywhere else, she would stay with her, a gesture which, if discovered, could put all her family to death.

I got all the necessary documents ready for Leon, who was now going by the name of "Antoni Mierzwa," and the Arbeitsamt in Kalwaria Zebrzydowska—with the help of my useful brother-in-law Józek—sent him to work as an agricultural laborer on the Polanka-Haller estate, near ours. His new name was genuine; his birth certificate came from the town of Miechów and had belonged to a young hired hand who had long ago immigrated to America. My invaluable friend Pawel Kroczewski got me the real Antoni Mierzwa's certificate of marriage to a certain Maria, as well as *Kennkarten* for both Leon and Sara under their new names. (In general, whenever possible I tried to obtain genuine birth certificates because with these one could apply for genuine *Kennkarten*.)

"Antek," as we now called Leon,* rode into town every Saturday to get the clean laundry for the following week; on the estate they jokingly accused him of going to see his girl friend. One day I had a chance to see how he was getting along on the job. I was on a visit to my acquaintance Sigfried Kepper, the estate manager at Polanka Haller, described in Chapter 4.

After greeting each other and exchanging a few polite phrases, Kepper and I strolled into the stableyard toward the cow barn, as he wanted to show me a prize bull he had just bought. Along the way one of the laborers shuffled past us, a grubby individual wearing tattered trousers several sizes too large for him held up by a rope for a belt, a ragged shirt, an oft-washed vest of indistinguishable color, and a straw hat, beneath whose brim I spotted an unshaven face and bristling mustache. He was poking along noisily through the sandy soil in broken old shoes.

---

*Antek is a typical Polish peasant name, heightening the contrast between his present and former self.—*Tr.*

Chapter 18

As he passed us he doffed his straw hat and bowed. "The Lord be praised," he said, in the standard peasant greeting. "For ever and ever," I responded automatically.

As I walked on, the man's voice nudged my memory. Turning my head I took another look. Yes, there could be no mistake: this was my brother-in-law Leon! I asked Kepper who he was.

"You think I know?" he shrugged. "They come here, work a couple of weeks and then disappear. The Arbeitsamt just keeps sending them. Lazy bastards, every last one of them," he added as we entered the barn.

Kepper had purchased a fine three-year-old bull, which already weighed over five hundred kilos. He had great expectations for him and told me that he hoped some day to have nothing but breeding stock, as we did on our estate. I was curious to see his bunkhouses, so he took me into the largest of them. It was quite dim inside, illuminated by a single bulb hanging from the ceiling by a wire. The earthen floor was littered with old straw mattresses covered with horse blankets. A large hook screwed into the wall above each mattress served as wardrobe for personal belongings. This was the extent of the facilities that Kepper provided. I had seen enough; I exchanged a few additional pleasantries with Kepper and promised to visit him again soon.

"Here is an original picture," I thought to myself as I left. "One fellow arrives like a lord in a carriage with a liveried coachman, only to meet his own brother-in-law shuffling along in rags, working as a menial laborer, and hired by his other brother-in-law in the German Labor Office!" What a shock this life must be for Leon, I thought. Before the war he had been a well-known Cracow sportsman, an excellent skier and swimmer. Once he paddled all the way down the Vistula to the sea in a singleman kayak, a distance of more than one thousand kilometers. The person I had just seen was but a shadow of that man.

Because "Antek" was obviously wasting away, growing weaker in body and spirit, I began looking for a more suitable occupation for him. By luck I saw in the *Krakauer Zeitung* (the German daily newspaper) that the army canteen in Krosno was looking for German-speaking Poles to serve as waiters and counter help. The salary, which was fixed for all Poles, was low, but the job included food and lodging in the canteen building. It seemed an ideal position for Leon and Sara because of their excellent German. When Leon came to town for the laundry on Saturday, I showed him the advertisement. The job looked promising to him too, so on Monday, instead of returning to the Haller estate, he went to Krosno. He made a good impression on the canteen manager, a German, and was hired as a counter man, and Sara was offered a job as waitress. Overjoyed, he got on the train back to Cracow to tell us the good news.

Roundup on the Train

On Leon's return trip a dozen or more SS men got onto the train and began to examine the passengers' documents and baggage. Those without proper papers were taken aside and placed under guard. When Leon surrendered his papers, the SS man examined them carefully, one by one, and then looked Leon over from top to bottom. Unfortunately, although Leon was blond, he had a slightly hooked nose. The SS man looked at him steadily, then shouted, "You're a Jew!"

Leon pretended not to understand, but the SS man repeated, "You're a Jew!"

He had to respond, and so he said, in broken German, "Jew? No!"

The SS man took another look at Leon and motioned for him to follow. He took him to the lavatory and ordered him to drop his trousers. Leon again pretended not to understand, but the SS man pointed to his belt and gestured to him to unbutton his trousers. Leon had no choice. The SS man took a piece of tissue paper which he had handy, tucked under his belt, for just such an occasion. He held Leon's penis in the paper and examined it, then decided: "Yes, you're a Jew!"

"No! No Jew!" Leon insisted.

Leon buttoned up his trousers, and they returned to the corridor; the SS man kept Leon's documents but ordered him to return to his seat while he checked the other passengers. Several travelers were detained and placed under guard while Leon sat in his seat. He was well aware what this meant: the others were not suspected of being Jewish, so their situation was not nearly so dangerous as his.

Luckily he did not behave as one might expect a Jew to do when caught. He made no attempt to argue or escape but sat quietly, looking out the open window, desperately wondering what to do. The only thing he could think of was to try to escape as soon as they started to lead him away. If he were fortunate, they would shoot him on the spot rather than torture him to extract information about the whereabouts of his relatives. Everyone in the little band under my protection, including myself, was resigned to the idea that arrest and recognition meant death. It was the sacred obligation of any one of us who was caught to think only of the others—to do everything in his power to deprive the Germans of the chance to extract information about the rest from him.

The train pulled into Tarnów, and the SS man led away five men detained from Leon's car and added them to those people arrested in the other cars. Leon remained in his seat; the SS man was busy herding his other victims onto the platform and arranging the lot in columns. Had he not been busy and in a hurry, the matter would probably have moved to its bitter conclusion. The conductor whistled; the train was ready to leave. Leon was quiet in his seat, holding his breath. No one called him, no one came after him. The train gave a jerk, the wheels creaked and started to roll. No one was paying the slightest attention to him. As his car creaked past the SS man who had detained him, the German looked up to the window, gave Leon one last penetrating look, made a quick decision, and tossed his documents through the window into the train.

There they lay on the floor of the compartment. Leon sat motionless, too paralyzed with fear to think. He had given himself up for dead, and his sudden change in fortune caught him unawares. He could not realize that a miracle had occurred, that he would not be tortured, that he was out of danger. The train rattled on for ten minutes or more before he could unclench his hands enough to pick up his papers from the floor. Never, then nor later, was he able to explain the behavior of the SS man.

In three days the "Mierzwas" departed for their jobs in the canteen. They lived there safely to the end of the war. After the war they left Poland to settle in Israel with their young son, Uzy. Leon died there at an early age of a heart attack, leaving his wife Sara and Uzy, a tennis instructor.

Chapter 19

The Old Count Mellows

Count Antoni Potocki—"the old count"—lived, as I have recounted, on his Olsza estate on the outskirts of Cracow. I knew little of his life before the war, only that he had had an estate somewhere in the east before that property was expropriated by the Russians. Before the Russians took it over, he somehow managed to save almost all of his beloved purebred Arabian horses. Some of these animals were sold; others he kept at Olsza. I had heard that the Rymanów-Zdrój spa also belonged to him before the war.*

The property in Olsza looked old and neglected; the buildings were dilapidated and the workers mostly well along in years and unused to hard work. Even before the war the count had found it difficult to keep up Olsza properly, but that was nothing compared to the problems he was facing when I met him. Despite the hard times he did not release any of his workers, but he was unable to hire any new ones. In addition, he had the burden of his recent lease on Borek Szlachecki.

Old Count Potocki was an astute farmer, and it did not take him long to notice that we were accomplishing miracles at Borek Szlachecki. We never asked for help, had more than enough of everything, were not required to fulfill military quotas, and frequently even offered help to the other estate at Olsza. Up to now the old count had refused any

*Rymanów-Zdrój was a somewhat out-of-the-way mineral springs resort between Krosno and Ustrzyki Dolne, in southeastern Poland.—*Tr.*

assistance. He guessed, of course, that we were bending the rules but never asked for details. He knew only that we enjoyed excellent relations with the myriad government offices and bureaus involved in our affairs and that I was an energetic and capable manager who seemed to be the right man in the right place at the right time.

At first my weekly meetings with Count Potocki lasted only about an hour. I gave my accounting, answered his questions, and noted down his orders for the next week, all purely routine. In time, however, our relationship warmed, and the count began to show interest in various matters not strictly of a business nature. At first I was reluctant to discuss any aspects of my "wheeling and dealing," but as time went on I told him about some of my devices to get around the bureaucracy, and he gradually became familiar with my "management techniques." Our meetings grew longer and longer, and the count greeted my arrival and the news I brought with increasing interest and pleasure. I, for my part, came to see that his curiosity was combined with kind intentions and ceased to conceal anything from him concerning Borek Szlachecki.

I was aware of the cool relations between Count Antoni and his two sons: he disapproved of both their marriages. Little by little I attempted to make inroads on his conservative way of thinking. Whenever our discussions touched on a subject of a social or political nature, I stressed my belief that the greatest redeeming human virtue was liberalism, by which I meant that each person had the right to his own views but not at the expense of anyone else. Hitler's way was to force his convictions on others, I said, and we were seeing now the inevitable result of such a policy. One could not castigate dictators on the one hand and express intolerant views on the other. Times had changed and, with them, the views of the younger generation. His sons undoubtedly respected his beliefs but at the same time had their own ideas. This was the very essence of liberalism, I thought—to act according to one's own convictions while respecting the opinions of others.

The count returned to this subject again and again. It seemed that he was no longer certain that everyone who did not hold the same opinions as his own was a fool. The triumph of my proselytizing was shown in the interest he began to take in the lives of his son Jerzy and his daughter-in-law, the details of which I often regaled him with. I liked the young Potockis and considered them deserving of their father's love and respect. Increasingly he turned our discussions to their activities, news of which had a rejuvenating effect on him. Almost imperceptibly he opened his heart. He found in me a patient listener, and his long-standing bitterness little by little began to melt away.

One day I mentioned the troubles his son had had with the former steward and went on to discuss his replacement, not glossing over the fact that the man had half a dozen children. He laughed heartily at his son's fright over the number of youngsters but promised to be always on guard and never to ask his son about the family life of our new steward.

I Play Real-Estate Broker

I came to like the old count very much, and he reciprocated my affection. One day he confided to me that his greatest concern was a lack of ready cash to meet even the most urgent current expenses. While the war continued, selling parcels of his land was not an option (land sales had been frozen by the Germans), but no other idea had occurred to him. I mentioned that I had a friend who had sold some property in spite of the war and said I could find out exactly how this had been accomplished. (Of course, I had no such friend, but was reluctant to admit that I myself knew how to do it.)

I waited for several weeks before returning to the subject. "I had a talk with my friend who sold the property we talked about," I told the count one day. "It was arranged in such a way that the lawyer who drew up the deed of sale left blank the signature of the notary and the entry into the county records, to be completed after the war. If you approve of this kind of arrangement and can locate a buyer who will agree to these conditions, I can take care of the transaction for you. I know a lawyer who is a specialist in property law who can handle it for you, even though presently he is not in active practice."

The count found the idea very attractive indeed. Before the week was out he provided me with all the necessary information concerning the piece of land and the purchaser. I promised to get in touch with the lawyer and to bring all the required documents for his signature within two weeks' time.

Of course, I prepared all the papers myself and several days later delivered them to the count. Count Antoni looked them over and was pleased. He asked about the fee, but I replied that the lawyer was not interested in being reimbursed at the moment but would prefer to wait for payment until after the war. The count was pleasantly surprised and never suspected for a moment that I was the "lawyer friend." A week or so later I learned that he already had his cash in hand and was delighted with the whole arrangement. The wolf had been driven from the door. Half jokingly and half seriously he told me, "You yourself, my friend, are entitled to an honorarium, for you spent your precious time working on this matter, which really doesn't fall within your duties." I assured him earnestly that I wouldn't even know what to do with the money, that my salary on the estate was a mere formality because in practice I could take whatever I needed and as much as I wanted.

From that day on I began to handle various administrative matters for Count Antoni. The manager at Olsza, Director Miętka-Mikołajewicz, was elderly and rather infirm. I was encroaching on his territory, but only in order to facilitate the necessary contacts with the appropriate government offices. I mentioned none of this to Count Jerzy, and I sensed that the old count appreciated my discretion. Later, when I realized that my days in Borek Szlachecki were numbered and that I would be leaving sooner than I had anticipated, I tried each day to be of even more help to him than the day before. Of course the old count had no notion of my situation.

Jerzy and I Grow Apart

In Borek Szlachecki, in the meantime, nothing had changed, at least on the surface. I worked as hard as before—no, I worked twice as hard, trying to make up for my lack of enthusiasm with an excess of effort. I told myself that part of the reason for my lassitude was the increased responsibility for my family and worry over my mother's health, but at heart I knew the real reason, and it was something I could not do anything about. I had put everything into my work for the sake of the manor, while basking in the warmth and appreciation of the young Potockis. They were triply delighted with me: first, because they had found a Pole who could deal efficiently with the Germans by finding loopholes in their regulations and making good use of them for the good of the estate; second, because a mere agronomist had shown himself capable of outwitting even the best legal minds in the bureaucracy; and third, because this paragon of a steward spoke excellent German. To all his other accomplishments was added the aura of heroism—this marvel had snatched a condemned person from the very jaws of death. Best of all, their praise and admiration merely made me work harder. Now all this had come tumbling down: I was nothing but a clever Jew.

Perhaps I judged Count Jerzy too harshly, but I couldn't put such thoughts out of my mind. I tried to explain away the young count's behavior. He was basically a kind and good person. It was not his fault that he had been raised in a world far removed from the social problems that oppressed most of us, that he had never been taught to respect persons of different religious persuasions. This was why, at the test, he had failed. On the other hand, I could not but resent bitterly being lumped together with "that old swindler Schneiderman," as Count Antoni called him, even though he used the expression in a friendly way. Had Count Jerzy himself come to me and said that his attitude toward me had not changed, I would have tried to mend our bridges. I would have tried to explain that the terms "clever as a Jew" or "sly as a Jew" referred not to racial characteristics but to traits that were developed as a result of the Jews' continuing struggle for existence. Had Count Jerzy been born into my own family and had to fight all his life for survival, he would have developed traits similar to mine. It was all a question of upbringing and environment. But the count never came to me. Perhaps he thought that it was sufficient that his wife had asked my forgiveness.

My relationship toward the count now took on a formal aspect. We were more or less the same age and used to enjoy riding into the fields or going into town together, sharing private jokes and "secrets." But now in his presence I became tight-lipped and official. He was the boss and I was his employee. Thus it remained to the very end.

The Potockis never learned more than this one secret. They did not know that the forester in the green uniform came to the manor not to discuss allotments of wood for military quotas but to bring news of my dying mother. They had no idea that the frequent telephone calls from the Arbeitsamt were from my brother-in-law nor that my whole family was living nearby. I never departed from my principle of not confiding to the Potockis any more than they needed to know, and, conversely, I was never curious about what did not concern me. The less I knew, the safer it was for everyone.

House Guests

Both young Potockis were very open and hospitable. We often had house guests on the estate. Once a Princess Lubomirski from Lwów came to stay with us for several weeks. She was a young girl, around twenty years of age. Our servants outdid themselves in finding occasions to use her title. One end of the house to the other rang with "Yes, Your Highness," "No, Your Highness," "If you please, Your Highness." One day I met her in the manor yard, and we started to talk. I told her: "Dear Miss Hanna, if we are going to have a conversation, I must ask your forgiveness, because I am unable to use your title. I am not used to talking that way and I am sure I'd get mixed up."

She laughed heartily and told me a story. Once, when she was seven, her French governess told her to do something. She stamped her foot and shouted, "Who are you to give a princess orders?" The governess complained to her mother. Her mother took a stick, grabbed her, put her over her knee, and in an old-fashioned way, by hitting her hard in a famous place, drove once and forever from her head the word "Princess." Hanna spent three weeks on the estate and proved to be a most charming and cultured young lady.

On another occasion a couple came to visit us and took such a liking to the countryside that they decided to settle permanently nearby. The count and countess gave them a hectare of land* to use for raising vegetables, and they rented a cottage from a local peasant. They hadn't one possession to their name. The Potockis provided not only material assistance but professional help as well. Our horses tilled their little plot, our gardener provided them with seeds and advice, and our manor girls did almost all the gardening work for them. Neither one had any experience on a farm, and they hadn't the slightest notion of how to raise crops. The wife, Zofia, was a pleasant eighteen-year-old girl from the city. Her forty-year-old husband, a count, with a dark complexion, a monocle, and thinning hair, was also city-bred. He spoke out of the left side of his mouth with a kind of grimace. I could never figure out where he came from. Once it was Kłajpeda (Memel), another time Wilno (Vilna). Then I heard that his mother was Austrian and either lived in or had properties in Vienna.

---

*A hectare is equal to 2.471 acres.—Tr.

The count was a wonderful storyteller, and it was a joy to listen to him spin tall tales. In fact, his stories would not have been nearly so interesting had one thought they were true. He loved to tell of his adventures hunting big game in Africa. One day it was wild horses in Kenya; the next day the same incident occurred during a lion hunt in the Congo; a week later we were in the Sudan. One never grew weary of his company; it is a shame that this kind of storytelling is a dying art.

The count used to drop in at my office around eight o'clock in the morning. He always opened the conversation in the same way: "You wouldn't have a cigarette, would you?" Each time I would open my desk, pull out a cigarette, and offer it to him. One day I had none. The count appeared on schedule. "You wouldn't happen to have a cigarette, would you?" he asked, according to the usual routine. This time I answered that I was sorry but I didn't. I'd like to have a smoke myself, but I'd have to wait until our purchases arrived from town.

"No matter, no matter," he replied, reaching in his pocket. He serenely took out a cigarette case, extracted a cigarette, and lit it, without offering me one.

Next day it was the same:

"You wouldn't have a cigarette on you, would you?"

"No, I'm sorry, I don't." I answered.

And then each of us, without taking the slightest offense, would reach for his own cigarettes. We would sit there calmly smoking, while I would wait for the stories about big game hunting in Africa to begin. I never tired of them.

Often, when recounting some heroic hunting escapade, the count would fumble for a Polish word and finally express his thought in French. Each time he did this I would feign total disbelief in his tale, which always threw him into a rage. In his attempt to convince me that he was telling the truth, he would always miraculously "remember" the correct Polish expression. He never understood my game, which was intended to stop him from injecting French words into his speech where Polish would do just as well. His eccentricities were harmless enough, and in any case he more than compensated for them by his colorful stories, rare histrionic ability, and fertile imagination.

Chapter 20

The Hunt

The old count was not accustomed to receiving Germans at his Olsza estate. The estate was at the edge of the city and was of minor economic importance. When the Germans had any business with him—for example, some kind of inspection—they took care of the matter by telephone or handled it through the manager, Miętka-Mikołajewicz, who had offices in his home at the manor. It was known that Count Potocki did not meddle in the administration of his estate and was also in failing health, so the Germans had no reason to visit him.

The situation was different at Borek Szlachecki, which was located at some distance from Cracow. The Germans considered this area the "provinces," and whenever they came calling, they expected to be treated like visiting royalty. My office was located on the first floor of the manor house, so I met the Germans there to do our business. If the Potockis were at home, should they fail to come downstairs to greet their "visitors," the Germans were apt to take offense. It behooved them to receive these visiting Germans graciously and to chat with them in German. The Potockis were far from happy with this situation but had no other choice: delicacy, tact, diplomacy, and intelligence were their only defenses.

It was a day in late November, 1942. The crops were all harvested, and the fields to be sown with winter crops had long been ploughed. The weather was dry but icy; although the cold winds and rains were still a month or so away, one could sense winter in the air. We received a telephone call from Cracow informing us that the Kreishauptman (the German county superintendent) had decided to have a rabbit hunt at Borek Szlachecki that Sunday and had invited some thirty of his friends to take part. He wanted the estate to prepare everything necessary for this entertainment. In the meantime an order went out through regular administrative channels requesting the village to supply a hundred men as beaters. Obviously, we had no choice but to agree. Since there had been no snow and the ground was still dry, it promised to be a good hunt. There were rabbits in abundance, as no one had been permitted to hunt them for the past three years. Hunting rights were at the disposal of the Kreishauptman, and this was the first time he had arranged a hunting party.

Sunday arrived. Before seven o'clock in the morning a crowd of boys and young men appointed by the village elder had begun to assemble in front of the house. In accordance with the German instructions, each of them carried a pole and some kind of metal pan for beating and making noise. The count told some of the people to wait; the rest were to come back at noon for the second phase of the hunt.

The Germans arrived exactly at seven, dressed in Tyrolean hunting outfits—wool socks, hiking boots, leather jackets, and green felt hats with little feathers stuck in them. Some of the younger men actually looked picturesque in this getup, but older men with spindly legs and bulging paunches looked downright ridiculous. Each of them carried a double-barreled shotgun. The Kreishauptman, as a polite gesture, had brought along two hunting pieces, one for himself and one for the count, whom he invited to take part in the hunt. Young Potocki wriggled out of this diplomatically, explaining that while he would be delighted to do so, no one on the place except himself had any idea how to beat game and he would have to see to the details himself. The superintendent expressed regret but did not insist.

The count had prepared the following plan. The hunt was to begin exactly at 7:15. The hunters and beaters would be divided into two groups. The first, guided by the count, would start encircling the area to the north of the Skawina road, while the second group, under my direction, encircled the southern part of the area, drawing the circle together near the forest. The beaters would be stationed at intervals along the perimeter of the line.

We set to work, and in less than two hours the circle had been closed. The hunters took up positions in front of the beaters and had instructions to shoot only straight ahead. At a given signal the beaters began to bang their pots and pans. Shouting and whistling, they moved slowly forward, gradually shrinking the circle, while the frightened rabbits raced madly back and forth. Whenever they ran toward the line of beaters, the hunters fired, rarely missing. The beaters finished off the wounded ones with sticks. The circle grew tighter and tighter; the rabbits grew increasingly frenzied; and the shots rang out without interruption. Finally the circle had become so small it was no longer safe to fire for fear of hitting the other group of hunters. The German "master of the hunt" sounded his horn, and the hunters withdrew outside the circle and stationed themselves with their backs to the beaters, who now drove the rabbits out of the center. When a rabbit broke out of the circle of banging and shouting beaters to the open field, he ran into a murderous line of fire.

Soon the Germans declared a break for lunch. Around noon we began a second encirclement, even larger than the first, which lasted more than three hours. By four o'clock the hunters were back at the manor house, having bagged 167 rabbits and 3 pheasants. Our lads carried the game. The rabbits were tied by their hindquarters and hung upside down on stakes in bundles of twenty-five. Each hunter stood in front of a bundle of hanging rabbits to have his photograph taken as a memento of the hunt. Then they lit a great bonfire in the courtyard, dragged out the bottles of beer they brought with them, and wolfed down the mountains of food we had prepared for them, bragging all the while about the exploits of the day. They left for Cracow with their game around midnight, leaving us a dozen or so rabbits for our table.

Jews and Rabbits

That evening I took a walk through the fields where the slaughter had taken place. The earth was brown, the color of a rabbit's pelt. Early in the morning, when the beaters were still fifty meters apart and there were large gaps in the line, a rabbit stood a chance of staying alive just by crouching close to the ground, very still, using the protective coloration nature had given him. Once he started up from his spot and began to run, his fate was sealed, but the longer he delayed his escape, the harder it was for him to escape the tightening circle.

It was the same with us Jews. At the beginning of the occupation it was still possible to escape, not for everyone, of course, but for those who had the necessary "protective coloration," that is, those people who did not look like Jews, spoke Polish perfectly, and were familiar with Polish customs. But suddenly it was too late: the circle had closed. The Poles subjected each newcomer to careful scrutiny and suspected everyone, whether correctly or not, of being a Jew. Once such rumors started, there was no putting a stop to them until that person—if he actually was a Jew—was exposed and caught.

It was my habit to walk into the fields after supper, lie down in the grass, and think things over. I loved to lie on my back and stare up at the heavens. I luxuriated in those peaceful evenings, breathing in the earth's heady fragrances, gazing up at the stars overhead. One evening as I lay at ease I was startled by a sudden noise. Two large male hares had appeared near me and were fighting over a female. She sat up rigidly nearby, bright-eyed, observing the battle waged over her charms. From her movements it was clear that the rivalry was exciting her. The males fought with increasing ferocity, leaping on one another, tearing at each other's stomachs with their powerful hind legs. Fur flew in all directions as they tore away, so oblivious in their rage that one could have easily captured them with one's hands. The fight lasted ten minutes or more. Finally the weaker of the two gave in and hopped shakily away, leaving the field to the victor. The excited female continued to sit up stiff as a board, chattering and casting sparkling glances at the winner, who began to dance around her in circles. He circled faster and faster until the female began to circle slowly around too. Finally they both had enough of formalities. The male interrupted his dance, hopped off a little way, stopped, and waited; the female obediently hopped off after him.

People generally assume that rabbits are a mixture of timidity and gentleness and can't imagine these creatures capable of cruelty, violence, or even self-defense. However, nature in its own way provides them, too, with the tools necessary for survival.

Gypsy

December arrived, and the earth was enveloped in a dazzling white coverlet of snow. A blissful calm settled on our world, as the snow muffled and dampened all sounds but the clear ring of sleighbells. The

214

week before Christmas I lost my best friend. During his lifetime I never really realized how much he meant to me, so accustomed was I to having him near me. He no longer shared my meals, slept at my doorstep, listened eagerly to my intimate confessions. Everything reminded me of him: the path through the fields, the eaves of the building, the places that we alone knew.

He had turned up one day in 1941 while the estate was still in the hands of the previous landlord. No one knew where he had come from; he simply appeared in the yard and made himself at home. Nothing startled him or aroused his curiosity: it seemed that he had seen it all before. He found me, took me immediately for a long-lost friend, and almost never left my side from that day on. During meals he would sit by my table; at night he kept watch outside the door while I slept. I never could persuade him to come indoors; he had a natural aversion to closed spaces and loved freedom, movement, and the outdoors.

A mongrel, black, without any distinctive markings, he was built like an English setter, had the coat of a collie, and the adroitness and grace of a panther; yes, more than anything else he reminded me of a panther. Long black forelocks covered his eyes. His long furry tail usually was at half mast, but whenever we saw game it stiffened. He never walked; he glided silently along, recognizing neither paths nor roads but keeping to the fields, boundary strips, and other invisible pathways known only to him. When he was near the farm buildings he would skulk along stealthily in the shadows, almost invisible. Always dignified, he never barked, never fawned, never allowed anyone to pet him. Even I, his best friend, would never dare to lay a finger on his magnificent tail, a tail which, amazingly enough, he never was seen to wag.

He did not care for the food we ate at the manor house. If I passed him a tidbit of food during a meal, he would take it slowly and gingerly, as though to humor me. His main occupation and primary source of sustenance was hunting—for rabbits in particular. He did not bother the barnyard fowl or even notice them. However, once I saw him attack an enormous bull which belonged to the estate. Suddenly, for no apparent reason and without even a warning bark, he shot across the barnyard toward the bull, leaped up onto his back, and fastened himself on the poor animal's hide. From there he worked his way down to the tail, which he clamped firmly in his powerful jaws. The bull was wild with pain and rage, but there was no separating him from his adversary, so we all stood by, fascinated. After a few minutes he released the

215

bloody tail of the bull, jumped down, and sauntered calmly away, as though he had been only a spectator at the fray.

Wild and untamable, he recognized only my existence but even so would not obey me, but always did as he pleased. I called him Gypsy, though he responded to the name with a marked lack of enthusiasm, making it clear that he was doing me a favor by allowing me to call him that. He was such a shadow that often I did not know that he was with me. Once a neighboring farmer stretched out his hand to greet me, and before I knew that he was there Gypsy dashed between us and caught the farmer's hand in his massive jaws. I cried out in alarm, and the dog, sensing that he had done something wrong, let go at once. Amazingly, the man's hand was not even scratched.

Whenever I took the carriage to town Gypsy would be lurking nearby, and by the time I arrived at my destination he would be there waiting; he always knew where I was going. He knew I objected to his following the carriage, so he never did; he arrived before I did by taking his invisible shortcuts across ditches and under fences. He never came near the carriage but kept a protective and watchful eye on me from a distance. By the time I returned to the estate, of course, Gypsy would be there, waiting in the yard. It was no good locking him up; he could escape from any enclosure.

He preferred to hunt at night. He would lie silent and motionless in a ditch, by a boundary marker, or in some other well-concealed location until a rabbit hopped by. As soon as this happened it was all over. He had a sixth sense for the spot where the unsuspecting rabbit was jumping and would head him off, fall on him, and crush his spine in one bite of his powerful jaws. Then he would trot off with the dying beast to consume it in private. He was ferocious and unrestrained at such moments; I tried in vain to break him of his hunting habits and accustom him to regular dog food. He didn't fraternize with the other dogs; they avoided him, and he did not seek their company either. He preferred to go with me into the fields where the two of us were alone. I would talk and he would listen, lying beside me, placing his head on my chest, staring into my eyes. It was clear that he understood everything I said.

I often went home to my family for the weekend by train. One Saturday evening on my way home I entered the Skawina station and there on the platform was Gypsy waiting for me. I was in a quandary; the cars reserved for Poles were hopelessly overcrowded. I generally rode on the steps of the train hanging on by one hand wherever I could. What in the world could I do with the dog? My only choice was to use the next car, marked "Nur für Deutsche" ("For Germans Only"). I opened the door of that car, and Gypsy understood and leaped inside. It was dark, the car was almost empty, and I hoped that no one would notice his presence. In any case clever Gypsy kept still. At the next stop, Cracow-Swoszowice, I opened the door of the car and out he jumped.

We walked to my apartment together, but I entered alone, for he did not know any of the people inside. However, after a moment's consultation with my wife I invited him in. Then I took my three-year-old daughter Elusia by the hand and led her up to him. "Gypsy! This is a little girl! Take care of her!" Predictably, Gypsy understood me perfectly. He went over to a corner of the kitchen and lay down quietly. I relaxed and began to talk with Basia in the other room, forgetting that I had left Elusia and Gypsy alone. Suddenly I heard a peal of laughter. I rushed back into the kitchen and stopped, frozen at the sight. There in the center of the room stood Gypsy, with his tail straight as an arrow, motionless, statuesque, bending slightly forward to keep his balance, while my daughter hauled on his tail with all her strength. This was the first time that anyone had even dared to touch Gypsy's tail, much less tug and pull it! It was an unforgettable sight. A little while later I saw that he was letting her pull him around by the hair, the tail, the muzzle; he even offered her his head so that she could twist his ears. This was my Gypsy—noble and protective, wise and gentle. He slept that night right next to my daughter's bed, and the next day this outdoor animal never left the apartment, but played with Elusia with great gentleness. We returned home that evening, I riding on the steps of the railway carriage for Poles while Gypsy traveled in splendor in the car marked "Nur für Deutsche."

As I mentioned, the hunting rights on our land belonged to the Kreishauptman, the county superintendent. On one of his tours around our property he must have seen Gypsy hunting, for he warned me once that if I did not keep my dog under control he would shoot him. However, there was no way to change Gypsy's nature. One day our stable boy came running from the fields shouting that Gypsy was dead, that the Kreishauptman had shot him—in fact, he had fired both barrels of his shotgun into my dog at close range, letting the rabbit he had caught get away.

I ran across the railroad tracks to the fields, where I could see a black spot against the snow. Gypsy had died in flight, his forepaws stretched out, his head buried in the snow, his tail in its hunting position, straight out behind him. The snow made a bloody halo around his head. I put back his long forelocks. His eyes were glassy, dead, fixed on some distant point; they were no longer the intelligent eyes of my friend. Perhaps they were already looking at another world. His body was so stiff that he must have been lying there for several hours. I asked the boy to go for a pick and shovel, and when he brought them I sent him away.

I dug a grave near the boundary strip of the field, in the place where he loved to run. I was dressed in a winter jacket and flannel shirt; I unbuttoned the shirt, wrapped Gypsy in it, and laid him to rest, enveloped in the scent of my body. Kneeling before his grave I said a prayer that God grant him a better and richer life in the hereafter, where he would be free to roam and hunt wherever he pleased, far from all Nazis. Several days later I found a large plain boulder in the forest and brought it to decorate the mound which covered my faithful friend.

Chapter 21

My Intelligence Network

By late 1942 I had learned to greet all military communiqués from the war theater with skepticism. Both Germany and the Allies either lied outright or blew up the actual facts beyond recognition, ignoring or distorting any developments which would reflect unfavorably on them. But my fate and the fate of those near to me depended on our knowing the real state of affairs, so I established my own personal intelligence network.

Before long I became a specialist in interpreting the military situation on the Eastern Front. (I had no interest in the Western Front—what did I care what was happening in North Africa? One day the Germans were routing the Allies and the next the Allies were chasing the Germans; one day Tobruk belonged to Germany, the next to the English. None of these battles had any bearing on my own problems.) I had access only to the BBC news broadcasts from London, to which I listened under the very noses of the SS, at the firebrick factory, over an excellent German eight-tube radio; sometimes I read the texts of the BBC communiqués in the underground newspapers.* The English reports on the situation in the east were sparse. They may have had scant information, or they may simply have been uninterested in our part of the world, preferring to tout only their own military exploits.

---

*Throughout the war, and increasingly toward its end, the underground press flourished throughout Poland in both the Polish and German languages.—*Tr.*

219

It may seem surprising that I could gather information about the war in such a remote spot as Borek Szlachecki, but the process of intelligence-gathering, I found, is not as it is depicted in spy stories. One need not be a Mata Hari; anyone with a modicum of intelligence, common sense, and a flair for deductive reasoning can form a pretty accurate impression of situations and facts.

Letters from Magda

Since the Western news broadcasts said almost nothing concerning the Eastern Front, I began to collect information on my own. My best informant was my colleague Siegfried Kepper, the manager of the Polanka-Haller estate, whom I have mentioned. He was from East Prussia; on my frequent visits to him I expressed my "concern" for his family and farm back home, near Olsztyn. My questions gave him a rare opportunity to unburden himself, for few around him spoke German. For me, our "friendship" provided my closest link to the situation at the German-Russian front.

I learned through Kepper that the situation in the east was grave indeed. All workers able to carry a rifle had long ago been taken away from his estate and sent to the front, and the entire property had been turned into a repository for machines and materiel bound for the east. His barns had all been requisitioned by the army. At first he had been able to maintain some semblance of order, but now supplies and equipment were lying helter-skelter wherever there was room to put them down. No one had any idea where to send these goods: if the destination were known, as likely as not the shipment would be canceled anyway because the locality had been cut off by the enemy or because the Germans themselves had relinquished it in an attempt to "consolidate" their front lines. To make matters worse, Kepper had run out of enough true Germans to maintain order. They had been replaced by Latvians, a disorderly mob of men who loitered about the estate by day and at night attacked the local villagers in their homes, plundering, pillaging, and raping. Poor Kepper did not even have anyone to complain to about these troubles.

As a young man, I learned, Kepper had been a hired hand for a wealthy farmer and had married one of the daughters. He was given forty hectares of prime farmland together with a plump wife named

Magda, several years his elder, who never let him forget that he had once been her father's hired hand. She made him work like a horse. When the Nazi movement began, Kepper was the first in his village to join and soon rose to head the local Nazi Party organization and to be a member of the draft board. All the local youths tried to find work on his farm because it was up to him whether or not they went into the army. He paid them starvation wages, and they slaved for him as he once had slaved for Magda.

When the Russo-German war broke out, Kepper was certain that Russia would surrender in a matter of weeks. He had heard that there were some beautiful hereditary estates in former Poland which could be had practically for the asking. For the time being, these lands were administered by the German government, but later, after the war, they would be distributed either free or for a nominal sum to deserving private individuals. Kepper counted on being among those deserving persons: he had belonged to the Nazi Party from its inception and had accumulated a good record of service to the community. He therefore decided to go to the occupied area as quickly as possible to choose a nice piece of property for himself. Apart from this intention, he was also probably enticed by the prospect of escaping for a time from the clutches of his possessive wife.

When Kepper arrived in Cracow, he was shown a list of possible estates to administer. He took his time looking over the prospects, trying to find the best possible property. He finally settled on Polanka-Haller, a property larger than his own in East Prussia—a veritable hereditary fiefdom, in fact—with a milder climate as well.

Enthusiastically he set to work on his new farm, but from the very beginning nothing worked out right. In the first place, he spoke no Polish and his Polish workers spoke no German. At first he had a Silesian bookkeeper as a translator, but that man was soon drafted, and Kepper was left on his own. In his opinion, Polish workers were worthless. They moved slower than molasses in January, not like his German lads at home who had jumped at his every command. The Polanka-Haller workers either did not understand or pretended not to understand what one said to them, and both entreaties and threats were useless. Kepper's love life had not prospered either. One day he tried to get his kitchen maid into bed, and she raised such an uproar that he took flight and never dared show his face near the kitchen again. Now he had to fear the wrath of the Polish partisans for trying to rape a Polish girl. Worst of all, he was no longer sure that the estate would ever be his—he even began to doubt that the Germans would have any Polish estates at all after the war. The Blitzkrieg, that "lightning war," was not going as he had expected. Communications from Magda back home indicated that Hitler's expedition for the golden Russian fleece had run aground. Kepper's dream of becoming a rich landowner began to fade, and after consulting Magda he began preparations to return home. However, it now appeared that this was not as easy as he had thought. The authorities would not permit him to abandon his post; he was to remain at Polanka-Haller and carry on his work. All his local connections and years of service suddenly were meaningless; his superiors treated him superciliously, and his disenchantment knew no bounds.

To Kepper I was nothing but a *verfluchte Pole*—a "damned Pole"—but at least he could talk to me in German. Besides, I was not his subordinate but his equal in rank, as I was in the employ of a count. The worse his superiors treated him, the greater his bitterness grew and the more he unburdened himself to me. During my first visits to Polanka-Haller, we talked exclusively of farming. Gradually Kepper began to discuss his personal life. I listened attentively, and that was all the encouragement he needed. He came to look forward to my visits, brightened at the sight of me, and poured out all his grievances. He even read me his letters from Magda. The letters were balm to my soul; they raised my spirits and gave me strength to carry on. Among other things I learned from them that the unbeatable German army was becoming demoralized. It was an ironic situation: Kepper was grateful to me for taking an interest in his personal life, while I was grateful to him for all his cheerful news.

One day, around New Year's, 1943, I paid a social visit to my would-be squire. He had just received a long letter from his expansive Magda and gave it to me to read. Those were the best New Year's greetings I could possibly have received. In brief, the letter said, "I'm afraid to remain in Prussia. Don't return; I'm coming there."

Deciphering the Trains

Another kind of news was brought by the trains passing through our area, more comprehensive than that provided by Kepper, for it concerned both the Eastern Front and the "actions" carried out by the

Germans against the civilian population. The tracks leading from Skawina westward to Oświęcim, which was about thirty-five kilometers
away, ran through our own fields. During the Russian occupation of
Przemyśl, while working on the railroad, my job was to record the passage of thousands of cars of different sorts. The Przemyśl station was
busy around the clock with trains going east and west, to Germany and
back. It took a day or more for the frontier guards to search the cars,
after which the train was allowed to travel on down the line. My task was
to record the numbers of the cars after the search. Before long I became
quite adept at accurately assessing the contents of particular shipments.

I now put my knowledge to work "deciphering" the loads traveling through our estate. The Oświęcim-Skawina line had never been a
major route during the war, as the main thrust of the German military
machine had been directed north, toward Leningrad and Moscow. By
1942, however, especially in the last half of the year, the Germans were
applying less and less pressure along the northern front, and in fact
shortened it and turned south toward Stalingrad. The Oświęcim-
Skawina-Cracow line became clogged with transports headed east. The
same line led to the Oświęcim extermination camps. Often the smaller
railroad stations had insufficient sidings to accommodate the increased
number of trains, and they would be forced to stop on the line and wait
for the all-clear signal from the railway station, which gave me the
opportunity to make precise observations.

Immediately after the outbreak of the war with Russia, the soldiers traveling east acted as if they were going to a picnic: the cars were
decorated with colorful streamers, and the soldiers sang rousing patri-
otic songs as they rolled along. When the trains had to stop on the tracks
and the soldiers hopped out to stretch their legs, they were handsome,
well cared for, self-assured. But as the front grew longer and longer in
the winter of 1941-42, as I mentioned, the bitter cold was the main victor. Little by little, the German cannon fodder began to give out. The
trains that now passed through our fields were no longer decorated, and
there was no more singing. During the forced stops only gaunt-faced
older men climbed down from the cars. The longer the war lasted, the
more the Germans had to pay in men and materiel. Now storms, snow,
mud, and overextended supply lines, along with the stiffening resistance
of the Red Army, gave the Germans a new outlook on warfare.

Accompanying the army east were trains loaded with military
equipment. In the beginning we would see agricultural machinery among

the goods being shipped east, for the Germans dreamed of occupying these vacant lands, turning them to the plough, and gathering in the harvest. This bubble had long since burst in the winter of 1941; now the passing trains carried strings of platform cars loaded with tanks, tanks, and more tanks—not merely hundreds but thousands of tanks were being sent to that insatiable Eastern Front. One day we would see trains loaded with artillery of various calibers, unsuccessfully hidden beneath tarpaulins; the next day there would be an entire shipment of armored personnel carriers; and so on.

These instruments of modern warfare were too large for boxcars and had to be shipped on open platforms. From the vast number of shipments traveling east day and night I could easily deduce that this war was not the Blitzkrieg the newspapers still talked about. Military shipments could always be recognized because they were escorted by the army. Furthermore, these were not regular trains made up of cars of different sorts and sizes (boxcars, coal cars, tankers, and the like) but transports consisting of a single item—for example, fifty flatcars convoyed by soldiers.

Trains carrying provisions for the army were also easy to spot: instead of being under army escort they were guarded by civilian railway workers, and if the train stopped for a while in our fields I could even make out roughly what the shipment contained. It was amazing: here on our estate, in this little village far from the center of action, I could tell with considerable accuracy what the war was costing the Germans, how their military operations were faring, and even what kinds of equipment were most needed at the front.

Transports traveled west as well, of course, at first carrying prisoners of war in closed cars with tiny screened windows. Later the trains carried civilians caught in street roundups or ordered to forced labor in Germany by the Arbeitsamts. The windows of these cars were not wired over, and the railwaymen would even open the car doors from time to time to let in fresh air.

Trains went to Oświęcim as well, from the east and west, from almost all the countries of Europe, as far as German authority extended, transporting Jews for hard labor or extermination. These shipments, escorted by special detachments of troops, took priority even over military transports headed to the front. Their windows were barred, and no one was permitted near them, but weak moans from the cars could be heard over the fields. The great number of such trains showed clearly the enormity of the Nazi crime.

Finally, one could observe the effects of the fighting on the Eastern Front from the hospital trains. In the beginning these transports were made up of specially reconditioned first-class Pullman cars. They traveled along slowly, and through the windows one could observe the wounded lying in upper and lower berths beneath clean white sheets. In time the number of hospital trains headed for Germany increased, and there were no longer enough Pullman cars to fill the need. Ordinary passenger cars were converted into infirmaries on wheels, and by the end of 1942 even regular freight cars, with large red crosses painted on their roofs, were carrying the wounded back to the Reich.

Official News

Besides Kepper and the trains, my third intelligence source was the newspaper *Krakauer Zeitung*, in which military communiqués were printed daily, including information about conditions at the Eastern Front. Listening to the BBC news from London and reading the German reports, I was struck by their essential similarity—including the exaggeration of successes and playing down of defeats. For example, from the Nazi military communiqués in the second half of 1941 one learned that German power had been so overwhelming that the war with Russia would be over in a matter of days—that the entire Russian army was in disarray, that all the larger cities up to the very outskirts of Moscow were in German hands, and that Leningrad was surrounded. Then came the harsh winter, and neither Leningrad nor Moscow was taken.

In 1942 less attention was devoted to the northern front in the communiqués and more to the southern—to the march to the Black Sea and the Volga. We heard that the Germans would cut off the Allies by capturing the Suez Canal, that they would join up with Rommel's army marching east through Egypt, that the Russian supply base would be destroyed through occupation of the Ukraine, the Caucasus, and other distant territories stretching from the Volga to the Ural Mountains. The communiqués now proclaimed that there was no sense trying to capture Moscow and Leningrad; that road led nowhere, and capturing these cities was more a matter of prestige than of real military significance. It was better to withdraw troops from the north and throw them into the southern action, we were told: instead of occupying the Russian capital the German army would capture Stalingrad and the mouth of the Volga, giving it a stranglehold on Russia from which the Bolsheviks could never escape. The Germans did get as far as Stalingrad, of course, and even occupied it. We read that here and there a few isolated insurgents were still trying to defend the town, but that even this futile resistance would soon be over. Winter came, and the German army was still "stamping out the last remnants" of the Russian resistance in Stalingrad. Small groups of partisans operating behind the lines continued to harass the German troops, but these last-ditch attempts were said to be doomed to failure.

I realized, of course, that the Nazis had suffered heavy losses and could no longer conduct the war along such a wide front so far from home, but one thing seemed clear from all these reports: Russia no longer had an effective force with which to defend itself. The Red Army would do what it could to hinder the Germans, maneuvering them into shortening the front and withdrawing to a position closer to their supply lines, perhaps even as far back as eastern Poland, but there the Nazis would draw the line. I came to the conclusion that the war would be reduced to the level of a protracted affair of mutual harassment which could drag on for many years. Before this dog fight was ever concluded, I thought gloomily, my family and I would long be in our graves.

"The Overwhelming Might of the Enemy"

In the memorable first days of February, 1943, the Nazi papers reported as follows: the Sixth Army of General Paulus (who only the day before had been named Field Marshal) had surrendered to "the overwhelming might of the enemy." I was thunderstruck: what "overwhelming might"? Surely not those pitiful bands of partisans harassing the Germans from the rear at Stalingrad? But there it was in black and white in the *Krakauer Zeitung*: "the overwhelming might of the enemy"! My hands began to shake; I stepped out of my office to get some air and collect my whirling thoughts.

What a fool I had been! Despite my innate skepticism, I too had been totally taken in by the barrage of Nazi propaganda about the collapse of the Red Army. Now what would the German people say? Up to now they had been told almost daily that the German army had never lost a war, not even World War I—that it was the German Communists who persuaded the soldiers to lay down their arms in 1918. And now the

Sixth Army of General Paulus, a quarter of a million soldiers whom only the German military genius could have concentrated in a single spot, that invincible army with all its masses of equipment and a general staff composed of the most formidable military brains in the world, had yielded to "the overwhelming might of the enemy"! I felt a spark of hope kindled within me—faint, but hope nonetheless—that I and all those with me might live to see the end of the war after all.

The news struck the Germans like a lightning bolt. The surrender was so improbable, so absurd an idea, that it took them some time to fathom it. Some Nazis in our town suddenly turned "human," explaining that they had never meant anyone any harm, and that if they had acted badly it was under orders from their superiors. Others vented their frustration on the helpless Polish population. They claimed that everything was the fault of the *verfluchte Polen*—had it not been for their resistance to the German invasion in September, 1939, this war which was now threatening to destroy the Reich would never have started. Roundups, mass executions, and "pacifications" broke out all over the country. Still others reacted like common criminals by trying to cover their tracks. Several concentration camps were liquidated; prisoners still left alive were shipped to Germany; informers were shot. Despite the increased Nazi terror, Polish partisans now harassed the occupying forces with increasing boldness and frequency, often in broad daylight, in the open, from positions they had never before considered safe. Yes, Stalingrad changed everything.

The Ever-Changing Trains

The good old days, when no one knew who I really was and there were just the three of us to worry about, were gone forever. My "family" had grown five-fold and, with it, the accompanying danger by at least a thousand-fold. Our only hope, a mad hope at that, lay in the Russian advance. The Germans were still said to be "shortening" or "consolidating" their front lines. By now we knew that this translated into full-scale retreat. With each new withdrawal from one town or another, our faith in the approaching liberation grew.

In the meantime, the pattern of rail traffic to the east was changing drastically. Almost every German male able to hold a rifle was being shipped to the front, while the provisioning of the army was put in the hands of men too old and decrepit for war, mostly Austrians, it seemed. Military and supply transports moved across our lands daily. One had to ask why. Some of them, especially food trains for particular localities, would never reach their destinations for the simple reason that these places were no longer in German hands. In such cases, because the cars were needed back home for new loads, they would have to return, leaving the railroad workers no choice but to empty them anywhere they could. Eventually whole boxcars were being unloaded on Polish territory, creating one of the most lucrative and lively markets for profiteering imaginable.

The sellers were the railway employees; the buyers were the new Polish merchant class, former small tradesmen. At first only the contents of the last few cars were sold, for they were easy to detach from the rest of the train. German marks, of course, were still the medium of exchange. No one even knew what was inside the cars; one simply bought a "surprise package"—a number of wagons crammed to the brim with no one knew what. Later the sales agreements underwent modification: purchasers would no longer buy a "pig in a poke" but demanded to know the contents—a reasonable enough request, since the railway workers generally had a pretty good idea of what was inside each car. Still later, purchasers actually began to place orders with the railway people for specific items.

No one was interested in arms, and in any case they were shipped by special trains. For agricultural machinery, somewhat surprisingly, there was no market either, but all other goods were classified: some cost more, others less. It was standard practice for the railway workers to post a list of the contents of each car on the last car of each train. Some products had to be sold quickly; others could be kept indefinitely. One could purchase deluxe Norwegian pickled herring for next to nothing one week; another week it was Belgian chocolates; once there were even live turtles from Greece. Everything imaginable was available, ranging from Danish butter to Dutch cheese to all manner of preserved meats, sausages, and ham to German jam, marmalade, zwieback (German military crackers), sugar, chocolate, and condensed milk. Articles that had to be consumed quickly were valued highly but were often cheap, while any kind of canned meat or sweet was more expensive, since it could be stored. There was another class of items such as dry goods—dishes, pots, pans, utensils, light bulbs, oil lamps, and other household things. Dry goods such as sheets, towels, pillow cases, dishrags, blankets, undergarments, and army uniforms were in particular demand: wool blankets and uniforms were dyed various colors and made over into warm winter clothing for men and women.

There was almost no family or household that did not buy goods from these German transports either first- or second-hand, or even third- or fourth-hand. Furthermore, I am sure that there was not one arm of the German railway establishment, including the Railway Police, that was not involved in this trade. The Polish purchasers must have been exceedingly well organized to have at their disposal substantial amounts of German marks, warehouses for storage, and ways of transporting the goods from the railroad line to the warehouses, where they were hidden, and from there to retail stores. I heard of no case of an illegal shipment being confiscated, nor of any official, high or low, suffering any consequences. The profits were so enormous that there was enough money to buy everyone off.

This was one of the ironies of the war, I thought. On the one hand, the terror on the streets of Cracow and throughout Poland had assumed unprecedented proportions, and roundups were an everyday occurrence. Not only young people but everyone was fair game for the police. They tore work permits out of people's hands and loaded them onto army trucks. It was no longer safe for anyone to walk the streets, ride the trolleys or trains, or gather in any public place. But on the other hand, the same police force, or another branch of the German security forces, was providing protection for Polish profiteers by transporting German stolen goods and doing big business.

Although I myself did not buy any of these contraband articles, I studied the list of available items whenever I could. The assortment made me realize that the German economy was beginning to come apart at the seams, and my frail hope that somehow we would live to witness the arrival of the Soviet troops was strengthening.

A Dangerous Rumor

With each passing day I felt in greater and greater need of being rescued. It was bad enough to be a Jew; now, I learned, I was stuck with the additional label of belonging to the Polish underground. Whether the director of the Arbeitsamt, Joachim Mann, started the rumor or whether my frequent absences at night to see my family started people talking, from various hints in conversations I deduced that people took me for an important link in the resistance movement. More than once in response to my casual query, "What's new?" I received the reply, "You tell *us* what's new: *you* ought to know!" On one occasion the Czech director of the firebrick factory, Wasenda, approached me cautiously and said that it was none of his business what I was doing but that he had heard rumors that I was active in the underground. As long as his workers kept it to themselves there was no need to worry, he said, but if the story ever leaked to the SS men quartered in his factory buildings, the game would be up.

What could I do to counter these rumors? I couldn't very well walk about with a sign on my back proclaiming that I was not a member of the Underground Army. I began to wonder which was worse, being a Jew or being suspected of belonging to the underground, and I decided it was probably the latter. I concluded that it was time to disappear from Skawina, and the sooner the better. All that stood in my way was Basia's condition: she was six months pregnant.

Chapter 22

Unpleasant Surprises

People usually like anything new and out of the ordinary, a change in one's routine, humdrum existence, whether the surprise is something small, like an unexpected letter, or more important, like the return of a long-absent friend. One's heart beats faster, life seems worth living, and the day flies by, leaving a sense of well-being. However, should anyone ask me what unpleasant effects of my wartime experience persisted the longest, I would answer without hesitation: fear of the unforeseen—more specifically, fear of being surprised, caught unprepared by some unexpected event or person, and of being forced to react instantly, intelligently, and decisively. My unmasking by Miss Liebeskind in the home of Countess Potocki's family affected me deeply, and the shock and apprehension created by that incident did not fade away. There were other such incidents later, and by the end of the war I had had more than enough surprises to last a lifetime. My wife also received a series of shocks independent of mine, and, because she was unaccustomed to struggling along in times of violence and cruelty, the effort to ward off these blows was incomparably greater for her than for me; but more of this later.

A Friend from Cracow

It was the end of February, 1943, a bitter cold day. Snow covered the ground with a crisp white blanket that cracked beneath the runners of my sleigh. I had been to Cracow on business and was on my way home. By the time I reached Skawina I was chilled to the bone and decided to stop at the local café for a hot drink. It was dusk as I entered the dimly lit café, looking like a bear in my hooded brown greatcoat. I greeted the proprietress gaily, went up to the counter, chose a pastry, and ordered a cup of tea. As I waited at a table by the window, I suddenly heard a man at another table, whom I had not noticed, call out, "Why hello, Counselor! How are you? What brings you to Skawina?"

I was caught completely off guard. There sitting in the gloom I beheld none other than my old friend Judge Białas, from the Cracow municipal court. He was a tall, lean man with dark hair, shaggy brows, and swarthy complexion—an Armenian type, I thought. One leg was shorter than the other, and he walked with a slight limp. He was about my age, perhaps a year or two older, an immensely serious individual who rarely smiled, but I had liked him well enough.

I tried to gain time to think: "What do you mean, 'What brings me here?' What are you doing here yourself, Judge?"

He replied that he was still at the municipal court in Cracow, had come to Skawina to try a case, and was now waiting for the train back to the city.

A warning bell sounded in my head: he's working in the court? That could be dangerous. It was only a low-level civil court, but nonetheless. . . . I had no more time to think. I had to deal with the situation quickly and calmly.

I took my tea over to his table, sat down, casually extracted my cigarette case, and offered it to him. We lit our cigarettes, and I said in an off-hand way, "I don't feel like working in the profession just now. It's more peaceful living here on my father's estate."

He looked at me in utter astonishment. He knew my real name and he knew that I was a Jew. Something wasn't right about this, he was thinking: there were no Jews here. What was this business about living on my father's estate? Could he have confused me with someone else? No, that was impossible: he knew me perfectly well and I knew him.

I could read all of these questions in his face but did not want to give him a minute to come to the logical conclusion. Instead, I bombarded him with questions about himself, hoping to keep him off balance. He still had half an hour before his train left, and I prattled on about how our family had a large estate near Skawina, how at the beginning of the war I had tried to keep up my practice, but my father had fallen ill and someone had to look after the farm, so I had settled out here in the country and now was more than satisfied with my choice. I kept telling the judge how delighted I was at our chance meeting and brushed aside all thoughts of leaving before his train arrived. It was just luck that no one who knew me in Skawina came into the café and said something to me that would have given me away.

Finally it was time for the judge to go. He wanted to pay the bill, but I waved him away with a smile: "Please don't bother. It's taken care of."

"What? When?"

"It's nothing, really. The bill has been put on our account." (This last was the truth, for I had given the owner a quiet signal which she understood without our having to say anything to each other.)

As we stepped out into the street, my driver jumped down from the carriage, unsnapped the rear door flap, and lifted the bearskin carriage robe for us. I motioned the judge inside, but he declined, saying he preferred to walk, that the station was not far away. When I insisted, he finally climbed inside. "To the station," I commanded. The horses stepped out briskly, and in a few minutes we were there. The station-master greeted me effusively. By now the poor judge was completely baffled. I kept close by him until he was safely on board the train. As we parted, he invited me to visit him whenever I was in Cracow, and naturally I said that I would be delighted to do so. We embraced cordially, and he departed at last.

I met Judge Białas again only after the war. At that time he was a judge on the Commission for the Investigation of Nazi Atrocities. I apologized for my trickery during the war in Skawina, explaining that it had been a matter of life and death and that I had seen no other way out of the predicament. He, of course, said he understood and that he certainly harbored no ill feelings about the matter. He had only one question: what would I have said, he wondered, if he had asked me directly whether or not my name was Schatten? I replied that I would not have denied it but that he would still have been in the dark—he would not have been certain whether he had been wrong in taking me for a Jew. If he had actually asked me whether I was a Jew, I would have denied it, I told him, and the circumstances which surrounded our meeting—the sleigh, the driver, the stationmaster's greetings—would have only bolstered my denial. "In either case, Judge, you would never have solved the puzzle," I concluded. He agreed, and added, "Counselor, from what I knew of you before the war, I never would have imagined you to have such nerves of steel." With this we parted on friendly terms.

My Father's Emergency

Two other incidents, though not exactly "surprises," in the sense that this time I had more than a couple of seconds in which to react, nonetheless demanded swift and resolute action. The first of these took place one day early in March, 1943, when the days were growing longer, the sun was warm, and the snow was melting rapidly. I was sitting in my office just after lunch when the maid came to tell me that an elderly gentleman by the name of Nowak wished to see me. I knew that this was my father, and told her to have him come in. He had never come to see me here before, so I guessed that some crisis must have arisen. After exchanging a few social pleasantries to look convincing before the maid, we strolled out the door into the yard so that we could speak freely. I asked him what had brought him here. He had had an "accident," he told me, greatly agitated.

In these days after Stalingrad the Germans were on the defensive and had returned to the strict enforcement of blackout regulations. The night before some German soldiers had passed by our house in Borek Fałęcki and apparently made a fuss about some windows not being properly blacked out. They noted the address and next day handed the complaint to the Blue Police for further action. Later that morning the local police chief came to our house and officially informed Basia about the complaint. She could not understand it, and showed the officer that our windows were indeed properly blacked out. The officer realized that the soldiers must have been looking at the apartment next door, belonging to Mrs. Proszkowski. Unfortunately for us, no one was at home at that apartment, so the zealous chief began to check the papers of everyone in our apartment—a totally gratuitous act on his part, for all he found was Basia's mother, an old invalid lady; my father, around seventy; Basia; and our little daughter.

My father, although officially a resident of Skawina, liked to move around and often came to visit us; the fifteen kilometers between the towns were an easy walk for him. However, his *Kennkarte* was issued in Borek Fałęcki, not Skawina, and this inconsistency especially upset the policeman. He carefully noted the number and date of issue of the card and left, saying that he would look into the matter of the conflicting addresses first thing next day. My father's *Kennkarte* was false, and we knew that as soon as the police chief checked with the town hall in Borek Fałęcki he would find that no such card had ever been issued.

In spite of the grave danger, I tried to reassure my father that we still had time to act and that I would see that the affair was hushed up. I took him to my apartment, brought him some supper, and warned him that I might not be home that night. He was not to worry—he had had a long trip to see me, and it would be best for him to relax, go to bed, and get a good night's sleep.

Returning to my office, I sat down and pretended to work. It was clear what had to be done: the policeman must be bought off and that miserable slip of paper on which he had so diligently recorded the information from my father's *Kennkarte* retrieved. I did not know the man's name or address, but I had contacts in the Skawina police department who could help. Our gardener drove to town once or twice a week to sell seeds, vegetables, and fruit. He found a ready market, for the manor produce was first-rate and cheap, as it came straight from the farmer. However, sometimes he did not sell his whole wagonload. At this point the Blue Police would appear in the market, and our gardener had instructions to give them free whatever remained in the wagon. Their gratitude was always evident, and they should be prepared to do the manor a favor in return. Well, that time had come.

I telephoned one of the officers I knew and asked him to get the name and home address of the Borek Fałęcki police chief, adding that I was in a hurry. I had the information in fifteen minutes. Next I ordered the carriage and two fast horses to be brought to the house for a trip to Cracow. I asked the head cook to pack up a couple of large links of hunter's sausage and four one-liter bottles of vodka. For good measure, I added a ten-kilo sack of pearl barley and one of peeled barley. (All this produce was prohibited from sale on the open market.) Thus armed, I set off to pay an evening call on the chief of police. For safety's sake, I drew up and took with me an official stamped permit slip stating that I was transporting this food to another estate in Cracow.

I found the address easily. The chief lived on the second floor of a house right across from the town hall. I went up the stairs and knocked, and the man himself opened the door. I introduced myself and, before he could say one word, insisted that he come downstairs with me to get a few small items which I had for him. Together we carried the goods upstairs, and he called his wife in to see what the bountiful heavens had rained upon them. Her eyes grew wide at the sight of these wonders.

As I expected, the atmosphere warmed, and the chief asked me respectfully to take a seat. He himself walked around the room, not even attempting to conceal his delight at my treats. After we had exchanged a few pleasantries, I came to the point and asked him whether he would be kind enough to take care of the complaint about our apartment which he had recorded. He assured me that the matter was only a trifle; there was no need to go to so much trouble over it, no need to bring all this wonderful food. I insisted that I had not gone out of my way at all; I had been in Cracow on business and had merely taken the opportunity to drop by to see him on my way home. For us there on the estate, this food was really nothing to make a fuss over.

The chief's wife was listening with one ear while carefully stowing away in the larder all the precious things I had brought. In a moment she set out three little glasses and a plate with a dozen or so neat slices of my sausage. The chief uncorked the bottle, filled our glasses, and called for a toast: "To the health of our honored guest!"

We tossed it down in one gulp, as etiquette required, and he filled up the glasses again. The chief and his wife had probably just finished a hearty supper, but I had had nothing to eat since luncheon and was not used to drinking in any case, so even the first glass hit me hard. I tried to hide my condition as I confided modestly, "I've never had much to do with the authorities before, so I am relieved to learn that you consider that little trouble about the window hardly worth mentioning. I'm not so much concerned about us as I am about poor Mrs. Proszkowski—she's such a dear old soul; I would hate to have anything unpleasant happen to her."

"Don't you worry. Nothing will happen to her," he assured me amiably. "The report was handed in by German soldiers, not by my men, so I don't have to file a follow-up report on the matter. It's mine to handle as I see fit, and I assure you I consider the matter closed."

I was satisfied with his reply. By now we were on our third toast, my face was on fire, and I was drenched with sweat. The chief finally noticed my condition and warned me in a fatherly way that I had had

236

enough; after all, I had a long trip home. Even now I was not so drunk as to forget the real reason for my visit, however. "Fine, I'll be on my way presently, I'd j-j-just l-l-like to have a l-l-look at the notebook where you wrote everything d-d-down," I stuttered.

I could see that he was surprised at my remembering the notebook in my present state, but I kept at him with the dogged determination of a drunk: "Every policeman carries a n-n-notebook. . . . I'm n-n-not going to go until I s-s-see it!"

He could see no other way to get rid of me, so finally he took his thick official notebook from the pocket of his uniform jacket on the back of a chair and showed it to me. Still I kept insisting: "I want to read what you wrote!"

Now really annoyed, he found the page and showed it to me. "I'm nearsighted—bring it closer. . . ."

He thrust the notebook at me and I caught sight of my father's name. The report on him was the only item on the page. I stared and stared at the page, laughing stupidly, then, quick as a flash, I tore the offending page out of the book, crumpled it up into a tiny ball, and asked for one last glass of vodka.

The chief was plainly running out of patience. "I won't go until I have one for the road," I badgered him. "Come on!" Finally, to get rid of me, he poured me another glass, and, to his astonishment, I gulped down the ball of paper along with the vodka. Only then, having consumed the dangerous document, did I consider my business concluded.

"I'll help you downstairs," the chief offered, sympathetic to anyone this drunk. Indeed, I did need his help, for I started to fall as soon as I tried to stand up. We staggered down the stairs with arms wound around each other, and at the carriage he asked me whether I thought I could drive home.

"Oh, don't worry about that," I assured him. "This won't be the first time; the horses know the way home by now." He dragged me into the carriage, I waved a drunken goodbye, and started home. The road led up a steep hill. At the top stood a church; the road to Skawina curved to the right. As I turned the horses to the right I was suddenly overcome with nausea and dizziness. I tried to stand up to get out of the carriage and almost fell out on my head, so I lay down on the floor on my back and inched myself out onto the roadside, feet first. Safe on the ground at last, I gave in to the spasms. As my stomach had been empty, I could bring up nothing but vodka, bits of sausage, and, I suppose, the wad of paper. As soon as one attack subsided and I lay panting, another would rise to take its place.

It must have been more than half an hour before I could drag myself upright by the carriage straps and climb back in. Shivering and clammy, I covered up with whatever I could find. Doubled over, groaning and trembling, I shook the reins and the horses started on again. I was wracked by a burning thirst; someone was pounding on my head with a hammer. All the while the horses ambled along, and after centuries the estate loomed ahead of me and this dreadful excursion came to an end.

I crept down from the driver's seat, dragged the harness off the horses, and staggered off with them to the stable. When I got into the house, I looked in a mirror in the hall. My face was bloodless—I looked like a ghost. I fell heavily into the armchair in my office and sat there staring; I could not fall asleep until four o'clock in the morning. When I woke, I went to tell my father that the coast was clear and that he should go back home and reassure Basia. Then I went back to the manor house and told the maids that I was going to bed, for I had an attack of influenza. I lay in bed sick, shivering, and almost delirious, with cold compresses on my head, for hours. At last I crawled back to my office to try to take care of the usual business. For the next three days I could eat nothing, and by the time I was up and about again I had lost more than ten pounds.

Shutting Mann's Mouth

May arrived, the snows were gone, the damp black earth was giving off a heady fragrance. Primroses were in bloom, cattails were poking up, and everything was coming alive again in the warm rays of the spring sun. On one such morning the telephone jangled; it was my brother-in-law Józek calling from Kalwaria, asking me to come to see him. Next day I dropped by. He told me that his superior, Joachim Mann, kept hinting that he was a Jew. Józek said that Mann kept baiting him. Sometimes it was "Come on now, admit it! You're a Jew! Say it: *'Moyde ani!'*" (these are the first words of an old Jewish prayer for a good day). At other times he would simply taunt him: "Józek! You Jew!" Józek was terrified and wanted to know what to do. As always in such circumstances, I tried to calm him down and told him not to worry; I would shut Mann's mouth somehow. Actually I was quite worried, but I tried to conceal it.

On the way home I tried to work out a strategy. I did not know much about Mann except that he was a German by birth, from Silesia. When the Nazis occupied Poland and incorporated Silesia into the Reich, he automatically became a German citizen. Since he spoke Polish and knew his way around, he was appointed director of the Arbeitsamt in Skawina. These were fairly important posts in the German occupation network, as the directors were responsible for supplying a steady stream of workers to the Reich.

I had no idea what Mann's political convictions or attitude toward the Nazis were: around me he was dignified and reserved. Tadek Słomka handled the contacts with our estate, and he himself was not concerned with our affairs. In fact, Mann tended to let his underlings take care of most of the office work; he spent most of his time attending meetings in Cracow. I had observed him carefully since the time of the Jewish deportation from Skawina and had noticed nothing unusual in his behavior. I was sure only of one thing, that he had no desire to go to the Eastern Front to fight the Russians, but since all Germans I knew shared this sentiment, one could not attach any significance to that.

Mann and I were on fairly good terms: he needed what I could provide from the estate and I needed extra workers. He looked the other way whenever Słomka assigned extra workers to us, and I never forgot to leave some kind of delicacy for him in return. Lately we had even drunk *Bruderschaft* together,* so we were on a first-name basis, a dubious distinction from my point of view. Personally, however, he was a mystery to me. I couldn't understand why he was baiting Józek. And where did he learn the Hebrew words *moyde ani*? Was it his task to track down Jews? Surely not; if he really suspected that Józek was a Jew he would simply have handed him over to the Gestapo. It was true that Józek had a rather long nose and spoke German unusually well for a Pole, but those things alone were not enough to accuse someone of being a Jew. And if he did have suspicions, why not act on them instead of taunting his victim?

---

*Bruderschaft is a ceremonial passage from formal to informal address, roughly equivalent to going over to first names in English. When one drinks *Bruderschaft*, one generally links elbows across a table in a mutual toast, followed by a kiss on either cheek.—*Tr.*

I had no answers to any of these questions, but one thing was certain: I had to stop Mann from making dangerous jokes. If they did not stop, the situation could grow unmanageable and we might all perish. I could usually handle the Poles, even the Blue Police, but I knew that to enter into hard negotiations with a German, especially an official like the chief of the labor office, was extremely risky. Still, I could see no safer way to handle the problem, so the next day I paid a visit to the Skawina Arbeitsamt.

Mann had not yet come in. I told Tadek Słomka why I was there and asked him to hold all incoming telephone calls for Mann once he arrived and I was in his office. (Tadek ran their small switchboard and relayed calls to Mann as the need arose.) Finally Mann arrived and greeted me. "I have some business with you and I'd like to see you in your office," I told him. "Of course," he said. He gave some instructions to Tadek, picked up his mail, and unlocked his door, motioning me to enter first. I smiled and prodded him inside ahead of me.

When we were both in the office I took the key from the outside lock and locked the door from the inside.* Mann looked at me in surprise. "Some kind of secret, I suppose?" he asked.

Instead of answering I merely grunted: "Sit down!" I pointed to a heavy dark leather chair which stood against the wall beneath a portrait of Hitler.

Mann still stood there, puzzled, so I growled again: "Sit down!"

The blood rose in his face. He sat down heavily and I stood in front of him, fixed him with an icy stare, and barked out: "In the name of the Underground Organization. . . ."

Mann literally cringed under this blow. "What? What happened? What do you want?" he sputtered. "I'm not doing anyone any harm. I'm just doing my job, nothing more. I swear it."

I remained silent, staring at him, and he cowered in his chair, like a dog who expects a blow to fall any minute. "What do you want from me?" he whined.

"We have been examining your behavior. Until recently, in spite of your despicable job of sending our people to work in Germany, you have behaved more or less decently, but lately you have begun acting against our interests. You should really be shot, but we have decided to

---

*In Poland it is not unusual to leave one's office key in the outside lock of an inner office, both for convenience and as a sign that one is in.—*Tr.*

give you another chance. If you continue to work against us, your fate is sealed.''

"But I haven't been acting against your organization," he pleaded.

"Yes, you have," I shouted. "You are trying to turn one of your own workers over to the Gestapo."

"What? Me? To the Gestapo? That's a lie!" he protested.

"Yes, it is true," I said coldly; "You have been spreading rumors that your director in Kalwaria Zebrzydowska, Józek Górnik, is a Jew."

"But I was just joking, I swear it—that's just my little joke."

"It's no joke, you idiot," I said; "Górnik really *is* a Jew and is under our protection."

"My God, I had no idea of it!" he cried.

"Well, now you know," I continued relentlessly. "Górnik is a Jew, and I'll say it one more time: he is under our protection, and if so much as one hair falls from his head you'll be a dead director within twenty-four hours." I turned and headed for the door, but before unlocking it I whirled about and hissed at him, in a lower tone, "If you so much as mention our meeting to anyone, that's the last conversation you'll ever have on this earth." I stalked out of the office, banged the door shut, and whispered quickly to Tadek to keep a watch on Mann—if he should telephone after I left, find out to whom.

I left immediately for the estate. I had done what I could. Now all I could do was wait. Either the bluff would work or it would not: either the Gestapo would come for me or they would not. One day passed, and then a second. No one came to the estate. I decided my stratagem had succeeded. Mann was scared.

I telephoned Józek: "You can rest comfortably now; everything has been taken care of." He told me that the previous day he had received a telephone call from Mann, who had murmured over the phone, "Dearest Józek, I had no idea; I'm so sorry. Please forgive me." With these cryptic words, he hung up. And so the danger passed, and all was well for the present.

From that time on, Mann took care of Józek Górnik like his own brother—in fact, he even spread a rumor that Górnik was a relation of his. Once after this incident, when an inspection team from Cracow was coming to Kalwaria Zebrzydowska, he warned Józek about it the day before, and advised him to say that he was sick and to stay home. He was afraid that one of the inspectors might be suspicious, and remembered that his life depended on Józek's safety. The day of the inspection he himself went to Kalwaria and took the place of his "ailing" employee.

I was more relaxed now. Whenever Mann saw me on the street, he would either cross over to the other side or duck into an alley. From that time on I never had another conversation with him. What irony! Before that incident I had been afraid of being caught and tortured as a Jew; now I had the additional prospect of being imprisoned, tortured, and executed for belonging to the underground. I did not know which would be worse, but I had long since learned not to fret about trouble in advance. One had to let matters run their course and try to avoid danger only when it actually was sighted.

Basia's Encounter

At home in Borek Fałęcki the curtain of our apartment window was always drawn slightly to one side. At a touch it would fall back into place. That was our signal: whenever I came home I looked up at that window, and if the curtain was drawn aside I knew that I could enter in safety. Apart from her constant apprehension over my safety, Basia experienced "surprises" of her own at times, when I was in no position to intervene. One day she was walking down the street toward Swoszo-wice when she saw one of her old neighbors from the street where she was raised in Cracow coming toward her. They had known each other since childhood, although they had never been close friends.

Basia couldn't avoid the meeting. Frightened, she began to pray silently for God to help her somehow. Her old neighbor recognized her too, and surprise was written all over her face.

"Why hello, Miss Neulinger! What are you doing here?"

"I beg your pardon?"

"What do you mean? Don't you recognize me?"

"I'm afraid you've made a mistake."

"Don't be silly, Miss Neulinger. You don't have to pretend with me."

"I'm sorry, I'm afraid you've made a mistake. I don't know you." Basia walked on, and the woman stood looking back. Then slowly she too went on her way. At home, Basia burst into tears, shattered. Always open and straightforward, she was not used to playing such games.

Chapter 22

After the war she met her old neighbor again, and the woman asked, "Now do you recognize me, Miss Neulinger?"

"Of course I do, and I recognized you then too, but what did you expect? I wasn't going to lose my life over it!" The neighbor walked away in a huff without another word.

On another occasion in Borek Fałęcki Basia was crossing Zakopane Street near a small church. Some Jewish laborers in striped prison clothing were bent over cleaning out the gutter. When one of the female workers straightened up for a moment, she looked at Basia and then at Elusia, sitting in her baby carriage. Basia walked on by, her face drained of blood. That was the last she saw of Rózia, her eldest sister.

The war left its mark on both of us. We never watch war movies, never recall those times to each other, and never talk to our children about our experiences. Basia, today, knowing that I am writing down the history of those days, makes sure I have peace and quiet. Dawn often finds me at my typewriter. Sometimes she has to call me several times before I hear: "Bronek! Bronek! Time for breakfast!" And then I am jolted back to reality here in sunny California, separated from those nightmares by thousands of miles and more than thirty-five years.

Chapter 23

Mother's Last Wish

July passed, then August; in mid-September of 1943 we were in the midst of a golden autumn. Through my office window I saw a familiar figure in a forester's uniform coming over the fields, my brother Emil. I hurried out to meet him, for he did not make a habit of paying calls on me. He knew that I tried to avoid meeting friends and relatives on the estate grounds. Even in official meetings about wood supply quotas, some other forester would arrive to talk with me, not my brother. He told me that our mother had died that morning. Her burial was to take place two days later in the town of Kalwaria Zebrzydowska, outside Skawina, where she had been living with my sister and brother-in-law, the Górniks. My father had not been told yet, for he was away from home visiting Basia. We had been prepared for our mother's death for some time, but still it was painful news.

My first task was to go home to see my father before he left our apartment. I did not want him to come to the funeral lest he forget himself in his grief and give away his identity. I told Basia the news but asked her to keep it secret from my father for now, and then suggested to him that he stay with her for a few more days. She was about to have our second child, and I needed someone at home I could rely on while I was away at work. He could go for the midwife when the time came, care for little Elusia, and keep the household going. Father readily agreed.

As I returned to the estate I was thinking about the wish my mother expressed six months earlier, when she was still living in Skawina with the Górniks. At that time I received a phone call from Józek asking me to come over that very day if possible, and I did. "Mother hasn't gotten out of bed for a week," my sister Krysia told me worriedly. "She eats almost nothing and sleeps all day—actually, it's hard to say whether she is asleep or unconscious. You would think that she is unconscious except that from time to time she regains her senses. Since yesterday she has been asking to see a priest to confess. I think she's just raving, but she keeps bringing up the priest again and again. What do you think I should do?"

I looked in on Mother. As they said, she was either asleep or unconscious; there was no response to my greeting. I decided to take the opportunity to have a talk with Józek in the next room. Just then Krysia came in and whispered that Mother had wakened and wanted to see me. I sat on the edge of the bed and took her thin yellow hand in mine. She said, in a weak, faltering voice, "For two years now I've been nothing but a burden to all of you. I realize it and it makes me sad. Now I know I don't have much longer to live, but you mustn't worry about me. Think rather of yourselves. You must go on living. I feel in my heart that you will live to see the end of the war. As for me, I can only help in one way. I have thought this over for a long time. If I die without a priest in attendance, the neighbors will start gossiping."

She was quiet for a moment, trying to gather strength, then continued: "The priest is the representative of God—the same God in whom we all believe. I want you to bring a priest so that I may die like any Catholic. I need to make my peace with God, and it will give me comfort and strengthen my faith that you will all survive. I know what I am saying—you will all survive. I ask only one thing: when the war is over, if there are still Jewish cemeteries, I want to be moved to one. I don't want to be an outcast, lying where I have no right to be." She said one thing more, but so quietly that I couldn't understand her. Then she sank into a kind of sleep again. I kissed her hand and left the room.

I repeated our mother's request to Krysia—without mentioning her reasons—and promised to bring a priest to the house the following morning. I told her to lay the table in my mother's room with a white cloth and to have ready a bowl of water, candles, and an envelope with a donation for the church. When the priest arrived she was to light two candles.

Next day in the morning a priest came to give Mother the Sacraments. He was accompanied by an acolyte carrying a small lantern and bell. As he walked along the narrow street leading up to the Górniks' house people knelt at the sight of God's messenger. When he arrived, Mother was unconscious and could not be roused, so he anointed her with the chrism, prayed for her with all of us, and went away. Several days passed, and Mother seemed to feel better, as though the knowledge that her wish had been granted had been good for her, lifting a heavy burden from her heart. Now she was gone.

The Burial Procession

Kalwaria Zebrzydowska was a sleepy little town where, except in the pilgrimage season,* nothing ever happened. Consequently, the death of the mother-in-law of the head of the Arbeitsamt was something of an event. The day of the burial was bright and sunny, as though nature were trying to atone to my mother for all her days of sorrow. The air still felt like summer; there was no breeze, the sky was deep blue, most of the trees were still green, with only patches of purple and gold.

Almost the entire local population followed the coffin in a long procession to the cemetery outside town. At the head of the line a young acolyte held aloft a cross, almost too large for him to carry. Behind him walked the priest, eyes cast down, reading his breviary. Next came the people carrying the funeral wreaths, then the small pinewood coffin, borne by four husky men. Next to these pallbearers walked their reliefs, and alongside them, at the very edge of the road, the hired wailers.† After the coffin came Krysia and Józek, as next of kin, and after them the representatives of officialdom: in the center, the mayor; on his right, the chief of the German police force and his deputy; on his left, members of the Blue Police force, their chief, and his deputy; behind them, the representatives of the forestry service in neat green uniforms, in the persons of my brother Emil and Basia's cousin Bolek. Then came the employees of the Arbeitsamt, and finally, at the end of

---

*Kalwaria Zebrzydowska is the site of an old Bernardine monastery and the object of religious pilgrimages during the summer months.—*Tr.*

†In the Polish countryside, old women would often congregate around a funeral procession and offer effusive lamentations, in expectation of a small tip or a place at the meal after the funeral. A similar custom in Ireland is described by James Joyce in *Finnegans Wake.*—*Tr.*

the line, I walked with Cousin Ala, her young friends, and a motley group of idlers and the curious from town.

Every two or three hundred meters the procession halted, the priest turned and faced the coffin, the relief pallbearers took over the load, and the hired wailers raised their voices in loud lamentations. Then the procession would move on. I tried to concentrate on the ceremony, but all I could see from my spot at the end of the line were the fat gray behinds of the German police, their overstuffed breeches straining over their haunches, shifting their weight heavily from one foot to the other like drafthorses.

When we arrived at the cemetery, the crowd ahead of me gathered round the grave, blocking it from my view, and the priest began to extoll the virtues of the deceased. None of this could I hear very well from the rear, and I suddenly needed to get away. Unnoticed, I took a side path out of the cemetery. Beyond stretched golden fields of stubble from the recent harvest; farther on there was a small stand of trees. I walked over to the grove and lay down in the shade. A light breeze began to relieve the September heat.

I felt exhausted. Lately I had been feeling immensely weary, perhaps because I had not been sleeping well at night. I would toss and turn, trying to keep one eye open, and when I did sleep, I sometimes dreamt that the Gestapo had caught me and I was trying to get away, but my legs were leaden and I could not run, or that I was trying to hide but could not because I was wearing my armband with the Star of David, or that I was being dragged away by the Germans, leaving everyone I loved behind.

I thought about the funeral dreamily. Had those fat-bottomed representatives of law and order really been there, or had I hallucinated them in the midst of my Jewish mother's funeral procession? Had my mother really been buried in a Catholic cemetery at the site of a holy pilgrimage? Was the director of the Arbeitsamt really my brother-in-law Józek? Our cousin Ala his scullery maid? My brother a forester? And I manager of the Potocki estate? Did the mayor really believe in the Nazis? Did the police believe in Hitler? Perhaps they were all part of a giant hoax—perhaps *they* were all Jews too!

Somewhat inappropriately, a joke popular in Warsaw before the war came to mind. After the unsuccessful Warsaw uprising against the Russians in 1863, the Tsarist government severely repressed the instigators, most of whom came from the nobility. As a way of humiliating their owners, many of the oldest noble names were given to Jews. Half a century later, in the period between the two world wars, General Sławek-Składkowski, the prime minister, with the support of the marshal (speaker) of the Senate, Alexander Prystor, helped to start an anti-Jewish boycott. Jewish stores were boycotted and picketed, and the slogan of the day was "Don't buy from a Jew!" While all this was taking place, a petty landowner with a noble name, in Warsaw on a visit, took a walk down Marszałkowska Street (the main business thoroughfare) and saw pickets around the stores. This in itself did not surprise him, but what he could not understand was why storeowners with aristocratic names like Potocki, Lubomirski, and Zamoyski were being picketed, so he went into Potocki's shop. Behind the counter sat an old Jew with a long beard. The landowner, completely baffled, asked him: "Excuse me, are you Potocki?"

The Jew nodded his head.

"And that Lubomirski across the street, is he also a Jew?"

"Yes."

"And Zamoyski next door?"

"Yes, he is too," the old man answered.

"Jesus Christ of Nazareth!" exclaimed the landowner.

"He also," the old Jew answered calmly.

What would these policemen say if they knew that they were participating today in a Jewish funeral, that they were surrounded by Jews—in front, in back, in the rear, and on the sides? What would the priest say who praised my mother so highly without knowing her? Or the hired wailers, lamenting the loss of a Jewess? For that matter, who could imagine that I, a Jew, would be threatening a German, director of the Arbeitsamt, with death unless he looked after the safety of a Jewish worker? Perhaps everything really was a dream.

Helena

As I lay there on the grass, Basia's sister Helena came into my mind. After her daughter Ritulka died and her husband was taken to Oświęcim, Helena was placed in a forced labor camp in Tarnów. When the family heard about this, I went there to see whether it might be possible to get her out. When I arrived, I spent two hours surveying the camp. It was surrounded by three rows of barbed-wire fence guarded by

Latvian soldiers. I bribed one of them to let me inside, despite a horrible fear that I myself would never walk out of the gate again, and promised him more money when I left. My story was that I was a merchant trying to buy valuables cheap from the Jewish prisoners. When I found Helena, I tried to persuade her to leave; I asked her, reasoned with her, begged her. I swore that there was no danger: I had bribed the guard and I had Basia's identification papers with me; the two of us would simply walk out together.

She listened to all this, and her answer was, "Why? What for? Ritulka is dead. My husband probably is dead too. You have enough trouble on your hands without me. You've already saved my mother, my brother, and his wife. What more do you want? Your wife is my sister— I don't want to put you both in danger. As for me, life no longer has any value." She continued in this vein, despite all my arguments and entreaties. On my way out alone I passed the Latvian guard. Although he thought I was a Pole and a blackmarketeer, and was waiting for his money, I was terrified. I kept thinking, what would happen if they changed guards? What would happen if I couldn't get out?

After I was safely away from the camp I needed a cigarette, but my hands were shaking too much to light it. I am not cut out for these heroics, I thought. I am really a coward at heart. I'm like a soldier who loses control over his actions in the heat of battle through fright, performs insane deeds of valor, and is then decorated for bravery. My dying mother had told me she was sure we would survive the war. I tried to believe it. I reminded myself that today was September 17, 1943. We had survived four years of war, four years of privation and struggle. Mother had believed; I had always trusted her, so I too must believe.

By the time I got back to the cemetery everyone had left. The little grave was covered with earth and a cross stood at the head. A small plaque on the cross gave the name, the date of birth, and the date of death: this was all that remained of my mother. I began to pray silently: "Mother, you knew so little joy in life; but you never asked anything for yourself. Only in your final illness did a request pass your lips—that you be buried among your own, in a place that was yours by right, where no one could scorn you. I swear that it will be as you asked. Rest in peace here for now." I took a handful of earth and sprinkled it over the grave. After the war, my mother's remains were exhumed and transferred to Cracow, where she now rests in the old Jewish cemetery on Miodowa Street.

Irena's Christening

Five days after my mother's death and three days after her funeral, our second child, Irena, was born. Basia wanted a son, but I felt that things were fine just as they were. As I explained to my wife, the fewer boys there were in the world, the fewer wars. Women somehow knew how to relieve their feelings without coming to blows. The baby was beautiful. I helped the midwife deliver her, then sat up with Basia all that night before returning to work on the estate. My younger daughter received two first names, Irena, for her godmother Irena Misiołek, and Ewa, for my mother. She proved to be very quiet and well behaved; she just ate, slept, and grew.

Several weeks passed, and it was high time to christen the baby. The neighbors were beginning to ask why we were putting it off. The reason, of course, was simple: as I mentioned, I had no marriage certificate to present to the parish office, and I was not sure how to get around this difficulty. The young countess again came to my aid. One day, while we were chatting, she asked, "When do you intend to christen your baby?" Seeing my hesitation, she added, "Jerzy would like very much to be the godfather, if you wouldn't object."

I confided to her the reason for the delay; the countess thought for a moment and then said, "Don't worry about a thing. That's not important; what matters is that the child be christened. Leave the rest to my husband. The priest will write down whatever Jerzy dictates to him."

Two weeks later, on a Sunday, my daughter's christening took place in the parish church in Borek Fałęcki. Half the estate workers appeared for the occasion, dressed in holiday garb, the girls in colorful peasant costumes. The carriage horses were specially washed and curried and their manes decorated with ribbons. Right after Mass that day, Father Wieczorek announced that the newborn daughter of Mr. and Mrs. Szatyn was to be christened, and that the godparents were Irena Misiołek, from Borek Fałęcki, and Count Jerzy Potocki, from Borek Szlachecki. Most of the parishioners stayed on for the ceremony, curious to see Count Potocki and to be witnesses. The young count walked down the aisle carrying Irena in his arms, with Irena Misiołek at his side. After Father Wieczorek performed the christening, the count handed the baby to Mrs. Misiołek, took a tiny box from his pocket, and placed a golden cross and chain around her neck. Basia took the baby from Irena while the count went to the sacristy with the priest and dictated all the necessary information concerning the newborn, its natural parents and godparents. Father Wieczorek did not ask to see any documents; the word of the count was good enough for him.

The ceremony concluded with a small dinner. Our daughter wore her cross as a talisman throughout her youth. She only removed it upon her marriage, when her new husband placed a gift of his own around her neck. I preserve this cross and chain today as evidence of the nobility of human nature.

Chapter 24

Visit to the Mountaineers

The winter of 1943-44 was upon us, the fifth winter of this war. The Nazis were on a rampage, looking for foreign workers to replace the Germans sent to the front, so we began looking early for laborers for the following season. We had already learned from the Arbeitsamt (more precisely, from our friend Tadek Słomka) that it would be unable to provide us with enough workers. Tadek advised me to try to obtain farmhands from the Mountaineers ("Górale") near Zakopane. The Nazis had decreed the Mountaineers to be a separate "race," which they called *Goralenvolk*. Tadek told me that the pressure to send workers to Germany was less severe in the Mountaineers' area than in ours.*

I opened a lengthy correspondence with the *Goralenvolk* in Zakopane, and the latter finally agreed to provide us with eight to ten village girls for the following season. I made contact with the proper village authorities, and we arranged that I would meet them in the first part of December to conclude our agreement. On the appointed day I left the estate before daybreak and took the train to Poronin, the nearest

---

*The Górale speak a distinctive Polish dialect transitional to Slovak. Capitalizing on Slovak nationalistic yearnings, the Nazis had established a separate Slovak puppet state across the border. By considering the Górale to be a separate Slavic "race," "uncontaminated" (by Jews and Gypsies), and by granting them special considerations, the Nazis hoped to appeal to similar sentiments among these mountain folk. Indeed there was a certain amount of pro-Nazi sympathy among the Górale.—*Tr.*

railroad station to my prospective workers' village. I had been unwell for several days and felt languid and weak, but the appointment had been made so far in advance that I felt obliged to keep it. I thought that I probably would not find a place inside the train and might have to ride on the steps, so I bundled up warmly.

I arrived in Poronin in the afternoon. The weather was fine, bright and sunny, but the mountains, fields, and roads were covered with a thick layer of fresh snow from a storm on the preceding evening. I couldn't find a sleigh at the station to take me to the meeting place, high on a hill above the railroad station, so I had to set out on foot. Before long I had to leave the main road and take off across the countryside, heading straight uphill. It was incredibly hard going through the deep fresh snow; time and again I sank up to my waist. All the while the sun grew hotter and hotter, until I took off my sheepskin coat, then my jacket, and finally my sweater. At last I even unbuttoned my shirt. A light breeze blew from time to time, but it made no difference: I grew hotter by the minute. It took more than two hours to make the climb up the mountain.

The Mountaineers were waiting for me. They apologized for not coming down to meet me, explaining that the snow was too deep even for a sleigh to get through. We arranged all the formalities promptly. Night fell quickly in the mountains, and I began to tremble and shake even in the warm cabin where I had been housed for the night. During the night I lost consciousness, causing my hosts no little anxiety. By morning the road had been cleared sufficiently for them to carry me down the mountain. The fresh air revived me somewhat during the trip. The villagers wanted to take me to the local hospital, but when I realized that there they would undoubtedly undress me, I categorically refused and demanded to be taken to the train station.

I was delirious all the way home, alternating between waking and sleeping. I asked the passengers sitting near me to rouse me when we came to the stop at Cracow-Swoszowice, and fortunately they remembered to do so, but they had to shout and shake me for a long time before I could be wakened. They even had to help me off the train.

The snow was deep everywhere. I did not want to walk along the road, for the trip was farther that way, so I decided to try to take a shortcut across a field. I was so dizzy that I kept falling and picking myself up again, at times even dragging myself along on all fours. Finally, I stopped making the effort to get up again. I crawled home, resting every few minutes, guided by a single thought: "Don't lose consciousness; home is just ahead; then you can rest." The distance from the station to our house was not more than three hundred meters, but it took me at least two hours to crawl there. I don't even remember opening the door to the building and crawling up to our apartment door. After several attempts, I managed to reach the latch. Basia heard a noise outside the door, opened it, and there I was hanging onto the latch. The sight of her and the children deprived me of my last strength, and I fell unconscious.

I was in a delirium from an advanced case of influenza for two weeks. My temperature was so high that everyone despaired for my life, and worried about brain damage should I ever recover. When the fever at last broke and I regained some semblance of consciousness, I remember saying to myself over and over, "I have to get well. I am needed desperately; I *can't* die and leave everything to chance; I simply *must* get well." I am convinced that it was this thought which tipped the scales in my favor and returned me to life. Two more weeks passed before I became aware of my surroundings again, but I was still unable to move my arms or legs or even lift my head. I knew that I was lying in my own bed, ill and helpless, with Basia bustling about somewhere, but that was all. I remained sunk in a stupor; this state of semi-consciousness lasted for another week. Finally I began to notice things around me, albeit feebly and lethargically. I heard the sound of our children at play and my wife's voice, and sometimes I could even make out single words. Eventually I could understand what people were saying to me.

I now found that I had been unconscious for almose five weeks, and that it would be a month or more before I could expect to be completely well. Several days later a doctor came to see me. He had called on me several times during my illness, but I had no recollection of these visits. He was satisfied with my progress but recommended that I stay in bed for another couple of weeks. Even before the trip to Zakopane I had been in very poor physical and mental condition because of lack of sleep, my constant nighttime travel, and a multitude of worries; this illness had drained the last drop of my strength.

Little by little my health improved, and after two weeks I felt strong enough to get up, but it was fully ten weeks before I could make a first tentative visit to my office at the estate. I stayed there only one day before returning home. I was simply too weak to work, and it was two weeks more before I was strong enough to resume my responsibilities. It was now March. All had gone well on the estate in my absence. The new steward had managed very well alone, and any urgent administrative decisions had been made by the Potockis themselves. Fortunately, in midwinter there was not much work to be done on the farm. By the middle of March the Mountaineers I had hired arrived for the seasons's work.

My nearly three-month absence had been noted and commented on variously. Those on the estate knew that I was really ill and had no suspicions on that account, as did some others in the neighborhood, but most people suspected that my disappearance had political overtones and was connected with a recent marked increase in Partisan activity in the neighborhood. I was pleased that everything had functioned so well during my absence, for I saw that nothing stood in my way: it was time to leave the estate. My departure was all the more urgent because I had received several more warnings about the rumors that I was in the underground. At this rate, I thought, it was only a matter of time before I would be arrested by the Nazis.

Now I went to Wasenda's firebrick factory almost daily to monitor the news of the BBC. The factory continued to be the safest place to listen to the radio. The SS couldn't uncover our operation, since it was their own installation. Whenever they were called out on a "mission," Wasenda immediately turned on the set and we listened to the programs in utmost security. If the troops returned unexpectedly, a cooperative Czech guard at the gate would warn us by pressing a buzzer that sounded softly inside the building. We heard that Hitler's armies were suffering defeat on all fronts. Increasingly we heard talk of the imminent attack of the Allies on central Europe. The bombing of German cities had been stepped up: the British specialized in night raids, while the Americans attacked in broad daylight in such numbers that the German anti-aircraft batteries could no long protect the targets. Many German towns were already in ruins. Berlin was the prime target for these attacks, and almost daily the bombers were reducing the city to rubble, district by district. In the east, the Russians had at last routed the Germans from around Leningrad; the German northern army was in full retreat, and things were not going much better for them in the southeast. They were withdrawing from the Ukraine, the Crimea, and Wolynia—in short, they were on the run.

A Nazi Tea Party

Around five o'clock one day early in April, our maid ran into my office and announced in a frightened voice that two Nazi policemen in an open car had just driven into the courtyard of the estate. They were still sitting in their armored car when I went out to meet them. "Who are you?" one of them asked, as he climbed out of the vehicle. I gave him my name.

"Your occupation?"

I told him. "You're under arrest."

I was hardly prepared for this turn of events. It did not seem that they had really come to arrest me, for they asked my occupation, which would have been part of the dossier of a wanted man. Besides, they carried their machine guns so carelessly, like pieces of extra luggage, that their actions did not match their words.

I told myself not to be panicky. I forced a smile and said fine, if they wanted me they could have me, but first wouldn't they come inside? They made me enter the house first. Instead of taking them to my office on the ground floor, I led them upstairs to the Potockis' private quarters. The count was not at home; he had gone away on business the previous day. Only the countess was in the house. Hearing their heavy tread on the staircase, she came out of her drawing room to see who was there.

She saw me first. I must have looked very pale as I whispered to her that I was under arrest. Behind me the policemen pushed into the room. The first officer now barked at the countess, "Who are you?"

"I am Countess Potocki," she answered coolly.

"Where is your husband?"

"He is away on business," she calmly replied.

"You are under arrest too!"

Evidently the countess had sized up the situation, for she did not change her expression, and calmly replied that though she might be under arrest, she had no intention of disrupting her daily routine. It was now time for afternoon tea. Would the officers care to be seated and have a bite to eat?

At first the Nazis protested, but in the end they sat down. I had had no personal experience with the Nazis' manner of arrest, but I was familiar enough with their usual mistrust mixed with brutality and nervous excitement. The present "arrest" seemed odd, but one never knew. "Please ask the maid to set three more places," the countess told me.

256

Chapter 24

When I started to leave the room, the Germans made no attempt to stop me. Out in the hall, my first thought was to take my chance and flee that minute, but I realized that I could not leave the countess behind in that dangerous situation; besides, if I had this chance to escape, there would doubtless be another. In any case, how far could I get? And the very act of flight would show that I had something to fear.

In the kitchen all was in a hubbub. Trying to behave naturally, I asked the cook to prepare five o'clock tea for four people—the kind of a tea that *Germans* would enjoy, I said. She needed no further hint. I went back upstairs to find the countess sitting elegantly on a sofa while the two policemen lounged at the tea table, their machine guns propped against the wall, peacefully smoking the countess' own cigarettes. Soon the chambermaid brought in the tea tray. There was smoked sausage, slices of ham, butter, cheese, and two bottles of fruit-flavored vodka, along with a pot of tea.

Our "guests" fell on the tray, sweeping the table clean of whatever they could get a fork into, while the countess and I picked at our own food nervously. The policemen began to joke and laugh boisterously. As the level in the vodka bottle dropped, their faces grew redder and their voices louder; one might have thought they were sitting in the post canteen.

"How did you like our little joke?" one of them asked suddenly.

"What joke?" asked the countess.

"Oh, you know, that we came to arrest you."

The officer sputtered with laughter at his own joke, while the other guffawed with him. In a few minutes they managed to recover, and spoke more to the point. They had been having trouble lately riding in their open car, one explained, for they were vulnerable to an ambush. On several occasions they had actually been fired upon. They had come to the estate to requisition our carriage because they felt that a closed vehicle would be safer to travel in.

So that was it! An expression of relief swept across our faces. A moment of uncomfortable silence ensued. Then the countess very politely informed them that she would be happy to oblige, but that there was only one closed carriage on the estate, and it was the only one she could ride in—she was pregnant (as they could see for themselves), and that carriage was the only one with rubber tires. However, she promised to ask our neighbors whether any one had the sort of conveyance they required.

257

Seeing the looks of disappointment spreading across their red faces, I jumped into the conversation. "If I may say so, it seems to me that these gentlemen enjoyed our modest fare just now, and I dare say they might appreciate having something for the journey as well."

I rushed down to the kitchen and told the cook to put together two large packages of food and to take them out to the car. When I returned, the officers were just rising from the table and adjusting their belts, which they had loosened at the sight of all that good food. They picked up their guns, saluted us both, and, wobbling slightly, tramped down the stairs. I went out to the car with them and stood waving after them as they drove away.

When I returned to the house, the countess was still standing by the drawing room window smoking a cigarette, with white face and trembling hands. Her recent strength had suddenly vanished. We did not say a single word to each other: what could we say?

I went outdoors to get some air: nature was always the best medicine for me when I felt upset. It was quiet and peaceful in the fields; only the skylarks continued their evening trill. As I walked aimlessly along a path I realized that I could not delay my decision any longer: I had to put an end to a situation which kept the Potockis in constant trepidation and fear. Until now in my heart I had believed that liberation was almost at hand, after which I could come out of hiding. It would be dangerous to leave the peaceful and secluded estate for the unknown world outside. Where could I go? However, the events today showed me clearly that my behavior was indefensible. At the very least I was exposing people who had been kind to me to unwarranted terror.

I did not wish to say this to the countess; instead, I decided to put my resignation in a different light. Next day after breakfast I told her that I was still too weak to endure the kind of incident we experienced yesterday, and that I thought I would benefit from a short leave of absence. The countess didn't reply; possibly she was glad to hear the news. Very likely she and her husband had already discussed the matter; after all, they knew as well as I the penalty for harboring a Jew.

I asked the steward to bring a wagon to Borek Fałęcki, for I was going on vacation and wanted him to take us to our destination. I added that he was to keep this quiet. He understood. He had doubtless heard rumors of my "underground" activities and probably took this as a sign that I was dropping out of sight. He promised that he would come by for us.

Chapter 24

I left Borek Szlachecki on Friday evening, seeing the estate and the Potockis for the last time. I had spent more than three years there: it still remains etched in my memory—its fields, buildings, stables, barns, greenhouses, granaries, the house, and the grave of my beloved Gypsy. Even today, so many years later, I can smell the earth and remember every one of the people—their faces, gestures, mannerisms, everything.

The Potockis in particular have remained indelibly impressed on my memory. The old count: beneath his bluff exterior of arch-conservatism he was truly a noble spirit—just, generous, and self-effacing, a man who went into debt rather than deprive his workers of food to eat and a roof over their heads. The young countess: she gave me her photograph, which I treasure to this day—there she looks out at me with beautiful expressive eyes, enveloped in an abundance of luxurious blond hair. She was intelligent and wise beyond her years, kind, sensitive, direct, always willing to help others—a golden personality. And Count Jerzy—even if nature did not endow him with any particular strength of character, his instinctive kindness and nobility more than made up for it. I not only respected him but also liked him very, very much.

The scant information I could gather from abroad after the war was that even after the incursion of the Russian troops old Count Antoni continued to live on his estate at Olsza unmolested. But for the young count and countess, new times had come. Jerzy, by training an agronomist, left Borek Szlachecki for a job teaching urban gardening in Katowice. I heard that the countess was studying theatrical directing in Lódź. The sympathy and warmth which I felt for the Potockis has not diminished with the passing years. Writing about them today, I see them before me, just as they were then.

Chapter 25

Kalwaria Zebrzydowska

Sunday morning the steward arrived in a peasant wagon strewn with straw, and Basia, the children, my mother-in-law, and I piled in. We drove to Kalwaria Zebrzydowska, the only place I knew where I felt safe. I told our landlady, Mrs. Proszkowski, that I had received a vacation bonus and was taking my family to a resort in Wieliczka, a town in the opposite direction from Kalwaria. Kalwaria Zebrzydowska was really an overgrown village of no more than three thousand inhabitants, most of whom were farmers, furniture makers, or manufacturers of religious items for the summer pilgrims. Because of the fresh air and the abundance of rooms to rent, the town was something of a resort. I rented two tiny rooms in a pretty house on a hill overlooking a woods.

Since it was not yet pilgrimage season, I had no trouble finding lodgings. No one but the steward knew that I was in Kalwaria. I trusted the man and knew that he was grateful to me personally for hiring him and helping his family, and that he was glad to be able to return a favor. Even if someone came looking for me at the estate, the steward was probably the last person anyone would think of asking. He came to Kalwaria once a week during the entire period we were there, bringing us supplies of food and bread baked by his wife.

Now I cut off all contacts with the outside world, even the Górniks, although I did visit my brother-in-law at his office and learned the latest news through him, especially the tidings from the Eastern

Front. I calculated that if nothing prevented the Russian advance, the Red Army would be in Poland in another three or four months. We had survived more than four years; surely we would manage to make it through this final stretch as well.

Dragnet

One day I was returning from the nearby town of Lanckorona, where I often went to buy food, on my bicycle, with a dozen eggs in a string bag hung carefully over the handlebars. As I turned down the road leading to our house, a voice rang out from the bushes: "Hände hoch!" ("Hands up!"). I turned my head and saw the barrel of a rifle pointing at me out of the shrubbery along the road. Calmly I dismounted and explained, in German, that the voice was asking the impossible: how could I raise my hands while riding a bicycle? At the very least I would break the eggs I was carrying.

Out of the underbrush stepped a man of around fifty pointing a rifle. I recognized him as one of the recently mobilized German "old-timers" that were now being used to snare Poles for forced labor in Germany. I introduced myself, said that I was the manager of an important estate, and that I was working for the Germans (he had no way of checking this statement, of course). In other words, I explained, he and I were on the same side. I showed the man my stamped permit issued by the Cracow District Police Department and pointed out that it had been signed by the district director himself just so that I would not encounter difficulties.

The old soldier lowered his rifle and calmed down. I leaned my bicycle against a tree, carefully placed the sack of eggs on the grass, and offered him a cigarette. I was purposely prolonging the conversation in order to find out as much as possible about his mission, for I was certain that he had not dropped out of the sky onto my road all by himself. I learned that he was from the Tyrol and indeed had just been mobilized, as I had suspected. He and a dozen or so others like him had been assigned to help the SS in a manhunt in the area. He was at the very end of the party; the leader, a Sturmführer, was farther down the road with the main group. Most of the others were guarding Poles who had already been caught. He advised me that if I were heading in that direction I should go straight to the Sturmführer and show him my papers.

I thanked him and bicycled on. In a few moments I spotted the main dragnet several hundred meters ahead. The SS men were walking down the middle of the road with their machine guns at the ready. In their midst their leader, a tall young officer holding a revolver, marched along proudly. At the side of the road, under guard, the captured Poles were being herded along. The manhunt proceeded slowly, stopping again and again as the SS men fell upon the houses along the way and dragged out their weeping and wailing inhabitants.

I bicycled straight up to the Sturmführer; at the sound of my bicycle bell he wheeled around. I repeated my story, as the old soldier advised. He was listening intently when a sudden shout from one of the houses and then a commotion diverted his attention. He impatiently waved me on, then ran toward the house. I continued down the road. There was nothing I could do to save those already captured, but I intended to warn anyone else I could find. As soon as I was out of earshot, I began yelling that a roundup was under way back down the road. When I came to a house, I ran in and shouted my warning. Alfred Sęczkowski was at that moment standing in front of a mirror shaving. On hearing my warning shout he dropped his razor in the sink, leaped out the window with his face still half-lathered, and disappeared into the bushes. His wife, who was in bed, hid herself under a large feather comforter. When the Germans arrived her husband was gone, and she was moaning that she was in labor, about to give birth. The soldiers left her alone and went away.

The Sęczkowskis

A bit of explanation is in order here. I had met the Sęczkowskis not long before in the woods, out hiking with my family. When they crossed our path we stopped, introduced ourselves, and chatted a bit. They were from Łódź, they said, and were spending their vacation in Kalwaria not far from us. Lola Sęczkowski was around thirty, with brown hair, a pleasant, lively disposition, and a keen sense of humor. Her husband looked past forty. He was shorter than his wife, with a large elongated head and thick horn-rimmed glasses. He always wore long trousers, a jacket, and a tie, even when strolling in the forest. He struck me as something of a milksop: when he spoke he drawled out each syllable interminably and in general, I thought, behaved in a thoroughly artificial, almost theatrical, manner. Whenever I met him in the woods after that, he would bow politely—with exaggerated politeness, it always seemed to me. If I were on my bicycle I would never stop to chat—I just did not care to get into a conversation with him, for some reason. And this was the person whose house I had run to, to warn of a German roundup!

Two weeks passed, and once again I was on my way to town on my bicycle. There was Sęczkowski standing in the middle of the path blocking my way. I had to stop. "I'm very sorry to take up your valuable time, sir," Sęczkowski began, "but I desperately require your assistance." I didn't like this overture but waited to hear the rest.

"You see," he continued, in his drawling way, "I must begin by confiding to you that I'm a Jew."

I was astounded to hear such a confession from a mere acquaintance. I might have guessed that he was a Jew, but why was he stopping me in the middle of the woods to tell me that? It seemed to me that I had more than enough troubles of my own without being burdened with the confidences of this boring old phoney.

"Why the hell are you telling this to me?" I snapped at him. "What business is it of mine? Take your sins to the priest, not to me!"

I started to get back on my bicycle and pedal away, but he grabbed the handlebars. "Please don't be angry with me. I really do need your help. I had to go to the Arbeitsamt the other day to register. When I showed my identification card to the director, he acted as though something was wrong. I am sure he knew that my identification was false; I haven't slept for three nights worrying about it. I saw you talking to him a few days ago and thought that he must be a friend of yours. Could you please smooth things over for me? You seem to be a decent person who would not betray a fellow human being."

I stared at him in disbelief, wondering how he had managed to survive this long. If he blurted out his identity to any passerby as he had to me, he was extremely lucky to be alive. As I listened to his revelations I was stalling for time. When he finished, I told him he was mistaken. "It's true I was walking down the street with the director of the Arbeitsamt the other day," I said, "but I don't know him well, probably no better than you do. As far as your problem is concerned, if they were going to come for you or cause any trouble, you may be sure that they would not have waited this long. Since nothing has happened to you so far, your fears must be imaginary. My only advice to you, if you value your life, is to hold your tongue. No one needs to know your innermost secrets." With that, I said a gruff goodbye and rode on my way.

Several days passed before I saw Józek again. When I did, I asked him straight out whether he remembered Sęczkowski.

"You mean that character with the false papers?" he said.

"How did you know?" I was amazed at his clairvoyance.

"Simple," Józek answered. "He must have gotten his *Kennkarte* the same place you got mine. You can imagine my surprise when I looked at it and saw the same information that I have on my own, right down to the address, 22 Tomasz Street. Besides, this Sęczkowski is dumb enough to say he comes from Lódź; then he shows me a *Kennkarte* issued in Cracow."

Only then did I tell Józek about my conversation with Sęczkowski. He admitted that he made a mistake by showing surprise when he examined the false papers and asked me to reassure that idiot somehow. I promised that I would try. I saw Sęczkowski several times after that but did not talk with him until a week or so later, when I met the couple out for a walk. I got off my bicycle, and we chatted casually about one thing and another. Finally, as I was leaving, I said to Sęczkowski, as if as an afterthought, "I told you you had a sick imagination. I ran into the director of the Arbeitsamt yesterday and mentioned you in passing. He didn't even remember your name." I rode off and from then on made a point of avoiding those people.

Chapter 26

The Front Moves

After a stop to regroup, the Soviet armies in the fall of 1944 were once more on the move. I was in a constant state of excitement. With an old map borrowed from Józek on my lap, I would sit for hours in the woods trying to calculate where and when the Russians would break through. In the south, the territory in which I was most interested, towns were falling to the Russians one after the other— Lwów, Drohobycz, Przemyśl, Jarosław, Sanok, Rzeszów. But then the Russians came to a halt between Rzeszów and Tarnów. They were not more than a hundred and fifty kilometers away, but I, who had been expecting to be free in a week or two at the most, had to reconcile myself to the fact that I must be patient and even more cautious than ever.

Our steward continued to visit me faithfully once a week, bringing not only food but news. Unfortunately, none of it was good. He did not know what the Potockis believed, but everyone else took it for granted that I had gone away to join the underground. For the moment no one was looking for me, and work on the estate was proceeding as normally as could be expected when everyone's mind was on the Eastern Front. He had no idea what the Potockis would do when the Russians came, but he himself planned to stay, he said. Where else could he go? Doubtless most of the other farm workers felt the same way. In the meantime, the German labor roundups and dragnets went on daily.

My only remaining pleasure was to ride into town to visit Józek in the Arbeitsamt. There we read newspapers and shared the latest news from the front. Soon, however, even this treat had to come to an end, for Joachim Mann, Józek's supervisor, had begun checking up on him frequently, and a run-in with Mann at this time would have been dangerous for me. I was now convinced that he was the one responsible for spreading rumors about my underground activities. For example, I heard that one day in Kalwaria he ran into Zdrzałka, a forester he knew from the time when I worked at Borek Szlachecki. During their conversation he asked Zdrzałka excitedly whether he had heard the latest news—that Szatyn, manager of the estate at Borek Szlachecki, had run away to join the underground. "You have no idea, Mr. Zdrzałka, what a dangerous sort that Szatyn is," he blustered. "He'd stab you in the back as soon as look at you. I had a run-in with him once, and I'll be just as glad to see the end of him."

Mann would have been horrified to learn that he was confiding in none other than the dangerous fellow's brother, and that I was close by at that very moment. In any case, my visits to the Arbeitsamt ended, but I still could not resist stealing over to the Górniks at night for scraps of news, from which I pieced together my picture of the progress of the war.

However, another matter now demanded my attention. As I mentioned, our house was at the edge of the forest. The living conditions were quite primitive, but that did not bother Basia or me. We were young, the late autumn weather was pleasant, and we spent most of the day outdoors, returning home only for meals and to sleep. It was a different matter for my mother-in-law, however. Her entire world was circumscribed by her narrow little room, constantly invaded by the screams and shouts of our landlady, Duscyna, who was bringing up two orphans and was always either swearing at them or beating them. My mother-in-law, a kindly woman, could not stand these scenes, and I knew that she was longing to get back to the peace of our home in Borek Fałęcki.

At first I was hesitant to take her back, for my address there was well known, but the front had stopped and one never knew when it would get started again and how long we would have to remain hidden in Kalwaria, so I decided to do so. Mrs. Proszkowski was overjoyed at her return, for her life had been a lonely one since we left. I was not worried about food, for Basia's mother had all five of our family's ration cards, and Mrs. Proszkowski promised to do all the shopping for her.

When I returned to Kalwaria, I told our landlady that we were giving up our rooms and moving back to Cracow; actually we moved to an out-of-the-way village near Lanckorona, in this way covering our tracks once again. The estate steward no longer knew where I was living, for I had instructed him to leave our food packages with a shopkeeper I knew in Lanckorona. With him I exchanged some of the food brought by the steward for other items I needed. The shopkeeper did not know my real name—I had given him a false one—nor did he know where I was staying nor when I was likely to drop by, for I never came twice at the same time. Not even my mother-in-law in Borek Fałęcki had any notion that we had moved. Fearing that these next weeks before the final German defeat would be the hardest, I began employing the same extreme security precautions that I took at the beginning. I cut myself off from the world and resolved to sit and wait patiently, hard as that was on our nerves.

Partisans

During this lull my only entertainment was to visit the Górniks to get the news. The Nazis were on a rampage: for all practical purposes the Arbeitsamt had ceased to function; the Germans were simply grabbing people off the streets or tearing them out of their houses. On the other hand, partisan activity was also on the upsurge. Large, well-armed bands of guerrillas were engaged in reconnoitering and then blowing up bridges, railway lines, supply dumps, and so on. Most likely these bands were Russian, for they never made contact with the local population; they struck and disappeared. Besides these guerrillas, local partisan groups were active in regions they knew well, attacking and disarming German units and requisitioning food from estates.

Any German capable of carrying a weapon had been sent to the insatiable Eastern Front. In their place, to guard the farms directly managed by the Germans, the Nazis stationed either Germans too old to fight or detachments of volunteers whose battle-readiness was questionable. Among the latter were Ukrainians as well as volunteer corps from Baltic states such as Latvia, Lithuania, and Estonia. These Nazi "warriors" were invariably commanded by SS officers. Some German-run estates adopted a policy of not resisting the partisan attacks. The soldiers would lock themselves up in their rooms and let the partisans rummage around wherever they wanted. In such cases the partisans did not attack the soldiers, and the Germans did not fire on them either. However, when the Germans tried to defend themselves by firing on the partisans and were overwhelmed, there was no pardon or pity. They were forced to undress and hand over their uniforms, boots, and weapons. The rank-and-file German soldiers were usually let go, but all SS men, Ukrainians, Baltic volunteers, and the like were summarily executed.

It was a grim battle, with many victims on both sides. German military patrols more and more kept to the main roads and feared to go into the smaller villages or the mountains. Along the more heavily traveled roads I used my work permit stating that I was the estate manager at Borek Szlachecki. Outside Lanckorona and nearer to home I put this away and showed only my identification card, for the Germans were afraid to set foot here and my challenges would come from partisans.

One day I was on my way home on my bicycle when a partisan "policeman" appeared on the road and flagged me down. He was dressed in a long German overcoat and boots and a civilian cap and was pointing a German automatic rifle at me. "Halt!" he cried. I rode up to him, stopped, and got off. Out of a ditch by the side of the road crawled several other partisans, wearing various bits and pieces of German uniforms and carrying a strange assortment of weapons.

"Are you Polish?" asked the one who stopped me.

"No, Chinese," I answered.

"Oh, a wise guy, hey? You know, I could easily shoot you right here and now." The voice came from behind me. I turned and saw a young partisan around twenty years old, dressed like the others in German boots and military overcoat, but with a black beret with a silver star indicating that he was a second lieutenant. Next to the star was a red-and-white ribbon. I concluded that he must be their leader.

"If your man calls out to me in Polish and I answer him in Polish, then the conclusion must be that I'm Polish," I said.

"That doesn't prove a thing. You could just as easily be a German Silesian or a Góral. They speak Polish too."

"That is true, Lieutenant, but I don't have a Silesian or Góral accent," I replied.

"Well then you could be a Volksdeutscher. They know how to speak it right."*

---

*The Volksdeutsch category had been improvised by the Germans at the beginning of the occupation. Any Pole legitimately claiming German ancestry could apply to the German authorities for German food rations, certain privileges, and the promise of German citizenship after the war.—*Tr.*

Chapter 26

"You have just convinced me, Lieutenant. I'd better show you my passport."

"Right," he answered.

I handed him my identification card, and he studied it carefully. Then he returned it and turned to the man who had first stopped me. "Let this citizen pass," he ordered.

I was about to mount my bicycle when I had a thought. "Lieutenant!" I called. "Teach your man how to recognize a Volksdeutscher. You do it by smell."

"What do you mean?"

"I mean they stink; they stink of betrayal."

The lieutenant suppressed a smile, while the other men laughed out loud. I got on my bicycle and rode off down the road.

Several days later when I visited Józek, I learned about the advance of the Allies in the west, but almost nothing about the Soviet front. Thus we spent the months of September through December waiting. The fields and forests were covered with snow, but I, probably for the first time in my life, was numb to these changes. I was obsessed with a single thought: when would the Eastern Front start moving again?

There were barely a dozen houses in our village. It was really more a little mountain hamlet than a real village. Each morning I liked to climb to a nearby mountaintop and peer off into the distance. To the east I could see Kalwaria Zebrzydowska; to the west the land slowly rose toward Wadowice. One morning I was on my mountain enjoying the view. The date was January 17, 1945. Suddenly a light breeze picked up, and there was a deep rumbling from far away. Enveloped in my own thoughts, I paid no attention at first, but then the sound became rhythmical and louder by the minute. There could be no doubt of it: it was artillery fire! I climbed higher to the summit. The sound of the guns was clearer from here, and it was coming from the direction of Cracow. The front had moved! The front was coming closer! No doubt it was already close to Cracow!

I ran and stumbled and fell down the mountain as fast as I could, ramming through the deep snow like a plow, to our house. "Basia!" I cried. "The front has begun to move! I don't know when, but it did! The Russians may already be in Cracow!"

Basia remained frozen to the spot. "How do you know?" she asked softly. I don't remember what I told her; I do remember falling into a chair panting and feverishly contemplating the new situation. All

269

my energy returned: I felt that I had to do something. "It isn't dangerous to stay here," I thought to myself. "The front will never come this
far but will follow the valleys down below. But Basia's mother is in
Borek Fałęcki, right in the path of the advance. She will be in danger. I
have got to get to Cracow to get her."

I called our landlord, a young peasant, and warned him not to
leave the house for any reason whatever: he was to stay put and look
after our two families. "It is too dangerous to be out and abroad with
things as they are," I said. "I myself will go to Cracow to scout out
the situation and be back in a few days. It is safest for all of you to
remain here."

The Rescue

It was too late to leave that day, but on the following day I set out
at the crack of dawn, pushing my bicycle. In Lanckorona everyone was
talking about the Soviet advance. Keeping to the back roads, I got to
Skawina and from there rode on toward Borek Fałęcki. I avoided the
main roads, expecting that they would be full of troops. Only when I
was near Borek, at a spot between a tiny church and a small estate, did I
venture out onto the main road leading to our house.

The highway was in an uproar. The Germans were in headlong
retreat from Cracow. They had been expecting an attack from the east in
the direction of Tarnów, and when the first expeditionary units struck
from the west, the Germans fled in panic without trying to defend the
city or to blow it up, as had been their plan. The scene on the highway
reminded me of our escape in 1939 magnified ten-fold. People were fleeing in all kinds of contrivances—automobiles, trucks, motorcycles,
horse carts, on foot, carrying bundles in their arms, dragging suitcases
behind them through the snow. Soldiers, civilians, women, children, all
were running—not walking, but actually running down the road. Apparently the Soviet army was just behind them.

I ran into our house and found our apartment in a horrible mess.
An artillery shell had hit the yard that morning, and the explosion had
shattered all the windows and the front door. Dishes were broken, furniture in both apartments was overturned. Fortunately, the two women
were all right; Basia's mother was in bed, covered with a quilt, her head

wrapped up in a wool shawl; Mrs. Proszkowski was looking after her. A bitter cold wind was whistling through the shattered windows, blowing snow around the room.

I went down the ladder to the cellar, which was still intact, and decided to get my mother-in-law down there, where it was at least a little warmer and out of the wind. I dragged a bed and mattress into the cellar. Now I had to figure out how to move my mother-in-law, for she could not get down the ladder under her own power. I got a mattress from another bed and put her on it; then I wound a clothesline around her, and the mattress, many times. It was an amazing sight, something like an Egyptian mummy, but it did the trick. I got the mattress as far as the basement ladder while Mrs. Proszkowski went down the ladder to help from the bottom. Next I shoved the entire package over to the trapdoor and began to work the mattress down the ladder, rung by rung. At the same time our dear landlady, without whose help I could not have managed, guided the foot of the mattress from the bottom. When the mattress and its burden was completely down, I untied my mother-in-law, who was then able to shift herself over onto the bed we had prepared. I moved another bed down for Mrs. Proszkowski and a day bed for myself, for we had decided that it was safest to spend the night in the cellar. We found some candles, and I lit a fire in the stove upstairs so that Mrs. Proszkowski could prepare our first hot meal of that day.

In the evening fleeing Germans could still be seen sporadically on the road, but by midnight even this trickle had dried up. I stood on the front porch and peered out in the direction of Cracow. There was no noise of any kind. It was silent on our street as well. I was about to go back inside when I glimpsed two figures, dressed in white, in a ditch, slowly moving along barely fifteen meters away. They crept silently, almost invisibly, in the direction of our house. As they drew closer a Russian voice asked me whether there were any Germans about. I answered in Russian that there were not. They asked me who was in the house, and I told them two old women, my mother-in-law and the landlady. They were in the cellar, I said. They came in, lighted their lanterns, and shone them over the trapdoor to the cellar to see whether all was as I described it. Then they muttered something like "Goodbye," slung their machine guns back on their shoulders, and disappeared again into the ditch like ghosts.

Our House at the Front

In the early morning we were awakened by the sound of traffic heading south: Russian tanks, trucks, staff cars, motorized caissons, and innumerable horse-drawn wagons loaded with provisions, ammunition, and other military hardware. This did not look like hot pursuit of the enemy to me: it was more like a military parade. Only later in the day did things take a more frenzied turn. More and more field pieces appeared, but they were now being pulled off into the fields at the side of the road. These were joined by increasing numbers of soldiers and ammunition wagons. Communications officers began laying down telephone lines, and we now began to hear artillery fire, not from the south, from Myślenice or Wadowice, but from the east.

If Cracow were already taken and the Russians were driving the Germans south, then what was this rumbling in the east? According to my calculations no Germans should be left there. Soon a line of cars drew up in front of our house. A female officer got out of one of them, came over, and asked whether I spoke Russian. I nodded. She told me that our house would be used as an observation and communications post and would soon be the site of a heated battle. She could see my amazement at this, and explained the situation. Apparently a column of the Russian army had unexpectedly broken through so far to the south that it had been able to encircle Cracow and capture it by surprise from the west, but now other German forces, having withdrawn from Tarnów, were once more threatening the city. The Russian aim was to force the retreating German column to bypass Cracow to the south, the route taken by the other retreating Germans. Thus the battle for Cracow was just beginning, and the sooner I abandoned this house, the safer I would be.

I tried to explain that there was a paralyzed old woman in the house in no condition to be moved, but none of my protests had any effect. The officers gave me twenty minutes to abandon the house, with or without my mother-in-law, as I preferred. The next thing I knew, a huge artillery piece was planted in our yard pointed toward Swoszowice. Other equipment was being set up in the field across the road, soldiers bustled about, and the communications officers hurriedly laid their lines.

In the midst of the confusion I remembered our neighbor had a wheelbarrow. I knocked on his door, but the house was empty. The barrow was out in the open beside his toolshed, and I commandeered it. I asked the woman officer to help me get my mother-in-law out of the cellar so that I could be on my way. She nodded to one of her soldiers—a stocky, well-built lad—to lend us a hand. In the cellar he got my mother-in-law up on his shoulders and carefully carried her up the ladder. I laid a mattress on the wheelbarrow for her to lie on, wrapped her tightly in a quilt, put a pillow under her head, and wrapped up her face in a wool scarf. Two soldiers helped me tie my parcel to the bottom of the wheelbarrow with rope to keep her from slipping off. Then I tore out a stake from our fence and tucked it in beside her.

After a hurried farewell to Mrs. Proszkowski, who was going to friends of hers in Borek Fałęcki, I roped myself to the wheelbarrow and headed toward Cracow—in the opposite direction from these troops. The road was slippery as glass, the ice polished by two days of wheeled traffic. However, without too much difficulty I made it as far as the little church at the fork of the road toward Skawina and Cracow. From here to the Solvay factory was a steep hill, and this is where the stake came into play: I stuck it through the spokes of the wheels to lock them and started down the treacherous path.

Across the Ice by Wheelbarrow

The middle of the road was empty, for motorized vehicles either drove over to one side of the road or stayed half on and half off to get traction. I alone was going down the middle of this glassy surface, concentrating all my effort on moving without starting to slide. When I was about halfway down I slipped; the next moment I was sitting on the ground and the wheelbarrow was going downhill sideways, dragging me after it by my harness. I was sure that the whole contraption was about to turn upside down with my mother-in-law underneath. Two Red Army men suddenly appeared; one grabbed the wheelbarrow, the other dragged me up onto my feet again. Then they helped me and the wheelbarrow over to the side of the road. I was shaking from the cold, the physical exertion, and my spill. "You'd better rest a bit," they said. "You look exhausted." I took their advice, but only for a moment, as I was afraid that it would soon be dark. I thanked the Russians for their unexpected help and crept on down the hill. The second stretch was not as steep, and I got to the bottom without further mishaps.

III: Fight for Survival, 1942-45

Pulling the stake out from the spokes of the wheels, I set off for Cracow as fast as I could. When I neared the Vistula, which I had to cross, I saw that the bridges were all blown up; only the iron tiers sticking up out of the water indicated where they had been two days earlier. Still I kept on toward the riverbank. I found a road leading downhill and was soon at the shore.

Before me was an unforgettable sight: from the other side of the river a steady stream of horsedrawn supply wagons flowed toward Podgórze across the ice. The dozens—no, hundreds—of wagons and the swarms of people made a sharp contrast with the gray strip of river and the rosy pink western sky. I stood for a moment weighing my chances of making it to the other side. I decided not to cross here, for I was afraid of being run over by the supply wagons; instead I walked downstream along the bank. After a hundred meters or so I spotted a path across the ice. "Ah, here's a crossing," I thought. "Other people have been across before me; it isn't as bad as I thought." The path was inviting me to cross, and I pushed the wheelbarrow onto the ice. The ice was covered with snow, and I made good progress.

When I was about halfway across, I heard a sharp crack like a pistol shot. The ice had broken under the weight of a supply wagon ahead of me. The rear wheel was completely submerged, and water from the hole was spreading over the ice in all directions. The soldiers whipped the terrified horses savagely to pull the wagon up, but their efforts were in vain. The animals were unshod, and they kept slipping back. In a minute there was another crack; more ice had broken; the wagon went under, dragging the horses after it into the depths. In the meantime water was pouring over the sagging surface.

Finally it reached me. At first I was walking in water up to my ankles, but before long it was over my shins. I stopped and looked around me like a castaway, water on all sides, the ice crackling everywhere. I could not go back: my only chance was to plow ahead, never knowing when the ice was going to break and swallow me up. I crept along gingerly, feeling my way. As soon as I felt the ice hold under my feet, I would move quickly forward several steps and then test it again. I don't know how long it took me to cross those several dozen meters—it could have been minutes or an entire hour. At last I got to a stretch where the surface was firm and dry. At that moment I heard a cheer from the shore. Hundreds of people were standing there on top of the Cracow embankment anxiously following my struggle with the elements.

In a moment I reached the shore, at the bottom of a steep and slippery embankment. I had yet to conquer this, but now the people on top formed a human chain, arm in arm, until it reached me, exhausted and almost unconscious. Someone drew back the scarf from my bundle and screamed with fright to see a person inside it. They pried the wheelbarrow out of my frozen hands and unknotted my homemade harness. They handed the ropes up the line and then slowly hauled up the wheelbarrow, then me. On top, I could not take a step. Someone gave me something to drink—vodka! Like a shot I felt that blessed warmth coursing through my body as I slowly began to revive and look around to see where I was. I don't even remember speaking to any of my rescuers, although I am sure I must have done so.

After only a short rest I warmly thanked the remaining people gathered around for their help and told them that we had to get on toward Cracow. At this moment a middle-aged man approached me with a younger man, his son-in-law, as it turned out. His manner and speech were simplicity and kindness itself. He said they had been watching my struggle on the ice and wanted to help me. Where was I headed? When I told him I was on my way to Bronowice Małe, where we had friends, he insisted that his son-in-law take up my burden. Without waiting for an answer, the young man harnessed himself to the wheelbarrow and set out. The older man pushed from behind; I walked alongside, hanging onto the side of the wheelbarrow to keep from falling. The long walk through the town was tremendously wearying, and, needless to say, I was at the end of my tether.

At last we limped into Bronowice, where a good friend of Basia's parents lived. He was Zygmunt Jaśko, a staff officer in the prewar Polish army and a tile-fitter by trade. Parting warmly with my chance friends, who had been so kind to us, I pushed the wheelbarrow the last few steps to the Jaśkos' house. They were overjoyed to see my mother-in-law and began fussing over her at once. As for me, I pulled off my boots, still full of water, my soggy socks, and my wet trousers. Somehow, my feet were not frostbitten. I collapsed in an armchair beside the stove with a feeling of immeasurable contentment and began to sip the hot tea which Mrs. Jaśko had brewed. I was too tired to tell them anything about our adventures. Night fell, and with it the temperature outside, but they bundled me into a dry, warm bed, where I fell asleep as soon as my head struck the pillow.

Chapter 27

I Cross the Front

I awoke early the next day, and after a hearty breakfast told the Jaśkos that I was going off to get Basia and the children. Jaśko looked at me as though I had lost my wits. "What do you mean, get Basia and the children? They are behind the German lines!"

"I know they are, but that's why I'm going. They're all alone, and I only came to Cracow to save my mother-in-law. Thanks to you, I needn't worry about her now, but I must return to take care of the rest of my family."

"You don't know what you're talking about," Jaśko cried. "The Germans are still holding out right there where your wife and children are. How do you expect to get through? The two most powerful armies in the world are fighting it out—thousands of men are dying every minute. Even if you make it up to the front without getting hit by a stray bullet, you're bound to be caught by one side or the other. They'll shoot you as a spy without a moment's thought. Do you think you can just walk through their lines as though you were invisible? Don't you think you'd better wait until the Russian attack succeeds and they get to your part of the country?"

"I appreciate your concern," I said, "but it's those few days before the Russians come that I'm worried about. These are going to be decisive days, and I can't leave my family unprotected. I'm not a fool. I know it will be dangerous, but I believe in predestination. If the Lord has guided me safely through the past five years, I don't think he will abandon me now. I am going to look after my family. I do believe that we will see each other again soon, with all of us safe and sound.'' Jaśko gave up, seeing that no argument could change my mind.

I left the Jaśkos at ten o'clock in the morning and headed for the Vistula. This time I crossed well above the place where the ice broke around me, and struck out across country toward Kobierzyn. From there I planned to head through Skawina, Kalwaria Zebrzydowska, and Lanckorona to our tiny village. Expecting that the main forces would be taking the well-traveled roads to Myślenice and Wadowice, I took a roundabout route to the east, on side roads through small settlements. As I marched briskly along, I saw no soldiers, although I could hear artillery fire in the distance.

Night eventually fell, illuminated by a full moon and punctuated by the sounds of war, now louder and nearer. When the sound of cannon fire grew too close for comfort I turned off to the side to avoid getting between the guns and their likely target. For the most part I kept to country roads or sometimes even paths, avoiding open fields and forests. Several times I heard the sound of motors in the distance—automobiles, moving along without headlights. I would jump off the road as soon as I caught even the faintest sound of an approaching vehicle and either hide behind a convenient tree or fall flat on my face behind some snowy hillock. Because they had no lights, I assumed that the passengers could not see much along the side of the road—I could not even tell whether the staff cars were German or Russian.

Usually it was dangerous to wander about at night in the country because of the village dogs, but that night they were neither seen nor heard. The noise of the guns and flashes in the sky must have frightened them. Dogs are usually silent before a storm, and I could imagine that for a dog it must have seemed like the rumble of thunder and lightning. I was in no position to tell where the firing was coming from, so I chose my path by watching the intensity of the explosions in the distance, as I thought it unlikely that the battle would be equally heated at all points along the front. Soldiers no longer fought with bayonets, I told myself, and these tanks and artillery were firing at one another from a fair distance. I intended to pass through the middle: while the shells were flying overhead, I would be hurrying along down below—at least this was how I reasoned.

The Battle of the Tanks

Suddenly I walked right into the thick of the battle. It happened so fast that there was no question of moving either forward or back, and I still cannot understand how I could have missed the sounds of the approaching tanks. Not far from Radziszów, east of the Skawinka River, as I was hiking along a road through the fields, I almost ran into a German tank, its barrel pointed north. From fifty meters away, the shells which it was hurling every thirty seconds sounded like the hissing of a gigantic goose. At each shot the tank recoiled, like a living creature in some sort of convulsion. I threw myself into a ditch, or rather a shellhole about a meter deep. To my right there was an abandoned house with a medium-sized tree next to it, but I dared not break cover and run for shelter.

I stared at the tank from my hole with a kind of fascinated horror. Then unexpectedly another tank appeared on the scene, a larger one. I saw a red star painted on the side; a Soviet tank. His turret with the cannon was reversed, and he was heading straight toward the side of the German tank. The Soviet tank struck with its entire force, right in the middle. The sound of the collision was frightful. The Russian colossus came to a stop, and it looked as though the two giants were preparing for battle, but no shots rang out. The Soviet tank increased its pressure, and now the German machine began to tilt. As the Soviet tank pushed, the German tilted more and more until one of its treads left the ground. The Soviet tank kept shoving until the German tank crashed over on its side, its turret grinding up the earth. As the Soviet giant towered victorious above the defeated German monster, a blue flame started to flicker from the fallen German machine. The Russians saw it and tried desperately to reverse away from the burning wreck, but without success; it was caught in the tangle of metal. Now the turret of the Soviet tank was flung open, and soldiers began to pour out of it and run toward the abandoned house. I was sure that I would be seen, and burrowed even deeper into my hole. The Germans struggled frantically to get their turret open, but it was buried in the dirt. Suddenly the ground rocked beneath me. I did not hear the explosion but saw a blinding flash, bright as a thousand suns, felt a hot blast of air, something pressing me down, then blackness.

I have no idea how long I lay there. Finally I was aware that I was face down on the ground. I tried to lift my head; no good. I tried to raise myself to my knees. Gradually I was able to pull myself up into a crouch and look around. The first thing I saw was the burning remains of the two tanks. Even after the explosion they were still locked in a deadly embrace. An enormous piece of shattered iron armor plate was lying right next to me. The old house was no more, and all that remained of the tree was a stump. The crackle of the burning machinery was the only sound to be heard. Not a living soul was in sight.

I tried to stand up, but fell back helplessly onto the snow. Soon I could not stand the cold any more and was afraid of freezing to death there in that field, so I made another determined attempt and managed to stagger to my feet. Half-conscious, I started to walk aimlessly— anywhere away from this spot. In the distance I heard dogs barking; there must have been houses nearby. As I was crossing a bridge over a small stream just before dawn, in the faint glow I saw a peasant wagon ahead. The peasant pulled up his horse as soon as he came alongside me. From his expression I could tell that I must have looked a fright. He asked me what in the world had happened. I tried to tell him about the tanks, but the words would not come; I was completely incoherent. The sympathetic fellow told me to climb in. He was going to Kalwaria Zeb- rzydowska and would take me there.

It was night again by the time I arrived home. Basia simply burst out crying at the sight of me. I told her right away that her mother was safe with the Jaśkos in Cracow. I said little about my wanderings because they were still too confused in my mind (in fact, it was a week before I could put the events of my return trip in some kind of order and could talk about them). Inside the house I drank three or four cups of hot milk and then began to scrub and soak the layers of dirt and grime. When the water in the tub got black, Basia would change it. Then I fell into bed to sleep the sleep of the dead. However, it was not to be.

The Fireworks Display

At the urgent request of our landlord, my wife woke me up around midnight. The noise of artillery fire could be heard nearby; the battle lines seemed to be drawing closer. I dragged on my warmest clothes and went outside. Our house was in a little valley, and I watched while the shells flew from one mountaintop to the other. Were it not for the whistling of the shells and the rumbling of the explosions, one might have taken them for flares. I must admit that it was a beautiful sight. I sat down on the front porch to watch: our landlord joined me, huddling quite close; I could feel him trembling. I took his hand and tried to calm him. "Nothing to be afraid of," I said. "Just try to imagine it's a fairy-tale; two fire-throwing dragons are fighting it out, with us as spectators. The fire on the left is Soviet; the Germans are on the right."

"How do you know that?" he asked.

"It's easy," I answered. "Mýslenice is on the left and Wadowice is on the right. The Soviets are trying to push the Germans west. Besides," I added, "look at the shells being fired from the left. They look like a bridge of fire. Those are the Soviet *katyushas*—'Stalin's organs,' they call them. They wreak terrible destruction; the Germans are terrified of them."

The landlord stared at me, impressed at my fund of information. Suddenly a misaimed or misfired shell from the German side landed about a hundred meters away, sending up a fountain of snow and earth, but not doing any damage. "You see?" I told him. "Deep snow is the best protection we could ask for. The shells don't burst on impact but bury themselves in the earth and then blow up into the air like a geyser. We couldn't be safer anywhere than where we are now."

In another half an hour the German fire weakened. The moments of silence between barrages grew longer. Finally their guns stopped altogether. The Soviets ceased fire too; they probably had already picked up and moved farther west. "The show's over," I told my landlord. "Time to go inside."

The War Ends

Earlier that evening my landlord had offered me a glass of beer, so I proposed that we have our drink now, recommending that he heat it up. He was bustling about the stove lighting the fire when a knock came at the door. Must be a neighbor come to gossip about the artillery, I thought. I opened the door and there stood a Soviet soldier, dressed in white. He came in, glanced around the room, and asked, "Any Germans here?"

"Nyet, Vsye poshli v Germaniyu" ("No, they've all gone back to Germany"), I answered.

He chuckled and was off as quickly and silently as he had arrived. I ran after to have a look. There were eight of them outside, all in white, all on skis. Our visitor snapped on his skis and they moved off down the road to the next house, single file.

I returned to the kitchen, where the hot beer was already standing on the table. Before taking a sip, I proposed a toast: "Here's to David!" I said.

"Who the hell is he?" asked the landlord, again amazed.

I told him I was thinking of the shepherd boy in the Bible who accepted a challenge to do battle with the giant Goliath and defeated him with nothing more than a slingshot and courage. I could see that he still didn't understand, but it was long past midnight, so I bade him goodnight and went across the hall to our apartment.

Basia was not sleeping either. Whether from the beer or the adventures of the past twenty-four hours, I could barely stand. Taking care not to wake the children, I whispered to Basia, "I'm going to sleep, and this time don't wake me up for anything." I had my first good night's sleep in five years. For me, the war was over.

Epilogue

Two days after the Soviet ski troops passed through our hamlet, I returned to Cracow to see how things were at our apartment. Even before I had left it, in the midst of the Soviet offensive and the German withdrawal, it was a wreck—broken windows, shattered window frames, a front door jammed, and frost in every corner. I dreaded to think what it must look like now.

Despite the bitter cold and deep snow I was traveling by bicycle. As I was riding through Kalwaria Zebrzydowska I met Alfred Sęcz-kowski, the man who asked me to help him with the matter of his false papers. Catching sight of me from afar, he took a stand in the middle of the road waving his arms like a windmill, impeding my further prog-ress. I was in no mood to tarry. It was January, the days were short, the snow was deep, making travel by bicycle next to impossible, and I had to get to Cracow before nightfall. Sęczkowski brought me to a halt, beamed at me, and began to carry on.

"Dear Mr. Szatyn," he exclaimed. "I'm so glad to see you alive and well. Thank God my wife and I are safe and sound too. I wanted to thank you once again for your brave intervention on my behalf with the Arbeitsamt and for not telling anyone that I was Jewish. I know that you're an important person in the underground, for I've seen you riding into the mountains all the time, and if you ever should need my help, I will swear to anyone how selflessly you acted during the war."

I was impatient to get away. "Thanks very much," I said, "but I don't need your help. I also am a Jew." Sęczkowski looked at me incredulously. As I got on my bicycle, I added for good measure, "And for that matter, that forestry officer in the green uniform you saw me with the other day is my brother. And to put your mind completely at ease, I should tell you that the director of the Arbeitsamt is my brother-in-law, and he is also a Jew." With that parting shot, I pedaled off, leaving Sęczkowski standing in the road staring blankly after me.

By chance I ran into the Sęczkowskis after the war in Buenos Aires, where they had settled. Only then did I learn that Alfred's real name was Albert Bukiet; his father was co-owner of a well-known company in Łódź, Bukiet Brothers, known mainly as manufacturers of head scarves. He himself was a chemical engineer who studied in Amsterdam before the war. During the German occupation of Poland Lola Sęczkowski, the Polish daughter of the factory engineer, fell in love with him and provided him with copies of her brother's identification papers. They hid in Łódź until it became too dangerous and then went to Cracow. Someone there suggested that Kalwaria Zebrzydowska was a safe spot, so they settled there, and that was where they came into my story. They were married after the war, and Albert resumed his real name. Of course, when I saw them later, they no longer had any doubts about my true identity.

I have only partial knowledge of the life after the war of the various other persons mentioned in this book. When the Soviet army entered Cracow, Joachim Mann, the director of the Skawina Arbeitsamt, fled to his native Silesia. Eventually Silesia was reunited with Poland and the inhabitants again became Polish citizens, Mann included. One day, I heard, he was recognized on the street; the security forces arrested him for crimes against the Polish people, and he died in prison.

At my first opportunity I tried to contact my friends the Kroczewskis, who helped me on so many occasions during the war. They had lived on Zwierzyniecka Street in Cracow. I went to the second floor and rang the bell of their apartment, and a young blond woman whom I had never seen opened the door. I asked for the Kroczewskis, but she claimed never to have heard the name. I insisted that this was impossible—that they were my friends and I had visited them often here during the war. She replied that I was mistaken; she had lived there for several years and had never heard of any Kroczewskis. When I went to check with the building superintendent, he said that he did not know the Kroczewskis and that no person by that name had ever lived in that building. Thus they disappeared without a trace.

I saw the Misiołeks frequently. Mietek Misiołek, as I have mentioned, worked in the Solvay chemical factory. Basia and I maintained contact with the Misiołek family until we left the country in 1945. I do not know what became of them after that. I never heard from or saw again my good friends from Przemyśl Józef Moskalewski and Professor Mylanko. Similarly, I know nothing further of Edek Garbarz, the cashier in the Cracow train station, or Tadeusz Słomka, the worker in the Skawina Arbeitsamt.

Recently I learned the names of the heroic young couple who risked their lives to save Maria Friede: they are Felicja Sikorska, now a physician in western Poland, and Jan Czopek, who still lives in Skawina.

Countess Potocki, the young countess of my narrative, got in touch with me when this book was published in Poland in 1983. She wrote that she was very happy to hear of me at last, that she was sure I would turn up somewhere sooner or later. We continue to correspond. From her I learned of the fate of the rest of the Potocki family. Her father-in-law Antoni, the old count, died on his estate at Olsza in 1952. Jerzy, the young count, took over the estate at Olsza and lived there until his death in January, 1983, at the age of sixty-nine. The countess sent me a recent photograph of Jerzy as well as her own. We promised to remain in touch.

My wife's cousin Bolek, the nightwatchman on the estate at Borek Szlachecki, and later the forester, married a local beauty after the war and must live in or around Cracow. I have not had any contact with him. Basia's friend Maria Friede still lives in Poland and is well. From time to time we get a letter from her.

Basia's brother Leon Neulinger (alias Antoni Mierzwa), his wife Sara (alias Maria Mierzwa), their son Uzy, born in Poland during the war, and my mother-in-law Gusta (alias Maria Szatyn) all immigrated to Israel. Leon and his mother both died there.

Basia's eldest sister Rózia died, several days before the cessation of hostilities, on the ferry supposedly transporting the Stutthof concentration camp prisoners to Sweden. Her husband, Samuel, and his two sons were taken to the camp at Mauthausen, where they were liberated by the American army. Samuel died of malnutrition and exhaustion twenty-four hours after the liberation. Both sons survived the camp, but never regained full health. They immigrated to Israel. Basia's other sister, Helena, survived the concentration camp at Ravensbrück, weighing seventy-seven pounds upon her release. Her husband, Leon, returned from Oświęcim only to die within the month. Their daughter, Ritulka, and Basia's father, Isaak, had perished in the Cracow ghetto during a Nazi roundup of children and old people. Helena lives in broken health in Israel under constant medical supervision.

With my own family I was more fortunate. They accepted my position that everyone should fight to the last moment for dignity and life. I said earlier that my elder sister Helena alone refused to come to us and perished without a trace. My mother, of course, died of natural causes during the war. My father, Joachim (Jan Nowak), immigrated with us to Venezuela after the war. He died in 1960 in Caracas, at the age of eighty-six, the victim of a mistaken medical diagnosis. My brother Emil (alias Kazimierz Zdrzałka, the gamekeeper) married his cousin Ernestyna Schwartz (the kitchenmaid Ala) after the war; they too immigrated to Venezuela, where they now live. They have two daughters and three grandchildren. My sister Krystyna (alias Janina Górnik) and her husband Józef (the director of the Arbeitsamt) also immigrated to Venezuela. Recently they moved to Florida, but their two sons and five grandchildren remain in Caracas.

My wife Basia (Barbara) and my two daughters, Elizabeth (Elżbieta) and Irene (Irena), and I eventually settled in the United States; I received United States citizenship in 1968. We have four grandchildren. Barbara and I lead a quiet and simple life. Each morning we take a long walk along the paths and meadows near our home in Palo Alto, California. We listen to the birds' songs, climb the nearby hills, and swim. I still ride my bicycle. We thank God for granting us the chance to live in a marvelous country in comfort, security, and freedom.

Bruno Shatyn holds master's degrees in both political science and law. He holds the doctoral degree in law from Jagellonian University, Cracow. A United States citizen, he is retired and has lived in California for many years.

Oscar E. Swan is a professor of slavic languages at the University of Pittsburgh. He holds the doctorate from the University of California, Berkeley.

The manuscript was edited by Jean Owen. The book was designed by Don Ross. The typeface for the text is Times Roman, based on a design by Stanley Morison about 1931; and the display face is Friz Quadrata. The text is printed on .55 lb. Glatfelter text paper and the book is bound in Holliston Mills Kingston cloth over binder's boards.